I0595048

The CEO's STAMP of Approval

T. Wiles Fowler

BusinessLeadership.com

The CEO's STAMP of Approval
Copyright © 2026 by T. Wiles Fowler
ISBN: 979-8-9936564-0-3

All rights reserved. No part of this book may be used or reproduced in any form or by any means, electronic or mechanical, including photocopying, recording, or any information storage and retrieval system, without the author's written permission and printed in the United States of America.

Printed in the United States of America
First Printing, 2026

B

BusinessLeadership.com Publishing
Sheffield Village, Ohio 44035
BusinessLeadership.com
StampofApproval.com

Acknowledgments

To…

My lovely wife, **Terri,** for
your sacrifice and love,

The **Reverend Jim Dubbs,** for
your consistency and teachings,

and

Thought Leaders
**Rafael Frontaura, Robert Hutcherson,
Mark Ladd, Jason Moore, Ganesh Siva, and Lee Winters**

To you all, I humbly give the…

Table of Contents

The CEO's
S-T-A-M-P
of Approval

Leadership is often described as the ability to inspire people toward a shared vision—but what if leadership could be understood as something more dynamic? What if it were a practical framework that intentionally integrates organizational culture, strategic execution, and human potential?

The CEO's STAMP of Approval is far more than a leadership book—it is a transformational blueprint for executives and leaders determined to elevate their organizations amid volatility, uncertainty, complexity, and ambiguity. Drawing from decades of hands-on leadership experience and academic rigor, T. Wiles Fowler delivers a compelling narrative that blends real-world insight, innovative frameworks, and engaging storytelling to empower leaders at every level.

This book challenges conventional leadership thinking by offering actionable strategies that redefine how leaders build teams, drive performance, and cultivate high-performing cultures. Fowler's approach places people—not processes alone—at the heart of organizational success, reminding us that sustainable results are achieved through alignment, trust, and intentional development.

Framed around the setting of a golf tournament, the story introduces the S-T-A-M-P framework—Support, Teamwork, Aptitude, Morale, and Performance—as a practical sequence for leadership and team development aligned with organizational vision. Through the experiences of HARDAWAY Tools and The Learning Center (TLC), readers see how situational agility, employee alignment, and continuous improvement can overcome inertia and organizational friction, transforming stagnation into momentum.

The book's use of memorable acronyms—such as L-E-A-D-S, T-R-A-I-N, and C-H-E-C-K—distills complex leadership and operational theories into clear, actionable steps. Fowler's extensive background, including his Lean Six Sigma expertise, is evident throughout, offering evidence-based strategies for talent development, team dynamics, and performance improvement.

Ideal for leaders navigating economic pressure, operational challenges, or organizational change, *The CEO's STAMP of Approval* provides a clear and practical roadmap to improve morale, streamline processes, and enhance profitability. Its balance of relatable storytelling and academic depth makes it both engaging and credible.

Clever, thought-provoking, and highly practical, this book offers value for leaders at any stage of their journey. Rich with real-world examples that bring the S-T-A-M-P framework to life, it also leaves space for readers to define their own leadership path. Without question, this is a book worth reading (and revisiting) for anyone committed to unlocking the full potential of their organization.

Robert Hutcherson, PhD, CEO/Founder – Optimize, LLC

By following the stories of HARDAWAY and TLC, the book makes complex and often abstract ideas feel practical and easy to grasp. Business leaders will easily find relevance with the STAMP approach and see themselves reflected in the four leaders we follow throughout the book. The book also does a great job of grounding its ideas in solid research, while sharing that research in a way that feels accessible and relevant to today's challenges.

It's a smart and engaging way to bring *leadership science to life*, especially at a time when the world needs ethical and effective leaders more than ever.

Dr. Dieter Veldsman | Chief Scientist: HR & OD, AIHR

Technical: *The property that causes all matter that is moving to stay in motion and all matter that is not moving to remain at rest until acted upon by an <u>outside</u> force.*

Practical: *The tendency to stay the same, a resistance to change. Tradition.*

Technical: *A force that opposes or slows the* <u>*momentum*</u> *between two surfaces in contact with one another.*

Practical: *Disagreement or conflict; discord. The clash between two people. Alternatively, parties of opposing views.*

Technical: *A by-product of mass and speed.*

Practical: *An idea or strategy on the move. <u>Hard</u> to stop.*

Introduction ...

Dear CEO/C-Suite, many of you are already skilled in running a successful business, yet the *STAMP of Approval* can enhance your leadership approach. Presented in an engaging story format, it empowers your leaders and teams to help preserve your wealth, embrace their responsibilities, and align more closely with your vision for the company. As you navigate each phase of the S-T-A-M-P, your understanding will become increasingly apparent, aligning their efforts while generating significant mission momentum. The narrative addresses the essence of system robustness and promises to be a valuable read. Academic support and industry best practices are highlighted as read-aheads for the story's characters and their learnings. You will be given the scientific rationale for all of the S-T-A-M-P principles.

...There are two ways to read this book!

If you prefer to focus on the background and academic research for particular topics, it is available as separate appendices at the back of the book. If your interest is in principles being taught through the story, I have you covered.

Thank you for taking the time; it will be worthwhile. In a world where customers and society value 'experience' more than mere technical specifications, the STAMP concepts bring customer satisfaction to life. For instance, even the most talented watchmakers may struggle with sales without the strategic marketing expertise of a brand like Rolex. The broader context (macro) fuels the profitability of individual endeavors (micro). Similarly, the STAMP transforms simple activity (inertia) into a dynamic, aligned strategy that advances your mission. The book's phases enable your leaders and teams to engage with the following essential CEO priorities and questions:

- How can I inspire my direct reports to showcase *situational agility* consistently?

- How can I ensure that my HR department cultivates *employee alignment* for sustainable momentum?

- How do I develop talent to embrace responsible autonomy from *self-actualization*?

- How can I foster strong *group interdependence* that collaborates through teaming-plus?

- How do we leverage *continuous improvement* to draw closer to my vision?

Swing away! Tim

Preface ...

This workbook boldly explores the enduring debate between autocratic Theory X and participative Theory Y management, seamlessly weaving in elements of golf club culture to establish a compelling, user-friendly management framework for the future. One character wittily labels this innovative concept *Theory Y2K*, showcasing a fresh perspective on traditional management styles. While it may take a moment to grasp both the vertical and horizontal connections within the template, the narrative featuring the golf course foursome powerfully distills the message, making it universally applicable to any organization.

It effectively demystifies human relations theories with striking graphics and unforgettable acronyms. This influential story-forward work is poised to revolutionize corporate thinking, much like *The One Minute Manager* did in the last millennium. It outlines a pragmatic strategy across five strategic fronts designed to tackle and eliminate the mediocrity that can plague organizations due to <u>inertia</u> and <u>friction</u>, ultimately empowering CEOs to clear the drag and resistance in their organizations.

These five phases offer a sequential, cohesive, holistic, end-to-end approach to building system improvement through:

SUPPORT: Leadership Awareness (Phase 1)
TEAMWORK: Employee Alignment (Phase 2)
APTITUDE: Self-Actualization (Phase 3)
MORALE: Dynamic Interdependence Alliances (Phase 4)
PERFORMANCE: Continuous Improvement Attainment (Phase 5).

This engaging guide invites leaders and teams alike to embark on a transformative journey, inspiring them to unlock their full potential and redefine how to leverage success. It provides a comprehensive framework for cultivating a vigorous, evolving organization. It aligns seamlessly with contemporary global development trends, delivering a remarkable surge of energy with minimal resource investment. More than just an acronym, S-T-A-M-P embodies profound change that honors human dignity and acknowledges the vast potential we all contribute to the tapestry of life, business, and organizations. The workbook's interactive nature promotes clear introspection for the reader.

Throughout their journeys, companies will inevitably encounter a range of challenges (economic downturns, energy scarcity, AI integration, workforce transitions, data security, supply chain volatility, regulatory pressures, improving customer trust, talent development, brand reputation, competition, disruptive technologies, and unstable demographic and geopolitical landscapes). While these considerations may appear daunting, they also present extraordinary opportunities for profound transformation. **The critical question for CEOs: How can you ignite your team's passion to engage wholeheartedly and sustain your vision during such turbulent times?**

Drawing on lessons from physics, we understand that inertia and friction are two significant obstacles to the conservation of momentum. In the business world, friction manifests as conflicts—be they interpersonal, departmental, value-chain disputes, or clashing ideas—while inertia echoes those all-too-familiar phrases like "That is how I have always done it!" Embracing change and overcoming these barriers fuels innovation and growth, turning adversity into advantage.

When departments—or specific leaders and/or processes within those departments—deviate from the company's implementation strategy, inertia can take hold. This inertia drains valuable energy from the organization, leading to wasted efforts and missed profit opportunities.

To overcome this challenge, leaders must clearly understand how each division supports and aligns with others from a *visual-spatial* perspective. This understanding cannot be achieved through an annual personnel planning exercise; it demands ongoing, real-time monitoring and engagement. Leaders should consistently articulate and revisit each department's path to success, ensuring that every team remains aligned with the broader organizational goals. Fits and transitions in the white space are often overlooked. Furthermore, each sub-leader must foster regular communication with their counterparts, viewing them as integral suppliers or customers within the profit stream. This will not occur naturally.

The seamless flow of interconnected processes is not a matter of chance; it requires careful attention and leaders equipped with confidence and robust coping skills. Inertia, often mistaken for work, can give rise to contentions between individuals and strategies, resulting in friction that hinders progression. This cyclical challenge can arise from innocent oversight or coercion. By recognizing and addressing these dynamics, CEOs can unlock their full potential, turning challenges into catalysts for momentum.

This captivating book takes you on a profound journey through potential bankruptcies, revealing an intriguing connection between inertia and friction at the heart of this complex issue. It is an indispensable resource for C-suite executives, visionary business leaders, and proactive HR professionals, offering practical strategies and transformative insights to unlock the human element of system improvement across transactional, traditional, and future-oriented settings.

Within each phase, there are five intervention modes, with movement from left to right indicating greater employee autonomy and increased trust from executives (i.e., system maturation).

With a golf-related, storyline-engaging approach, this workbook distills advanced-level insights on adult learning and human development theories into a holistic, memorable path that is both accessible and inspiring. We invite you to let these foundational concepts ignite your curiosity and motivate you to explore further within the S-T-A-M-P of Approval Series.

Uncover powerful revelations in Book 2 on Leadership support through situational agility, delve into Book 3 on progressive

Human Resources and Training, and be inspired by Book 4 on Individual Achievement and a wealth of other enriching topics.

However, for now, are you ready to put your stamp on it? If so, let us introduce you to our characters' dilemma...

Three months ago...

"No ... you listen!

They are not getting the job done; they have to go!

If the marketing group cannot sell the tools, the manufacturing folks cannot build them.

'If you build it, they will come' is nonsense, and it only works in movies, not real life!

Pass out the 300 pink slips now!"

DAILY TRIBUNE
SPORTS
Special------------Edition
Help TLC
The LEARNING CENTER
Celebrate 125 Years!
1st Annual Benefit
Golf Tournament
For the community to link with your business, your business should link with the community!
We Need Corporate Sponsorship!
Call 1 555 TLC-KIDS for details
NON PROFIT TLC IS PARTIALET FUNDED BY THE FEDERAL GOPERNMENT

CHAPTER 1 - THE LEADERS
A Common Handicap

"I have heard a lot of good things about TLC," comments Cindy Gray, the wife of HARDAWAY Tool's successful CEO, Chad Gray.

"TLC? What is TLC?" Chad yawns while reading the morning paper.

"It stands for The Learning Center, honey," Cindy replies. "Look, they are organizing a benefit golf tournament in mid-July to raise some money."

Suddenly, Chad's interest is piqued. "Did you say golf tournament? Where?" he asks, perusing the details in the advertisement. "Cindy, I have always supported local human service centers with our annual donations."

"Yes, honey, but it is more than just a tax write-off," Cindy responds. "These agencies need time and resources."

"I agree," Chad jokes, "like playing in the tournament."

"That is not exactly what I had in mind," Cindy replies. "But I bet it would be fun. It says here that TLC is a not-for-profit agency funded by the federal government."

"Yeah, but that is mostly for operations," Chad acknowledges. "They probably have many capital improvement needs. Given the business's experiences over the past year, incorporating sensitivity training on the realities faced by less fortunate individuals might help refocus the current HARDAWAY team. What do you think?"

"A little volunteer work might be helpful," Cindy agrees. "But how does that tie into golf?"

"We will sponsor a hole or something. Have a good time, meet some of the staff, and see where it goes from there. So, what is the number?" Chad asked. "I will have Bob Jiminez make the call after today's executive review."

"How is Bob doing these days?" Cindy inquired.

"Well, he is still leading our HR team and finished up his Doctorate in Strategic Leadership (DSL) a few months ago. His dissertation is entitled *Leadership Development Through Human Resources*," Chad replied. "However, his being away from work for the last few months has set us back. He is working on a leadership journal article based on his schooling. He thinks the concepts will help us, but I am not sure. He is under much pressure due to the concerns our employees have raised lately. I have been trying to handle the bottom-line issues since he is better with people," Chad admitted as he rushed from the table to prepare for the day.

HARDAWAY Tools was founded thirty-two years ago in the Gray garage. As a young man, Chad had always been handy and had a knack for making money. Starting with small garden tools, HARDAWAY Tools grew into a company known for producing the world's most durable industrial equipment, earning a reputation for toughness and sustainability. He applied the same approach to managing his employees.

Gray's ongoing theme was, 'Only high expectations produce high results!' For the first thirty years, that slogan proved effective. Profits soared, the townspeople earned a good living, and customers received quality tools.

However, recently, amid overseas competition and lower profit margins, HARDAWAY laid off nearly 300 employees from the residential manufacturing division. This left the remaining employees feeling disillusioned and unmotivated. The past year has been challenging, marked by pay cuts and no employee profit-sharing. Chad's tough exterior has softened in light of HARDAWAY's recent decline. For the first time, he felt helpless in addressing the situation.

On his way to the office that morning, he could not shake thoughts of the laid-off workers and their families. He wondered whether TLC had helped any of them and if his current employees could benefit from volunteer assistance at one of their agencies. His reflections were abruptly interrupted when a picketer jumped in front of his car at HARDAWAY's front gate. The sign read:

HARDAWAY'S LAYOFFS HAVE MADE THE WAY HARD FOR MY FAMILY

"Sure, you can go to work," the picketer yelled. "But I can only go to the unemployment line!"

"I have got kids to feed!" shouted another laid-off coworker.

"And Gray, you have not done a damn thing about it!" exclaimed another.

This interaction became a daily occurrence. Before he knew it, it was time for the monthly executive review. Chad entered the room, aware that the quarterly finance update would likely not meet his expectations; he feared a record decline. The expressions on his senior management team's faces spoke volumes. Morale matched the dismal bottom line.

Gray was unimpressed with any of his team's proposed solutions, nor did he have any ideas of his own. The meeting concluded with an assignment: to develop a strategy to improve the manufacturing and marketing divisions, increase profitability, and, hopefully, rehire the laid-off employees. Given Wall Street's skepticism, the team had only the next two quarters to devise and implement the beginnings of a plan, or more layoffs would be inevitable. Chad knew the stock price could not withstand further hits.

As the meeting concluded, Gray expressed the company's support for the upcoming TLC Tournament. He believed that sponsorship and volunteering would benefit his team and enhance HARDAWAY's image in the community, especially given the recent layoffs.

HARDAWAY HR Manager Bob Jiminez reached out to his counterpart at TLC, Pete O'Neil, to express their interest in becoming a corporate sponsor for the upcoming tournament. Bob first met Pete a few years ago at the state's annual human resources conference, where they were both doctoral students. Pete's dissertation was on *Talent Development and Teaming-Plus for Performance*. At the time of the call, Pete was enroute to TLC's monthly board of directors' meeting, accompanied by his Executive Director, Rob Lane.

Lane has been with TLC for sixteen years, starting as a part-time childcare worker while completing his master's in social work. After graduating, he was promoted to Residential Director of one of TLC's smaller facilities. His rise within the organization can be attributed to his determination and remarkable ability to foster an environment where his team is motivated to work hard for him.

Under Lane's leadership, the human services agency has experienced significant growth and success. He has built upon its rich, century-long heritage of providing quality care to the community. Currently, TLC offers a wide range of social services, including temporary housing for people experiencing homelessness, a food pantry, a counseling center, a low-income daycare, drug treatment centers, a school for students with learning disabilities, and 17 suburban facilities for individuals with physical and emotional challenges.

TLC operates on an annual budget of over $29 million, serving nearly 1,000 staff and clients. Lane strives to balance the demands of people management with fiscal responsibility but has recently found it increasingly challenging to maintain control of the organization.

Lane is likely to lose the board's confidence due to federal budget cuts and the unrealistic expectations of a few vocal board members. He still has the support of his staff and clients, but he knows that his days in the position are numbered without the trustee's endorsement.

At the beginning of the meeting, Lane shares the positive news of HARDAWAY's corporate sponsorship. However, this was the only highlight. The discussion quickly turns to several issues: delinquent debts from acquired properties, increased staff turnover, residents fleeing, and ongoing disagreements over the agency's mission and future outreaches. Lane hopes the upcoming tournament and auction will raise a quarter of a million dollars to help pay off some of the property debts. Unfortunately, the meeting concludes with many unresolved issues.

CHAPTER 2 – THE TOURNAMENT
In the Rough

As the big day arrives, the atmosphere at Bailey's Country Club is filled with excitement and anticipation for TLC's success. The CEO, Chad Gray, and the Executive Director, Rob Lane, are both avid golfers. They are joined by their respective HR Managers, Bob Jiminez and Pete O'Neil, who may not be strong golfers but are certainly enthusiastic.

"You are up, Rob," Chad calls out. "After all, this is your tournament!"

Rob Lane steps up to the number one tee, places the ball, and drives a straight shot down the middle of the fairway.

"Well, if your boss can do it, so can you, Pete!" quips Bob Jiminez.

Surprisingly, Pete O'Neil's drive starts straight but hooks to the right, landing just inside the midway bunker.

"Two HR professionals in a pod," Rob exclaims as Bob Jiminez's shot lands ten feet from Pete's in the rough.

"I am sure glad I brought that weed whacker in my bag this morning," Bob laughs after his shot.

"Yeah, I saw it in there," Pete observes. "It is a HARDAWAY, right?"

"It better be," Chad interjects as he approaches the tee. Chad's drive also lands in the middle of the fairway, just past Rob's.

"After we get back from the bunker hole," Rob suggests, "let us move my bag to your cart, Chad. It looks like these guys will be all over this course today."

"Sounds like a great idea," Chad agrees.

Jiminez and O'Neil continued to enjoy the scenic tour throughout the first nine holes. Meanwhile, Gray and Lane played just above par and engaged in superficial conversations about their respective organizations. Their dialogue was primarily focused on past accomplishments, as they felt no need or desire to discuss their current problems. They just wanted to play some good golf that afternoon.

In reality, both men were dissatisfied with their typical approaches to management and decision-making. Gray had set 'high expectations,' which, lately, had not been met by anyone, including himself. Likewise, Lane's people skills have not significantly improved TLC's bottom line.

After nine holes, the foursome took a break for a quick lunch. Rob Lane broke the ice by admitting his agency's financial concerns. This honest admission prompted Chad to share HARDAWAY's issues as well. Both men were surprised to discover the similarities in their challenges. "I guess for any business," Lane remarked, "to be successful, managing the human element is crucial. I am learning the hard way that non-profits also need solid business acumen to survive. It is all about balancing the objective and subjective."

As the two executives proceeded through the last nine holes, they began noting their shared concerns on the back of their scorecards. Their conversation revolved around management topics, and the event concluded with TLC raising nearly $200,000. Though it fell short of their goal, it was still a success.

CHAPTER 3 – THE PROPOSAL
Swing Away

That night, while organizing his paperwork for the following morning, Chad stumbled upon the proposal Bob Jiminez, his HR Manager, had given him in the executive garage the previous Friday night. He had slipped it into his briefcase and forgotten about it over the weekend. However, he recalled something about a stamp. The document was titled:

S-T-A-M-P of Approval! A HARDAWAY Business Process Template.

He recalled his earlier conversation with Director Lane and noted the similarities between HARDAWAY and TLC. Chad's interest was piqued as he began to see clear answers to many of the issues he and Lane had discussed. Although exhausted from the day's events, he found himself engrossed in the content for most of the next hour. Eventually, fatigue took over, and he drifted off to sleep.

"Cindy...wait until you hear some of this!" Chad said the following day as he sat down at the breakfast table.

"What stuff?" she replied while pouring his first cup of coffee.

"This is so good!" he continued excitedly.

"What, the Starbucks? Spit it out!" Cindy teased.

"Jiminez's approach to fixing the company's problems," Chad replies. "Listen to this: Bob says, 'Real leaders not only know their people, but they also know themselves. They genuinely examine their motives for every decision, which creates an atmosphere of openness among their employees.'

As tough-minded as Chad was, he recognized that the more straightforward a procedure is, the more likely it is that everyone will understand and implement it. His first rule was...

KISS with an extra S!
Keep It Simple, Stupid (and Short, too!)

"Honey, Pete continues, 'The first requirement for any organizational leadership is support for those value-adders—those who interact with the product or service, perform the job, and/or touch customers. Support is not passive; in fact, it is quite the opposite. It must be active to be effective. Ultimately, providing support fosters leadership development. For example, consider any department head at HARDAWAY. They can recite the latest corporate initiative word for word. However, they rarely take the time to walk the floor and discuss the current status with their supervisors or floor workers. Sure, they claim to 'support' the latest policy, but in reality, they only pay lip service to it in front of a crowd. In our company, support usually means, 'Sure, I will pay for it, but do not bother me with the details.' Real support requires time, effort, and two-way dialogue, where every mind is engaged at every level. After all, the floor staff are the only ones 'making' money for the company; everyone else is just spending it! So, get out there and lead with your feet!"

"The challenge of two-way support lies in the unpredictability of people," Chad concludes. "This reminds me of that old book from the '60s by Douglas McGregor, about the Theory X and Theory Y continuum."

Cindy jokes, "Well, now it seems more like a Theory Y-2K."

"Very funny," Chad replies, smiling. "Love you, dear. I have to go."

Later, at the office, HR Manager Bob Jiminez reviews the proposal with Chad, point by point. The discussion focuses on leadership. "Boss, here is how I see it at a high level: Organizational success is the goal, right? Everyone needs to pull in the same direction as you, the CEO. I consider momentum an output, while the team's concerted effort is the input. This process is smoother when there is solid alignment, which stems from strong leadership."

"The flow looks something like this…"

"That is quite a lot to digest at once, but I see your point," Chad said. "Leadership support at all levels is essential for our success. It all begins and ends with leadership. Why didn't you mention this on the golf course?"

"Because you are right, it is quite a bit to take in," Bob replied. "I wanted you to review it firsthand before we discussed it. Besides, you did not spend much time out of bounds while I was distracted by the poison ivy, did you?"

As Bob continued to speak, Chad reflected on his conversation with TLC's Director, Rob Lane.

"You know," Chad interrupted, "these concepts might work in the non-profit world as well."

"Really," Bob inquires, "what do you mean?"

"As you and Pete were driving around Baileys last week, Lane and I were comparing notes about our organizations," Chad explained. "I concluded that we have failed to manage the human aspect of the business. Rob felt the same way; he believes he is losing the board's support due to a lack of control over financial issues and hesitating to make difficult decisions."

"Where are you going with this?" Bob asks.

"Call TLC," Chad instructed. "See if Pete and Rob can join us for lunch later this week. I have an idea."

"Okay, I will handle that," Bob replied.

"Let me know their response as soon as possible," Chad said. "We are running out of time, you know!"

"Yes, sir!" Bob quickly agrees.

CHAPTER 4 – THE LUNCH
The Approach Shot

After confirming their schedules, the four met the following Tuesday at the Rose Garden, an upscale yet affordable restaurant well known in the community for business luncheons. It provided just the right amount of privacy for the meeting. They reserved a small conference room at the back of the building. Bob had prepared the S-T-A-M-P proposal in presentation format.

"Thank you both," Chad begins, "for taking the time out of your busy schedules to meet with us today."

Bob opens, "So you know, it is ironic. Half of these original concepts that eventually made it into this current *S-T-A-M-P of Approval* draft journal article were developed by Pete and me for our final doctoral projects. My dissertation paper covered leadership and human resources (which ultimately became the 'Support' and 'Teamwork' sections we have today), and Pete's academic paper covered talent development, group dynamics, and improvement, which have become the Aptitude, Morale, and Performance sections. So, I am glad both organizations are having this discussion now."

Pete agrees, "After we both were close to finishing our respective papers, we had a few study sessions together to discuss and finalize our concepts and formatting; we started to notice how each of the five topics supplemented one another. After our original papers were submitted and approved, we began meeting to refine and strengthen the connections and acronyms between the S-T-A-M-P phases.

Bob continues, "Yes, we were working on aligning the concepts for a leadership journal article submission when I first gave it to Chad for a possible solution for what Hardaway was going through; I was thinking, maybe a case study or something? Chad comments, "Yes, I had the paper but did not review it until after the golf tournament. I considered that both organizations could collaborate and work through the framework, but for now, let us have a meal."

After lunch, the men discussed…

1) Leadership styles and skills,
2) Training and placement,
3) Individual achievement,
4) The effect on (and from) the group as a whole, and
5) The lack of sustainability in innovation and continuous improvement.

"Thank you, Bob! That was excellent!" Chad transitioned. "Men, please take a copy of this partnership proposal. Over the next few days, see if you think this new approach will work for TLC, too. If it succeeds, many good people will be helped, which should hopefully improve our bottom line as well. What do you say? I want to keep us partnering with you, Rob."

In reality, Rob was desperate enough to consider any option. He knew his time was running short. 'This might just give us some breathing room with the board,' he thought.

"Sure, Chad," Rob responded. "We will do this with you. Let us consider the logistics of bringing both organizations up to speed on these concepts. Then we will need to cascade the information down through the ranks. Does that make sense?"

"Great," Chad replied. "I agree about the cascading and have some ideas. What is our next step?"

"What about a joint retreat?" Pete asks. "That way, our people can do a deep dive without distractions."

"Yes, good idea, Pete," Rob responded. "Earlier this year, we were given an old campground that we hoped would be an escape haven for our staff and their families. We cannot afford to pay large salaries, so TLC has always tried to be creative with other fringe benefits. However, it needs much work, especially on the grounds."

"Did you forget what we do? We will send a crew over right away," Chad volunteered. "We will spruce the place up before the retreat."

"That would be great… thank you, Chad," Rob acknowledged. "Why don't we also have our two teams work together on the place during the retreat? It should not be all book learning; let us also incorporate some hands-on activities."

"When do we want to do this?" Pete asked.

"It will have to be on the weekend," Rob replied. "Our people are used to working weekends. What about HARDAWAY?"

"Well, most of the time, we work five days a week unless demand increases," Chad explained. "As the CEO, I am going to insist that my team be there. Let us make it happen!"

"Great, which weekend should we choose?" Bob inquired.

"I know vacations are heavy in August, so let us wait until September," Chad suggested. "Maybe a few weekends after Labor Day. Things should settle down by then."

"That sounds like a good plan," Rob agreed. "It will give us time to understand the concepts and linkages better and prepare the agenda. We will inform our team. By the way, gentlemen, thank you both for thinking of TLC in this."

"No problem, Rob," Chad replied. "Bob and I had a great time at the tournament. We saw first-hand the excellent work you and Pete are doing. Besides, as hard as it is for me to admit, we, too, must also develop our people's skills. We are glad to help. How can we prepare our people on some of these concepts before the retreat?"

"How about we just give the draft articles to the retreat participants beforehand?"

Advance Reading for Participants.
To read in full, please see Appendix A

Bob Jiminez's Final DSL Research Paper
Academic basis for the <u>S</u>upport & <u>T</u>eamwork portion.
Enhancing Leadership Development Through Human Resources

Pre-Reading / Table of Contents

Advance Reading for Participants.
To read in full, please see Appendix B

Pete O'Neil's Final DSL Research Paper
Academic basis for the <u>A</u>ptitude, <u>M</u>orale & <u>P</u>erformance sections.
Talent Development & Teaming-Plus for Performance

Pre-Reading / Table of Contents
Abstract
Talent Development and Teaming-Plus for Performance
History of Talent Development
Stages of Talent Development (W-O-R-K-S)
    The <u>W</u>anderer (New & Idealistic)
    The <u>O</u>bjector (Reality is Different)
    The <u>R</u>esolver (Greener Pastures)
    The <u>K</u>eeper (Impact)
    The <u>S</u>enior (Longevity)
Result: Self-Actualization
Aptitude Self-Assessment Workbook
Teams, Teamwork & Teaming
Leadership for Teaming-Plus
Morale: Teaming-Plus for Dynamic Interdependence (G-R-O-U-P)
    <u>G</u>uarded (Where do I fit?)
    <u>R</u>esignation (Can I fit in?)
    <u>O</u>peration (Are we Good? Yes!)
    <u>U</u>tilization (Now, we are humming!)
    <u>P</u>roduction (Cooking With Grease!)
Result: Teaming + Alliances
Morale Self-Assessment Workbook
History of Organizational Performance
Lean as a System
Lean Thinking

CHAPTER 5 – THE RETREAT
Sink the Birdie

A total of sixty-seven people - forty from HARDAWAY and twenty-seven from TLC - arrived early Saturday morning for the joint retreat.

"I know we are all busy; thank you for your time this weekend," Molly Taylor, HARDAWAY's Director of Strategy and the facilitator for the weekend, began. "FYI team, a recent Gallup poll (2024) shows a 6-percentage point drop in employee engagement over the last 15 years. This certainly affects companies' bottom line."

"To start, we do not need another seminar on Conflict Resolution or How to Deal with Difficult People. What we need is an effective business process template. Most of you are familiar with the concept of a template. It provides an organized structure for data and digital information, defining where, how, and what is stored and released. We believe that the S-T-A-M-P of Approval is the first practical, *living* business process template that offers a simple foundational structure to guide our people and policies in today's competitive market."

"Hopefully, you reviewed the pre-reading. The S-T-A-M-P is more than just an acronym. It represents a framework for creating problem preventers rather than merely problem-solvers. It offers systemic, upfront analysis instead of a quick-fix approach."

"Although many of our employees possess the necessary knowledge (cognitive skills) and abilities (behavioral skills) to perform their jobs, they often fail to do so or perform at lower levels. Unlike machines, humans require reason and understanding to operate at optimal levels. They must value superior outcomes and high quality. Employees need to comprehend how they fit into the business, what their supervisors expect of them, and the systems that will drive activities within the organization. Content related to the affective learning component focuses on how to shift employees' attitudes toward outcomes that drive culture change. This is a clear result from applying the STAMP template.

"When an organization's culture is influenced, it is akin to building a barrier against substandard performance. Our two HR managers developed most of the material for this weekend's sessions, drawing on their educational backgrounds. You will receive the next-steps workbook late tomorrow. Over the next few months, your assistance in refining and applying these concepts will be invaluable. Teamwork is often defined by how well we collaborate, but that is just the result. True teamwork also involves inputs, such as properly placing workers within an organizational structure designed for success. It depends on leadership's ability and willingness to define everyone's roles and responsibilities for maximum impact. Regularly addressing issues such as redundancy, overburden, and a lack of process awareness and interconnectedness among functions is essential to reducing inefficiency."

"Teamwork can only thrive when 'boundaries' are understood, communicated, and coordinated by everyone in the organization. More boundaries will be discussed shortly. Your presence here this weekend indicates that the senior leadership at HARDAWAY and TLC trusts you to share these principles with your colleagues. In a sense, you are becoming a coach. So, coaches, here is your agenda for today and tomorrow. Thank you again for your time. Any questions?"

Saturday

8:00-8:30	Arrival/Continental Breakfast
8:30-9:30	What is a Business-Process-Template?
9:30-10:15	Facility and Grounds Tour
10:15-10:30	Break
10:30-12:00	**S** = Support (Situational Agility)
12:00-1:00	Lunch
1:00-2:00	Outside Activities
2:00-3:00	**T** = Teamwork (HR/Placement)
3:00-4:00	**A** = Aptitude (Individual Achievement)

Sunday

8:00-9:30	Full Breakfast & 5-Table Exercise
9:30-9:45	Break
9:45-11:00	**M** = Morale (Group Dynamics)
11:00-12:00	Lunch
12:00-2:00	**P** = Performance (Continuous Improvement)
2:00-2:15	Break
2:15-3:00	Result & People-Driven Behaviors

"After each main session, you will have a brief period to jot down notes regarding implications for your department."

As a thought starter, Molly transitions, "What comes to your mind when you hear the phrase 'culture change'?"

"We have a hard one!" someone exclaims from the snack table.

"I understand," Molly responds. "Business culture, like any culture, is made up of the routine behaviors of its members. These behaviors, when repeated, set in motion what we call tradition. Traditions, or norms, generally dictate the comings and goings of its people. Therefore, attempting to change culture is akin to convincing a fish that there is no such thing as water. Culture is the water. However, there are components we need to discuss. To extend the water analogy, I believe Boundaries are like the two parts, hydrogen, and Behaviors are like the one part, oxygen."

"We will propose this weekend, based on research from Bob's team, that culture is an outcome of behaviors. We believe behaviors result from what Bob calls 'Boundaries.' Boundaries encompass policies, procedures, organizational structure, management expectations, performance metrics, incentives, roles, responsibilities, routines, and other key elements. Thus, we can summarize it with the BBC Formula:

Boundaries + Behaviors = Culture

"And now," Molly concludes, "I will turn it over to Rob Lane, Executive Director of <u>T</u>he <u>L</u>earning <u>C</u>enter…Rob?"

8:30-9:30 Business-Process-Template, Rob Lane

"Thank you, Molly." Since many members of the HARDAWAY team are not familiar with the work at TLC, Director Lane begins by outlining the agency's vision, mission, and recent concerns that have led to today's discussion.

"I want to provide more details about our new business template. In this session, we will only cover the highlights, but we will dive deeper as the weekend progresses. We have tried to incorporate some group participation into the modules, so we are not always lecturing."

"You will notice," he says, directing the group's attention to the next slide, "that the five phases in the S-T-A-M-P framework are Support, Teamwork, Aptitude, Morale, and Performance. Each phase consists of five progressing modes, represented by a simple acronym. Do not worry; everything will be explained in detail over the weekend."

"Progressive means moving forward, successfully transitioning to the next level. Each phase has a logical progression in the following categories:

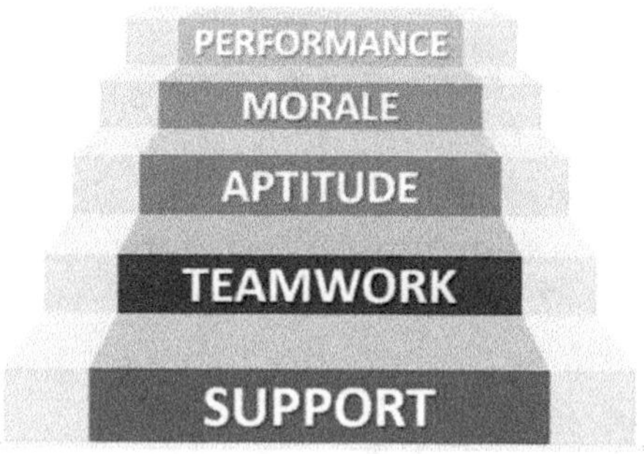

"Let us begin with the stair-step model, starting with support as the foundational first phase. It is essential to recognize that true teamwork cannot exist without a strong foundation of support. When team members are appropriately placed, their willingness to learn increases, enhancing their aptitude. These values can then become ingrained in the group's morale as more participants become willing to engage, thereby improving performance. I realize that this is too much information to take in at once. As you can see on the agenda, we have allocated sufficient time for each phase. This hour is intended to provide a simple introduction. Additionally, after each session, you will have time to jot down your thoughts in the end-of-session Review Notes and peruse real-world case studies that highlight the S-T-A-M-P concepts in action, demonstrating their metric effectiveness. Please feel free to review them and to take session notes for your later reference."

"Now, based on his excellent work, HARDAWAY's HR Manager, Bob Jiminez, will discuss what he refers to as the Big Mo' Talk, where Mo' stands for Momentum! Bob... or was it Curly or Larry?" Rob jokes.

"Very funny! Do you write your own material?" Bob returns. "Good morning, everyone! Seriously, though, picture a large ring in your mind. This ring has four long ropes and four workers positioned around it. I happen to have a ring with me today, and I need four volunteers to come up to the front—two from HARDAWAY and two from TLC. Do not be shy, or I will have to choose four people myself!"

In a quiet, clandestine manner, he instructs each person to grab the rope and make a run for it. However, since these directions were given in isolation, without any coordination or input from the others, they fail to build any collective momentum.

The crowd, buzzing with excitement, begins the countdown: "Ten, nine, eight, seven, six, five, four, three, two, one... go!" However, as their journey commences, they quickly come to a halt. Two of them cling to the rope so tightly that they nearly lose their balance.

The ring stubbornly remains in its original position. The four participants then discuss how their individualistic approaches ultimately hindered the team's success and the detrimental effects of misaligned goals. With a little nudge from Bob and a spirit of cooperation, they realign their focus, unite around a shared objective, and swiftly propel themselves in the intended direction.

"Momentum," Bob emphasizes as they return to their seats, "is the most challenging aspect to cultivate when operating alone. When you join others, however, it can become a powerful force."

"Please recognize that the Big Mo' is the powerful result of three essential elements: dynamic leadership, strategic alignment, and a concerted effort—each contributing to the momentum that propels an organization toward success."

"Allow me to elaborate. The cornerstone of any thriving company is impactful leadership, not mere dictatorship. Effective leaders possess the confidence to empower their teams, allowing them to make decisions within their scope of authority. When necessary, they also take on the responsibility of being decisive."

"This style of leadership forges alignment within the organization. Although 'alignment' has become a popular buzzword in the business world, it is essential to understand that, by itself, alignment (a mere input) does little for an organization. What it truly accomplishes is placing the right people in the right roles, ensuring they have a shared vision."

"Momentum (the output) truly takes flight when employees achieve their annual objectives by reaching departmental goals. At this stage, each individual participates in interconnected daily activities that contribute to the company's overall well-being. This symphony creates energy—the Big Mo—which drives continuous improvement and ultimately leads to exceptional organizational success. In contrast, companies that overlook this sequence often find themselves disjointed, grappling with traditional departmental inertia (such as HR, Sales, Design), resulting in friction and a lack of focused direction. Please refer to the slide for further insights."

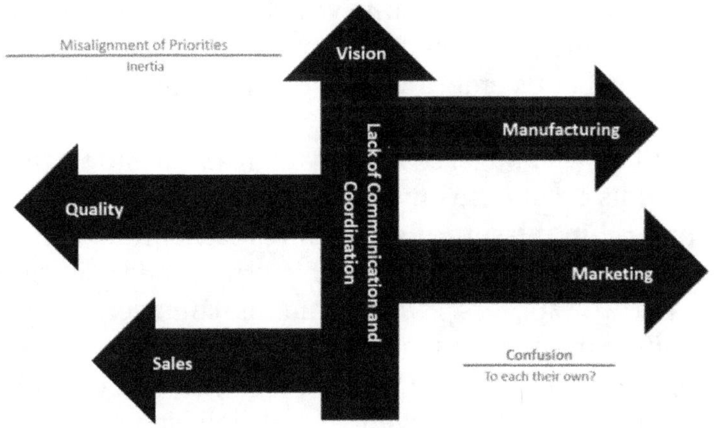

"This weekend, we will delve into several crucial concepts as we face the challenges of HARDAWAY's declining profits, escalating layoffs, and TLC's urgent need for refocusing. We believe that a well-structured template will be the cornerstone of our path to improvement."

"Pay attention—by tomorrow's end, you will see how the S-T-A-M-P phased approach directly ties to the organizational success I referenced earlier, unfolding step by step. We ask that you approach this with an open mind and a willingness to contribute your thoughts. Keep in mind this exercise: at the outset, every participant in the ring was brimming with energy and determination, yet they lacked genuine direction. Our challenge lies in maintaining a laser focus on the logical flow of this STAMP sequence, reflecting on it, and trusting that the benefits will reveal themselves over time."

"To illustrate this point," Bob continues, "let me draw on an analogy from the world of sports that underscores the importance of momentum. Consider the art of speed sailing coordination. In this exhilarating sport, momentum is generated when each crew member makes precise, on-the-fly adjustments to position the sails perfectly in the wind's path, creating powerful forward motion for the vessel. The Captain, from his unique vantage point, communicates real-time instructions to each crew member. While an individual team member may not immediately grasp the reasoning behind a particular directive, their responsive action—timed in concert with the collective effort of others on the crew—sets the ship on a course toward victory. Let us embrace this journey together!"

"Similarly, managers who strategically position themselves and their teams create the environment needed to deliver multiple instructions, all in pursuit of sustaining momentum. It is essential to recognize that momentum is both front-loaded and time-sensitive. The path to success often demands considerable effort, repeated again and again, to yield seemingly small results. However, over time, the momentum cultivated can lead to a cascade of outstanding outcomes from even the smallest, most deliberate choices."

"Now, let us move on," Bob transitions with enthusiasm. "At HARDAWAY, we feel truly privileged to collaborate with such an extraordinary group of individuals. I am sure many of you noticed the remarkable work our spruce-up crew accomplished this past week at the entrance. However, that is just the beginning! Director Lane would like to take us on a guided tour of the grounds to showcase the impressive progress. Rob?"

"We are incredibly grateful for your heartfelt dedication," Rob enthusiastically replies. "Let us take a moment to admire Hardaway's efforts!" With that, the group embarks on the tour.

9:30-10:15 Grounds Tour

This newly designated facility and its surrounding grounds provide a sanctuary for the TLC staff, offering them a serene escape from the demands of their draining human service work. Chad generously allowed the HARDAWAY ground crew to revitalize the area. With their top-notch tools and unwavering dedication, the TLC Center had never shone brighter.

Director Lane appreciated the help, especially when Chad volunteered to have his crew teach job skills to some of TLC's clients. This relationship was becoming a win-win for both organizations. If he could persuade the board to back off, he thought, this STAMP stuff might actually work.

10:15-10:30 Break

*The only test of **leadership** is that somebody follows.*

-Robert Greenleaf

10:30-12:00   Support, Chad Gray

Without any formal introduction, CEO Gray decisively launches into the next session: "I have been doing much serious thinking as we approach our meeting. My recent readings on leadership, especially regarding these STAMP concepts, have led me to a crucial realization. At HARDAWAY, we are averse to bad news. We sidestep it like the plague—investing countless hours preparing for a VP visit, combing through our data to uncover a single highlight of good news while expending double the effort to mask the bad news. This behavior stops now! We need to address the existing elements within our culture that promote—and even encourage—this toxic practice. As the leader, I must take full responsibility for this. The buck stops with me!

Team, I am making it clear: I have changed," Chad asserts. "We will not live like this any longer; I mean it! We will no longer look down on those who bring bad news; it is not bad news; it is the reality we face. It reflects our current state. Our metrics are underperforming—it is undeniable. We will confront this head-on and formulate a solid improvement plan...understood?

For far too long, we have emphasized the positives while downplaying the negatives. This distorted view may yield short-term benefits for individual promotions, especially if trends appear positive, but it can be detrimental to our long-term success as a company. Additionally, pressure from Wall Street to deliver quarterly results has only exacerbated this issue. We must change our approach now, no more myopia!

In my reading, I have identified key competencies among companies that consistently outperform Wall Street, such as Toyota, and it is essential to share how we can adopt this mindset. It is time we recognized the importance of our perspective on human nature. While avoiding pain may feel natural, it can lead to more significant issues. Pain, in a physical context, serves as a crucial alert wake-up call that demands attention. It signals that something is wrong and requires immediate action.

In the business world, ignoring what we perceive as painful in the short term only sets us up for greater long-term harm. We often operate contrary to what we should be doing.

Consider our manufacturing efforts: More often than not, operations are struggling, yet we do not admit this when 'heavy breathers' like me come to assess the situation. Instead, we put our best foot forward at every plant visit and hope no one asks about the troublesome data. This needs to change. By embracing transparency and honesty, we can leverage our workforce's creative insights to find real solutions. We must flip the script. Rather than hiding the bad news and presenting only the positive, we should confront reality when things are not going well and empower everyone to contribute to the solution. I urge all of us to adopt this approach. We must commit to supporting one another. Who is with me?

At HARDAWAY, when a manager declares, 'I support it!' it often translates to, 'Absolutely, I will cover the costs, but do not bother me with the details; it is your responsibility.' Moving forward, I expect my managers to take the initiative regarding support actively. This means implementing practices themselves and teaching the fundamentals through hands-on leadership.

Leadership is about providing clear direction and instilling a sense of belonging in a broader mission. Support is vital, as it acknowledges the power of 'followership.' It demands a focus on individual member issues and underscores the commitment a leader must demonstrate to secure loyalty.

True leaders do not restrict themselves to a single style; they adapt and remain flexible, which is essential for today's complexity.

Here are concrete ways to initiate support within your department—these are critical aspects of leadership that should not be overlooked:

- Reinforce loyalty among your new employees by consistently guiding them with visible examples. Authentic leaders are not hidden in offices. As employees grow more skilled and managers build confidence in their abilities, it is crucial to step back and let them thrive while focusing on other priorities. This strategy will be elaborated on in the Dynamic Interdependence section tomorrow.

- Identify and cultivate individuals with the potential to succeed and commit to their long-term growth.

-Avoid adopting a dictatorial style. Authority will always be apparent, but the approach you take is crucial. There are times when firmness is necessary, but it should not define your leadership style. Embrace soft skills to achieve results with your team, but remember that being firm when the situation demands is also vital.

Master the L-E-A-D-S continuum; it will sharpen your focus and adaptability. The overhead will highlight this shortly."

Chad asserts, "One of the core tenets of 'initiate' is teaching the fundamentals. In today's competitive business environment, a manager must communicate with clarity, precision, and simplicity—going beyond mere facts and figures to provide valuable instructional content and effective on-the-fly modeling.

Moreover, the ability to transfer knowledge to fellow managers is non-negotiable. If a CEO's yearly objectives do not prioritize 'teaching the management team', early retirement may be the best choice. We have moved past the era of the Lone Ranger and Tonto. That was a boomer joke, I guess?

A STAMP of Approval leader cannot rely solely on their personality. It is essential to utilize a diverse range of approaches rather than sticking to what feels comfortable, as I once did.

Leaders must understand themselves and strategically position their team members to foster a sense of belonging and a commitment to growth. Once your employees feel empowered in their roles, petty competition will fade. This shift will enhance group dynamics and drive superior company performance and efficiency.

In addition, when employees receive support that resonates with their social needs, they become more willing to follow. Let us revisit the crucial topic of followership. Managers must tune in to their employees' perspectives—specifically, what they need to 1) know, 2) feel comfortable about, and 3) remain loyal to the company or cause. Conducting assessments and anonymous surveys can be invaluable in this regard, demonstrating that their voices truly matter."

"Speaking of assessments," Chad transitions, "what about our multitude of performance metrics?"

"They are quite confusing to me," a voice calls out from the audience.

"Me too," Chad responds, nodding in agreement. "Having spent years in the tooling field, I find our metrics overly complex. The truth is, I am realizing that we only need to focus on four essential areas at the enterprise level: our internal customers (employees), external customers (consumers), the bottom line (profits), and quality—whether it pertains to our products or services.

Before we delve into the five modes of leadership, let me make one final point: any wise manager understands that an idea or policy is far more likely to thrive when it garners unwavering support from the lowest levels of management. Why is this? As we ascend the corporate ladder, we often lose touch with the realities our teams face on the ground. Upper-level managers must engage with their supervisors and frontline workers, as they hold the key to either the success or failure of any new initiative.

This brings us to the L-E-A-D-S acronym, which encapsulates the modes of progressive management intervention we like to call situational agility. Here, sensitive, adaptable, and perceptive managers transition into the role of hands-off leaders, empowering their teams to flourish.

The Leader mode stands as the most directive approach, gradually moving toward less direct involvement, culminating in the Screener role—whose primary mission is to clear away obstacles. When managers adopt flexible leadership—offering support precisely where and when it is needed—they can position employees in roles that truly highlight their unique gifts, talents, strengths, and areas for growth. I prefer the term 'areas of opportunity' over 'weaknesses' to emphasize potential rather than limitations.

Moreover, managers should cultivate the anticipation of support, signaling the readiness for a timely and appropriate response. This expectation embodies confidence that action will follow. The degree of employee compliance or endorsement serves as a powerful litmus test for authentic leadership."

Chad then concludes. "Now Director Lane will delve into the definitions of the support phase for clarity, along with a concise statement that encapsulates the essence of each stage, Rob?"

As Rob Lane steps to the front of the room, he begins, "Thank you, Chad. I have been reflecting on this evolution in thought—this exciting paradigm shift—and it inevitably draws my thoughts to the sweeping changes in business at the turn of the last century. I am not referring to the Y2K phenomenon we faced a few decades back; I mean the drastic transformations that occurred over a hundred years ago, just before the inception of TLC. Did you know that only a few carriage makers successfully transformed into the automobile supply business, while the rest faded into obscurity?

I do not wish to sound alarmist, but I genuinely worry that we could find ourselves in a similar predicament if we neglect to adopt this flexible approach to leadership. What are your thoughts?"

A member of the audience answers, "Isn't leadership style almost a matter of default? Does personality not play a significant role, often dictating our management approach?"

"It has," Rob answers, "and continues to in many cases at TLC. Chad and I are saying it does not have to. That is a good question. Let us examine the specifics of nimble leadership/situational agility. There are five modes; please see the screen."

--The **L**eader
Webster: **One who holds first place in rank or position.**
Practical Definition: One who commands policy, attention, and respect with minimal rationale for direction.
Statement: *"Do as I say!"*

--The **E**ducator
Webster: **One who plans the learning process.**
Practical Definition: One who directs, accompanied by a brief rationale.

Statement: *"Still do as I say, but here is why."*

--The **A**dministrator
Webster: **One who serves, ministers, furnishes, or supplies.**
Practical Definition: One who helps those who help themselves.
Statement: *"What do you need?"*

--The **D**elegator
Webster: **One who assigns power or function to another.**
Practical Definition: One who allows others freedom (within boundaries).
Statement: *"You are on your own for now… I will check back later."*

--The **S**creener
Webster: **One who sifts unwanted material from the wanted.**
Practical Definition: One who removes obstacles.
Statement: *"What is in your way?"*

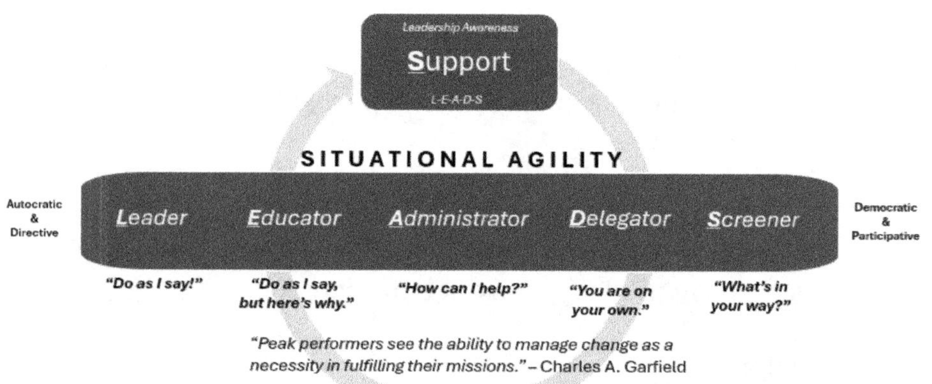

"We believe that this type of flexibility is what our organizations need, especially in developing our policy deployment: the strategic planning around yearly business objectives. This next slide shows how the L-E-A-D-S continuum lays a pattern for intervening along the planning and execution process.

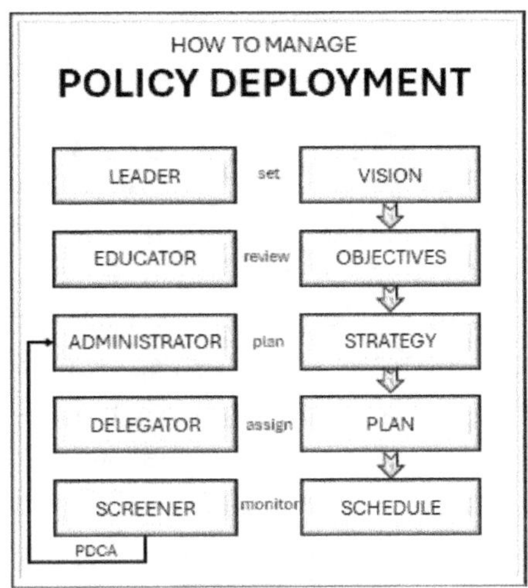

Isn't that a captivating slide? Now, let me invite you to reconsider the conventional wisdom around leadership for a moment. How often have we heard the adage, 'You manage things, and you lead people'? While I appreciate the essence of that statement, I caution against the notion that 'management' is somehow inferior or less noble than leadership. *At its extremes, a lack of management can turn leadership into tyranny, while a leadership vacuum can give rise to stifling bureaucracy.* It is a healthy culture of business that truly reflects this balance.

In the real world, a leader cannot inspire and guide without the essential art of management. For those among us who cherish the lessons of the Old Testament, think back to the figure of Moses. Picture Charlton Heston in *The Ten Commandments* [Film] - he was a remarkable leader who faced overwhelming challenges after leading the Israelites out of Egypt. Exhausted and burdened by the never-ending demands of thousands, Moses found himself on the brink of burnout. What did he do? He cleverly managed the situation by appointing 10 regional leaders to share the burden, ensuring the needs of the people were addressed efficiently. This initiative showcased his exceptional leadership skills, delegating tasks made the demands manageable and sustainable. It is not a choice between one or the other; it is about finding the perfect harmony with both."

"In closing," Rob beautifully sums up, "let us return to the concept of support that Chad elaborated upon earlier. The true essence of leadership lies in the ability to support others, which forms the backbone of an adaptable and effective leadership style. However, it is essential to recognize that this support is not always soft or gentle. Consider, for example, a vigilant teenager working as a theater attendant during a fire. His responsibility is to guide the moviegoers toward safety. While his tone may come across as stern in less dire circumstances, it is actually the most compassionate action he can take to ensure everyone's well-being. Indeed, support can sometimes wear the disguise of a sheep in wolves' clothing."

"Nice overview, Rob and Chad," concludes Molly. "Well, is anyone hungry? Which way do we go for lunch?"

"Just out this side door," answers Rob, "and straight across the field to the brown building. It is our cafeteria."

"Okay, folks, go ahead and fill out your session notes and review the support case study," Chad closes. "Enjoy your lunch. We will work later. I know the spruce-up crew did not finish the landscaping at the kids' playground. However, for now, let us eat!"

Review Notes—Section: ***Support***

The missing link in leadership is support. It is not a soft or touchy-feely approach to team building. The STAMP business process template emphasizes that support is essential to creating an environment where employees or groups are more likely to perform at an excellent level. This support must be flexible and depend on the leader's assessment of the group's level of autonomy. It can be autocratic and directive or trusting and subjective. A true leader understands when to be directive and when to allow more self-rule.

The five modes of progressive management intervention (situational agility) align with the L-E-A-D-S continuum:

1. Leader
2. Educator
3. Administrator
4. Delegator
5. Screener

In moments of crisis or when all opinions have been expressed without resolution, a manager ultimately has to make the decision; in essence, they must lead! Sometimes a manager recognizes that a brief rationale is appropriate. In the Educator mode, the manager understands the benefit of sharing the justification for a decision.

As the manager transitions to the Administrator mode, they have observed instances of self-directed autonomy within their department. This is the time for "ministering" or assisting the group as needed. I have noticed that as the manager works through these modes, control diminishes, and self-reliance is encouraged.

If a manager performs their role effectively, the natural outcome will be greater ownership among team members, allowing for a Delegator approach. The ultimate goal for departmental self-sufficiency is achieved in the Screener mode. This is where distractions are eliminated, enhancing solo leading. This sequence defines leadership *and is the first step to organizational **success**. Let us see about this leadership case study. I wonder if it really helped.*

1:00-2:00 Outside Activities

*Organizational **alignment** has become critical to achieving world-class performance. It is difficult, if not impossible, without a common language and communication system.*

-Chris Hart

2:00-3:00 Teamwork, Bob Jiminez

"Typically, most workshops I attend do not incorporate physical exercises," Bob quips with a smile. "It is a breath of fresh air to be part of one that stimulates not just the mind and body but also touches the heart. I truly appreciate the energy and effort you all brought to the last hour. Now, what better topic to dive into next than Teamwork, the next vital phase in the S-T-A-M-P? Your role will be to facilitate this, making it a breeze to encourage collaboration and granting everyone the freedom to shine.

Here are a few suggestions to consider:

- Training should be grounded in real-world examples and business situations (application), not just formal classroom education (content). The effectiveness of mere cognitive dumping is limited.
- Foster communication that transcends physical barriers and addresses the more subtle ones as well.
- Ensure accurate assessments for employee placement. Like professional sports teams that meticulously scout their

players, organizations should have a clear vision of what they seek in a candidate. Set clear expectations before embarking on the search and establish solid selection criteria.
- Lastly, embrace the progressive 'Human' Resource continuum using the T-R-A-I-N Model, which we will explore shortly.

Managers need to embrace the value of teamwork wholeheartedly and appreciate its true significance. For employees to genuinely feel like integral members of a company, managers must adopt an objective perspective, setting aside personal biases.

To illustrate this point, let us consider the scenario of a difficult employee—one who may annoy his supervisor but is nonetheless highly skilled and capable. This individual understands his job and executes it proficiently. In such cases, it is far more cost-effective for the supervisor to address any personal frustrations than to undertake the lengthy, often painful process of termination and retraining. The time invested in finding and training a new team member can be substantial, not to mention the potential legal expenses tied to hasty disciplinary actions.

Thus, the supervisor should recognize this employee's contribution to the larger picture and seek ways to channel their energy more constructively. Here are some impactful strategies to foster a spirit of teamwork:

- Begin with an organizational chart that outlines each employee's role during orientation, providing clarity from the outset.
- Engage in ongoing, iterative one-on-one conversations with employees to discuss their responsibilities and how they fit into the broader mission of the organization.
- Schedule regular meetings focused on role clarification and definition—both formal and informal. Feedback provides insight and shows support."

"By offering support alongside appropriate training and placement—what I like to call Progressive Human Resources—we can cultivate a highly competent workforce. This method is not only developmental and educational but also aligns with key theories of adult learning. It emphasizes not just cognitive understanding and knowledge acquisition but also the importance of practical, hands-on learning, effectively bridging the two for a cohesive knowledge transfer approach.

Let us embark on a transformative journey that begins with the intake phase—an engaging, information-based orientation known as the Tell/Teach mode. From there, we transition to dynamic 'On-The-Job' Review training, where we not only clarify initial expectations and responsibilities but also provide tailored assistance with essential job skills. Our seasoned staff play a crucial role, engaging in the process through thoughtful delegation and assignment. The culmination of this journey is the advancement training phase, where exceptional employees and their projects are nominated for promising promotions.

This cyclical approach fosters a genuine spirit of teamwork, as every individual contributes their unique strengths to propel the company forward. We refer to this ongoing method as the organization's 'training wheels.' In the early stages, it offers the necessary stability, gradually empowering our team to take calculated risks and embrace new challenges. To ride on their own, so to speak.

As each employee rises to new heights or transitions into different roles, this process rekindles, guiding them from a place of initial learning to one of high performance.

For our leaders, remember this invaluable lesson: you cannot teach what you have not mastered, nor can you lead others where you have not traveled yourself. A true vision fuels the organization's momentum on these training wheels, continually encouraging advancement while keeping a watchful eye on both speed and direction. If a leader ventures too far ahead, they risk becoming out of sight, leaving the team disoriented. It is vital to appreciate that progress unfolds at its own pace. We can cultivate a highly competent workforce by offering support alongside appropriate training and placement in these progressive human resources. The connections are detailed here."

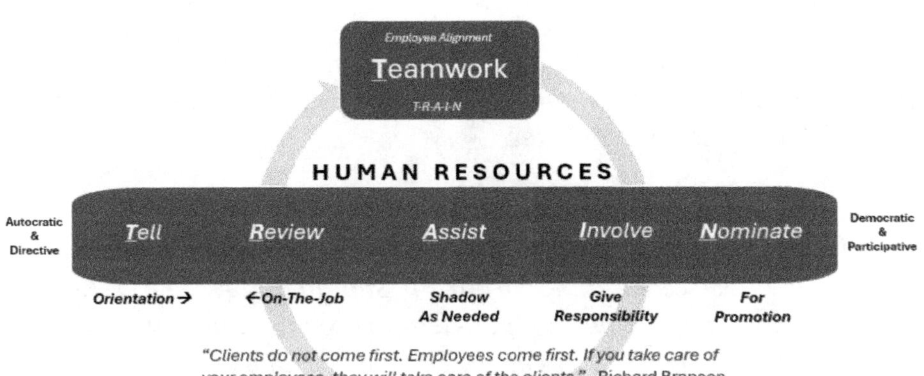

"Now, let us take the next ten minutes to craft our summary notes and review our case study," Bob concludes, "before we dive into our next session."

Review Notes---Section: *<u>Teamwork</u>*

I believe it would be naïve to think disagreements are always bad. People can be stretched to greater heights if challenged by a co-worker. I suppose the issue lies in where the energy is directed — to selfishness or to the mission's betterment.

However, Bob did make a good point—ineffective training and/or improper placement of our workforce lead to non-value-added, wasteful activities and policies.

Training, as well, should not be limited to the classroom. Actual training only begins with content, but it will be long forgotten if left there. An effective training program should follow the T-R-A-I-N Model, where departmental policies, protocols, and purposes are clearly outlined. This is the <u>Teach</u>/Tell aspect. Once delineated to the worker, that information needs to be <u>Reviewed on the Job</u> from time to time to ensure internalization. Progressing from heavy to less and less as the worker learns new responsibilities, as confidence and competence are fostered. Once a worker is comfortable with their standard duties, it is the manager's responsibility to <u>Assist</u> them in times of need. If a worker has been given the tools they need to perform, a wise manager will look for opportunities to <u>Involve</u> them in special projects that will bring out their best. A company can then <u>Nominate</u> this proficient worker and their projects for promotion, continually leveraging their abilities while stretching them to new heights.

This process is initiated each time a new worker is hired and applies whenever they are transferred to a new department or promoted to a new position. This developmental sequence considers the worker's comfort level with the new responsibilities, thus rotating from 'teaching' to 'nominating.' HR does not need to be so complicated.

I see how this fits into Bob's 'Big MO' talk. Leadership is the foundation. If the workers and the system are placed appropriately,

Alignment *is created. Has this worked in the real world? Let us take a look at the worker-health case study.*

Background: Several companies were studied to reduce cardiovascular risk factors in alignment with CDC standards. Financial considerations drove the study.

Intervention: Comprehensive Human Resource education, assessment, behavioral indexes and tracking were deployed, along with targeted health Programming focused on long-term health claims reduction.

Results: CVD risk reductions, $1.224.00 saved per employee, and return-on-investment resulted in nearly $5.00 per $1.00 spent. A double victory: Increased employee health for longevity and returns for reinvestment.

Boyce, I., DeVoe, J., Norsen, L., Smith, J. A., Anson, E., McGregor, H. A., & Singh, R. (2024). The Financial Impact of an Employee Wellness Program Focused on Cardiovascular Disease Risk Reduction. Healthcare, 12(23), 2358–2358. https://doi.org/10.3390/healthcare12232358

(Boyce et al., 2024).

*A **<u>concerted effort</u>** is applied when each employee performs a set of interrelated daily activities consistent with the good of the company.*

\- T. Wiles Fowler

"Next, we will look at our Aptitude," transitions Bob. "The facilitator will be my counterpart at TLC, Pete O'Neil. Let us welcome him... Pete."

3:00-4:00 Aptitude, Pete O'Neil

"Thank you," Pete begins with a warm smile, "Good afternoon, everyone. This is today's last session.

Effective leadership inspires individuals to engage fully; when they feel included and clearly understand their roles and how they contribute to the organization, their aptitude—essentially their willingness and ability to learn—flourishes.

Let us explore the concept of aptitude further. It represents a key aspect of one's ability to excel across various types of work and demonstrates proficiency. What we often refer to as 'talent' or 'skill' stems from this internalized aptitude. It is an innate capacity to perform specific activities that can be cultivated or left untapped. Importantly, aptitude is distinct from skills gained solely through learning; ability is a blend of both aptitude and the skills developed over time.

Allow me to step onto my soapbox for a moment. I firmly believe that the term 'aptitude' does not receive the recognition it deserves these days. We frequently hear discussions focused on attitude, but seldom on aptitude. Yes, nurturing a positive attitude among employees is vital, but let us be real - feelings alone will not drive profitability. In contrast, enhancing aptitude does lead to tangible benefits for many companies across the earth.

So, what is the pivotal role of managers in relation to aptitude? We argue that they must commit to continuously evaluating their employees' potential. This entails a conscientious effort to 'carefully assess the value of' each team member and recognize the unique contributions they can bring. Succession planning does not happen by accident.

Two-way performance updates are vital for fostering a thriving workplace. Partial appraisals (feedback) can be conducted quarterly to ensure that objectives are not only set but also clearly defined, such as 'aiming for an ambitious two percent increase in sales.' Furthermore, it is equally important to evaluate the more nuanced qualities of employees, such as interpersonal sensitivity and business social acumen.

Managers play a crucial role in highlighting their employees' strengths—defined as the ability to elevate their work and imbue it with meaning. Empathetic managers can skillfully identify and nurture their employees' unique talents and opportunities, highlighting individuals who can meet essential organizational needs. For a manufacturing example, an outgoing and articulate production line worker, well-versed in the intricacies of both the product and customer needs, would be ideally suited to lead monthly tours for vendors and the public.

This approach is part of Talent Development (Progressive Individual Achievement), a concept we will explore in greater depth later in this session. When employees feel comfortable and valued within the organization, their potential for growth and learning—what we refer to as Aptitude—thrives. This enhancement unfolds through five distinct modes, captured by the acronym W-O-R-K-S.

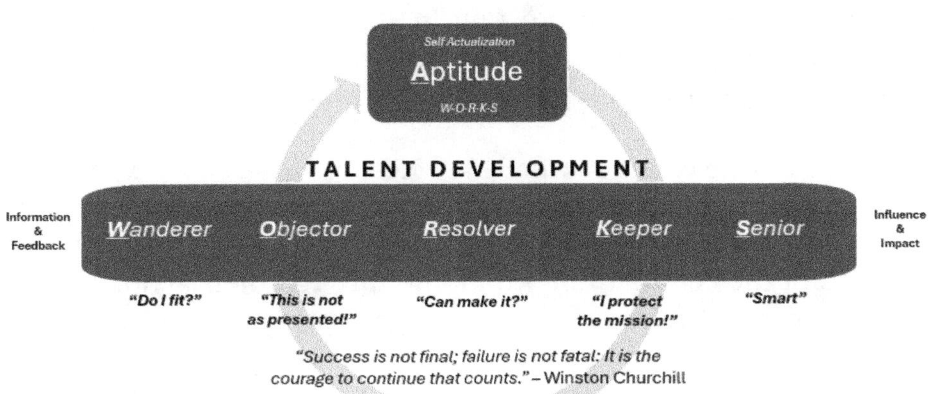

Now, envision a new employee stepping into your organization. At first, they may feel disoriented, wandering through their new environment and searching for their place in the bigger picture. However, within three to six months, many come to realize that the realities of work often diverge sharply from the idealized vision presented during their orientation. This inflection is critical; it can make all the difference in shaping whether an employee will survive or falter in their role.

Nearly all of us experience moments of dissatisfaction in the workplace, often feeling the pull to seek greener pastures. However, by engaging with those who share these concerns—whom we refer to as Objectors—you can guide them toward becoming dedicated, steady contributors, known as Resolvers. They recognize that, while their workplace has flaws, they have consciously chosen to navigate these challenges and remain committed to their role. Dispositional flexibility is evidenced by being both a realist and an optimist simultaneously. This journey marks an important milestone in their professional development. Sadly, many companies allow their talent to plateau here, with employees merely going through the motions instead of pursuing meaningful advancement and/or contribution.

The next level of development is becoming a Keeper. Keepers serve as guardians or gatekeepers, embracing the organization as something worthy of protection. In this phase, the employee fully commits to supporting and championing the company's mission, with a strong sense of loyalty at the forefront.

After they have succeeded as Keepers for a significant duration, these trusted individuals ascend to the Senior stage. Seniors exemplify consistency and political savvy, demonstrating a tangible impact on the company's bottom line through their actions. They have mastered the art of strategic organization, skillfully avoided unnecessary conflicts, and optimized resources.

In our last slide, we humorously illustrate this progression. We drew inspiration from some colorful examples provided by our HR department," Pete quips, lightening the atmosphere.

"I genuinely hope you found this session insightful. We recognized that today there is a lot of information. We know that repetition and feedback are essential for fostering adult learning. I would love to hear your thoughts!" The group then processes the information in a lively discussion, capturing the pluses and deltas for the day.

"Good discussion, team!" Pete concludes, "I am looking forward to seeing everyone bright and early. Until then, stay safe and enjoy your evening. We are meeting at Smitty's, a local pub on Main Street downtown, at 5:30 PM – so finish up your notes and case study – and then feel free to join us for some good company."

Review Notes--Section: *Aptitude*

It is crucial to place individuals in roles that suit their strengths. I recall Ken Blanchard, co-author of The One Minute Manager, saying, "People who feel good about themselves produce good results!" Business improvements occur as employees progress through the modes of their Individual Achievement (Talent Development).

The W-O-R-K-S acronym is straightforward and meaningful:

Wanderer - Objector - Resolver - Keeper - Senior

*Individuals begin to understand their unique roles once "alignment" is achieved through effective leadership and appropriate placements. When this understanding is harnessed, it results in a **concerted effort**. This is when an industry's best practices can emerge. Today was productive, and I look forward to learning even more tomorrow. What a great real-world case study from Harvard, too!*

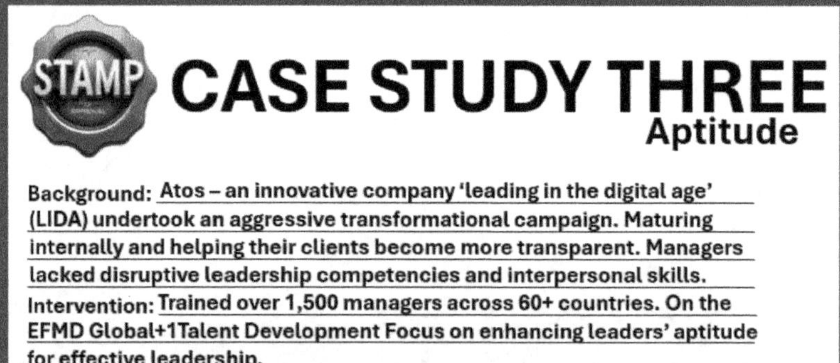

CASE STUDY THREE
Aptitude

Background: Atos – an innovative company 'leading in the digital age' (LIDA) undertook an aggressive transformational campaign. Maturing internally and helping their clients become more transparent. Managers lacked disruptive leadership competencies and interpersonal skills.

Intervention: Trained over 1,500 managers across 60+ countries. On the EFMD Global+1Talent Development Focus on enhancing leaders' aptitude for effective leadership.

Results: Seventy-five % reported making progress in becoming the leaders they want to be, and 94% of learners reported developing broader perspectives, increased confidence, and improved decision-making.

Developing Confident Leaders through Transformation at Atos. (2025, August 14). Harvard Business Impact. https://www.harvardbusiness.org/client-story/developing-confident-leaders-through-transformation-at-atos/ **(Atos, 2025).**

Sunday: 8:00-9:30 Full Breakfast & 5-Table Exercise

"Good morning, everyone," greets Molly Taylor. "I hope you enjoyed your breakfast. Once your caffeine kicks in, you will probably notice that the tables are arranged differently this morning. We have set the room up as an object lesson.

Each table represents part of the solution for every problem our two organizations may face. This approach was first developed in John Stuart Mill's System of Logic and later elaborated by Professor William Frankena* while at the University of Michigan in the field of education. We are going to expand it into the realm of business.

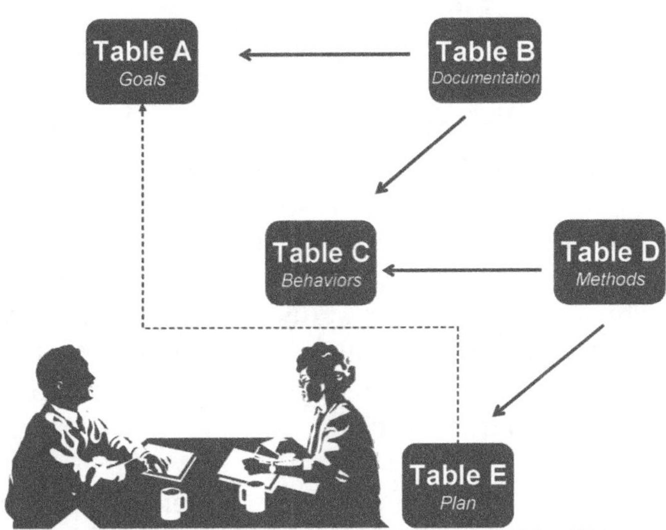

Frankena, William K. Philosophy of Education. New York: MacMillan Publishers, 1965

Without spilling a drop of coffee, take a moment to examine the bottom of your cup closely. There, you will discover a letter waiting for you—your options are A, B, C, D, or E."

"What if I cannot spell?" Chad quips, half-joking.

"I suppose TLC could find a place for you," Molly replies wistfully. "What do you think, Rob?"

"Could someone lend the boss a hand with his letter? Once that is done, I invite everyone to gather at the table corresponding to the letter on your cup. If you are not sipping a hot beverage this morning, please head to the serving area and pick up a cup. Afterward, sit at your designated table so we can dive in."

Here is how the room is laid out:

- Table A embodies the principles, purpose, and vision driving any endeavor.
- Table B provides the proof or premises behind that purpose.
- Table C outlines the resulting excellencies—characteristics or behaviors we aspire to exhibit.
- Table D details the methods to achieve those desired behaviors.
- And finally, Table E presents the action plan for putting everything into practice (praxis=applied theory).

Each table signifies a step in identifying, categorizing, and tackling the challenges we may encounter. We affectionately refer to this as our business philosophy. Philosophy, as you are aware, is a broad concept. It comprises four primary components. This may seem intricate, but I assure you, if you bear with me for a few moments, the point will become clear.

Let us take a moment to reflect. Yesterday, we explored the vital concepts of Support, Teamwork, and Aptitude, spotlighting each of you as individuals. Support encompasses the ways we give and receive assistance, while Teamwork concerns the resources you need for practical training and successful placement. Lastly, we delved into the environments that nurture and enhance your Aptitude.

Today, we are shifting our focus to a broader perspective as we embark on understanding a comprehensive business philosophy. What thoughts do you have when the term "business" comes to mind?"

One audience member chimes in, "Making money." Another responds, "Taking care of our clients."

"You both hit the nail on the head! It consists of four essential facets, which we will outline on the next slide."

A Philosophy of Business

1. The essential activity of making money.
2. The customer's perspective: "I want to do business with you."
3. The outcomes of effective practices: "He possesses sound business acumen."
4. The academic discipline dedicated to understanding business: "Do you hold a Master's of Business Administration or similar degree?"

"A vibrant business philosophy aims to examine all four facets to enhance quality and productivity, minimize costs, and uphold safety at all times."

"So, how can HARDAWAY and TLC embody this philosophy?" inquires a participant sitting at Table C.

"That is a great question," Molly replies, a smile spreading across her face. "And you are definitely at the right table."

"What do you mean, the right table?" they respond, curiosity piqued.

"Well, let us start with Table C," Molly suggests. "Why don't you read aloud what your card says, turn it over?"

The employee from Table C clears their throat and reads, "Table C is a list, with definitions, of Excellencies to be produced. However, what exactly are Excellencies?"

"They are simply a fancy term for behaviors," Molly explains. "So, to answer your original question, these behaviors are essential to reaching our goals. Now, speaking of goals, Table A, what does your card say?"

A member from Table A confidently responds, "Statement of basic ends or principles of ethics and social thought. Table A represents our mission statement, which outlines the core principles guiding our organization. That is why it occupies table A; it is our foundation, right?"

"Exactly!" Molly acknowledges enthusiastically.

Suddenly, a strong voice cuts through the chatter—it is Hal Jerra, a long-time TLC housekeeping supervisor. "We are Table B (and let me tell you) we are (get this) the 'Empirical and other premises about human nature, life, and the world!' This premise is crucial; it serves as proof, the documentation, the very rationale behind our goals. So, make way, Table A, for Emperor Hal!"

"Very amusing, your honor," Molly quips back with a laugh. "But you are spot on! Table B embodies our industry standard. HARDAWAY represents expertise in residential and industrial garden equipment. For TLC, it signifies the best practices in client care. Table B is the tried-and-true, time-tested path to excellence in everything we do!"

So," Molly asserts, "Table A clearly defines our goals, and Table B establishes our benchmarks. Together, they provide us with an essential list of characteristics and behaviors, which we will refer to as Table C, to drive our continuous improvement."

"What about those of us at Tables D and E?" a worker interjects.

"Go ahead," Molly insists. "Read your card from Table D."

"It states, Scientific knowledge about how to produce certain behaviors."

"What does that imply?" Molly challenges.

"I am not entirely sure, but we also have the word 'Methods' on our table. Could it mean that behaving in a certain way is similar to driving a car? In that case, the method would be... taking a driver's education course?"

"Excellent analogy," Molly affirms. "Now, let us hear from Table E."

"It describes concrete conclusions about what to do, when to do it, how to execute it, etc.," a Table E employee understands. "Ah, that is straightforward; our table outlines the action plan that connects the methods to the behaviors."

"Who would have expected this?" Molly acknowledges. "Some toolmakers and social workers are collaborating and engaging in meaningful sociological discussions."

"Molly, this all comes back to my number one rule," Chad interjects decisively. "All together now! *Kiss with an extra S*," everyone responds in unison.

"This is as straightforward as A, B, C," Chad asserts. "Molly, let us clarify this: Table A is our target, the goal we are striving for. Table B presents the evidence or data supporting this target. Table C illustrates the behaviors we need to adopt to achieve that target. Table D outlines the methods to encourage those behaviors. Finally,

Table E defines our agreed-upon approach to implementing these actions. Is that clear, Molly?"

"Could not have said it any better myself, Boss," she agrees. "And in addition, everyone, a line should be periodically drawn from Table E back to Table A. That is what we are doing right now, here, this weekend. Aren't we looking at our old action plan and calibrating a new standard?"

"That new standard," responds a participant, "is the S-T-A-M-P of Approval, right?"

"Excellent observation," Molly acknowledges. "We would like you to stay at your table for the day. In this way, you will meet some new people. I would like each area to begin listing some implications for your category over the next 20 minutes, and then each table will share these with the larger group. After, Director Lane will take us through the next phase before a fifteen-minute break at 9:30 AM."

"Sure will," prompts Rob, "looking forward to it."

9:30-9:45 Break

*The world is vast, and I will
not waste my life in friction
when it can be turned
into **momentum**!*

-Francis Willard

9:45-11:00 Morale, Rob Lane

"Good morning, everyone," Rob begins with an inviting smile. "As we discussed earlier, today is an opportunity for us to look beyond ourselves. We are part of a team, after all, right? While the players may feel restless, remember we stand united as one. Having spent seventeen years with TLC, I can confidently say we are more than ready to tackle any challenge that comes our way!

Chad has echoed a similar vision for HARDAWAY, and it is worth noting your impressive legacy of crafting exceptional tools. You are resilient artisans, turning out the finest instruments. With that said, let us dive into the matter at hand: Morale.

When workers find satisfaction in their roles, a wave of optimism begins to ripple across the team, enhancing morale among their peers—their G-R-O-U-P. This concept is known as Progressive Group Dynamics or the powerful force multiplier of interdependence. To connect back to Pete's insights from yesterday, remember this: A healthy attitude is rooted in a useful aptitude.

Just as individuals undergo developmental modes based on their aptitudes, groups of people do as well. A wise manager recognizes the profound influence—both shining and dimming—that a co-worker's actions and attitudes can impose on the entire team. This influence is powerful when it comes from a non-formal leader—someone without a formal title who commands respect from their peers. Their presence can significantly impact morale.

More importantly, it falls upon managers to exemplify positive morale. As cliché as it may sound, your attitude, shaped by your aptitude, ultimately determines your altitude. I know, I know—let us not dwell too long on these platitudes, laugh out loud ... but it is a valuable point to consider.

Great managers should also strive to direct morale—essentially acting as a guiding light. This is often accomplished by evaluating and nurturing the group's milieu—a psychological term referring to the climate shaped by the group's interconnected relationships. It is clear how each part contributes to, or detracts from, the success of the whole. They possess the insight to know precisely how and when to reposition individuals within their organization, ultimately crafting a more efficient and harmonious team. This transformative journey typically unfolds through five distinct modes.

"Proficient *teaming* often requires integrating perspectives from a range of disciplines, communicating despite the different mental models that accompany different areas of expertise, and being able to manage the inevitable conflicts that arise when people work together."
— **Amy C. Edmondson,**

The first phase, known as the Guarded phase, is characterized by a desire for safety. Individuals tread lightly, hesitant to take risks as they strive to carve out their roles within the group dynamic.

As frustration mounts and team members share their grievances, the team may transition into the Resignation phase. However, when these frustrations are validated and genuine, thoughtful changes are instituted, the group can rejuvenate and advance to the Operating phase. In this state, while the team performs their duties competently, their efforts—though sufficient—are yet to reach their full potential.

The next phase, though rare, is the illustrious Utilization phase. Here, a manager who embraces a Delegator style is confident in engaging their team in meaningful collaboration. This involvement not only elevates individual contributions but also maximizes the collective good for all.

Consider the world of sports: a shrewd coach recognizes and harnesses the unique strengths of each player. For example, in baseball, a speedy athlete with a powerful arm is far better suited to patrol the outfield than a shorter, stockier player who may excel as a catcher. By tapping into each player's bent and capabilities, the coach crafts a strategy that amplifies the team's overall performance.

The pinnacle of this journey is the Production phase, where each member's contributions culminate in heightened productivity, nurturing a vibrant and positive peer culture. In this phase, the team experiences a beautiful rhythm and coaction, a testament to the idea that none of us is as smart as all of us!"

"There are many ramifications to consider regarding selfish ambition and similar concepts," Rob concludes. "While there is nothing wrong with the desire to excel, it is unwise for an employee to believe that their accomplishments are solely the result of their own efforts. Ignoring other perspectives is shortsighted and, in reality, hinders one's own growth. It is said that former President Ronald Reagan had a saying on his desk: *'The secret of success is to be as excited about others' good ideas as you are about your own.'* This encapsulates the essence of the ladder Group Dynamic modes. Enjoy your lunch, and I will see you all at noon."

Review Notes--Section: <u>Morale</u>

I appreciate the simplicity of the G-R-O-U-P continuum. Our department is currently in the Resignation phase, following a recent transition through the Guarded phase, during which team members were apprehensive and reluctant to get involved. It feels like it is do-or-die time for our group now, as everyone seems quite discouraged.

If we can navigate through this phase and reach the Operation phase, where the team has resolved their petty differences, we will be able to perform our jobs effectively. Right now, I do not see much hope for progressing to the Utilization phase, where all members are placed according to their strengths. Wouldn't that be wonderful?

It is nice to dream about the Production phase, where team members are so interdependent that the whole is greater than the sum of its parts. I would love to be part of a group like that.

*I also think this is where **Momentum** comes into play. The result of an applied concerted effort through Dynamic Interdependence, or as Bob puts it, the Big MO! Does this work in the real world? It looks like it might. Who is Heidelberg, I wonder?*

Background: Heidelberg Materials (2025) struggled with silos, conflicting goals between asphalt and contracting. This misalignment hindered collaboration, caused friction, and limited business opportunities.

Intervention: Leadership launched a cross-organizational culture program that included workshops to surface the real challenges, added informal events (evening social activities) to build personal connections, realigned how performance was measured, and shifted metrics to shared KPIs that incentivized cooperation between the divisions.

Results: 14% increase in team engagement, accompanied by a stronger sense of unity. More productive collaboration. Financial impact: Heidelberg estimates that the collaboration improvements led to approximately $2 million in additional profit, resulting from fewer errors, more efficient scheduling, and better utilization of production capacity (Story, page 45).

INDUSTRY- LEADING CASE STUDIES 2024. (2024). https://businesscultureawards.com/wp-content/uploads/2024/12/case-studies-2024.pdf

11:00-12:00 Lunch

*The first law of **success**…is concentration, to bend all the energies to one point and to go directly to that point, looking neither to the right nor to the left.*

-William Mathews

An empowered organization is one in which individuals have the knowledge, skills, desire, and opportunity to succeed in ways that lead to collective organizational success.

\- Steven Covey

12:00-2:00 Performance, Bob Jiminez

"All right, everyone," begins Bob with enthusiasm. "We have reached the final phase—the powerful combination of Support, Teamwork, Aptitude, and Morale. This culmination is Performance, the driving force behind organizational success.

When I speak of performance, I am referencing several vital elements: Attaining continuous improvement, exceptional client care, enhanced quality, boosted productivity, reduced costs, and heightened efficiencies.

After all, what is our purpose in business? Regardless of our niche, we focus on people and value, and we strive to elevate the bottom line. It is our satisfied customers who guide our decisions, and sound choices that shape our processes. Ultimately - hopefully - these processes empower our dedicated, quality-driven workers in their daily practices.

A manager's role is to continually ignite a spark within their employees—to 'spur on or excite for action.'

They must also pursue perfection—to 'bring to completion or finish.'

The five intervention modes for Continuous Improvement are designed to stimulate and refine the services we provide for both employees and customers alike. The ultimate goal of any business is to craft a remarkable product, market it effectively, and drive sales. This last phase in the S-T-A-M-P Template will serve as your roadmap to achieving these outcomes. A *check*list, so to speak.

Our next slide unveils five essential principles that, when applied with unwavering discipline, have the power to elevate any company's quality program and enhance all performance improvement initiatives. Think of Six Sigma's Statistical Process Control as the skeleton of a business and Information Technology as its digital nervous system - then envision the S-T-A-M-P template as a powerful stair-master, living workout for your organizational framework! It is the application for our goals. i.e., where the rubber meets the road.

These five human interventions are meant to supplement a good quality program, not replace it. Researchers tell us that employees need to feel a sense of security and significance from an employer before they show loyalty. The C-H-E-C-K Model can enhance this relationship."

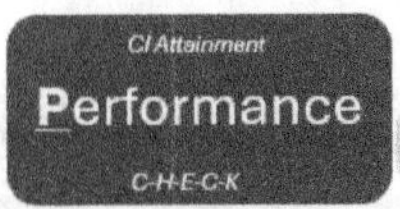

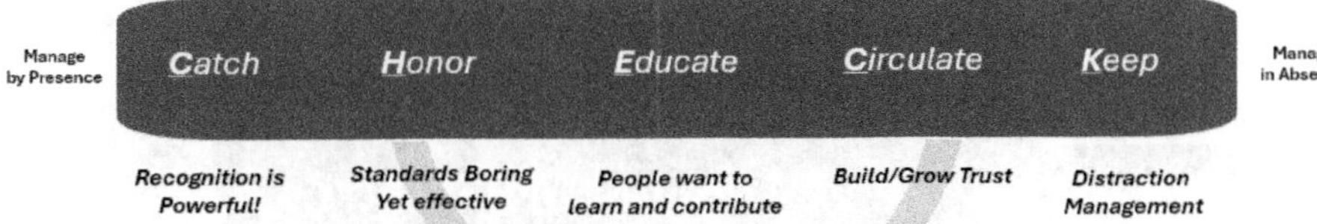

"Furthermore, now, Molly, please take everyone through the overview slides," Bob instructs. "This will clearly connect all the elements."

"Absolutely, Bob," Molly confidently responds. "I will provide an overview of how each previous level connects to the next.

We have already established the left-to-right progression, and now you will see the important vertical connections as well. The next six slides will effectively illustrate this progression in both dimensions.

The best way to stimulate your people to perform is by..."

_Catching...__employees doing things right!_

Regretfully, in most organizations, managers spend their time catching employees doing things *wrong*. Of course, directives for misguided behavior are sometimes necessary. However, due to mismanagement, the pervasive tone in many organizations is one of putting out their so-called 'subordinates' fires. I never liked the term 'subordinate.' It is very dehumanizing. Please see the slide...

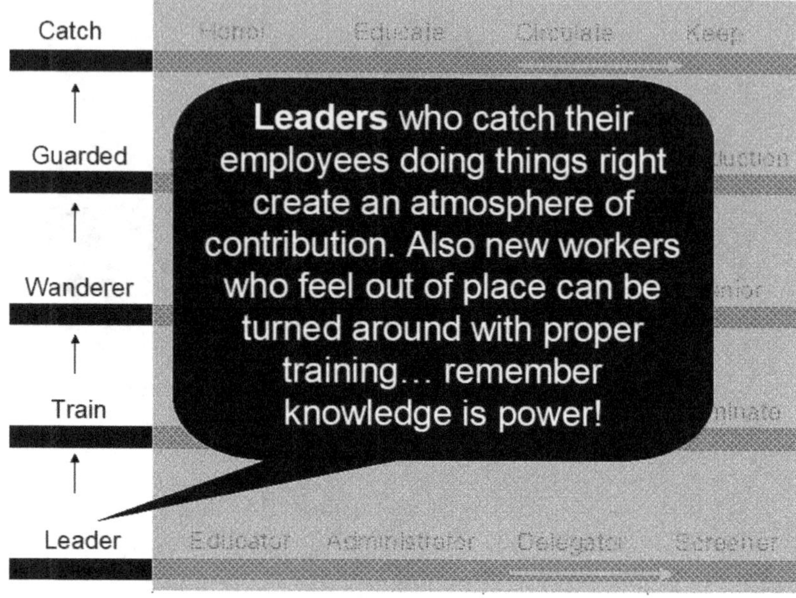

_Honoring__...standards and ideas!_

"The secret of standards lies in the foundation they lay for empowerment. If it cannot be measured, it cannot be improved. Honoring standards is more than understanding them—it is requiring their application with a sense of urgency. No exceptions! The standard is the initial measuring point. If the team can come up with a better idea, backed by data, a new standard is created."

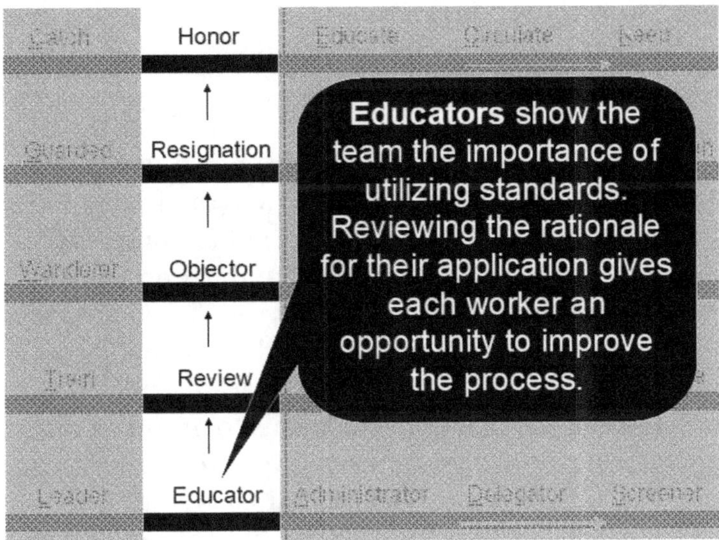

"Let me reiterate," Molly begins, her tone firm yet inviting. "Words and phrases like 'Empowerment!' 'Continuous Improvement!' 'Joint Effort!' 'You have a say!' and 'We want your ideas!' may sound inspiring, but they lack substance when treated as mere slogans.

"Companies that embrace this rhetoric while neglecting to establish standards as the backbone of their operations do a disservice to their employees. They create the illusion that small ideas can bring about significant change, all the while knowing that management will adopt only those that align with their existing agenda. I realize this may sound blunt, so allow me to elaborate.

"A standard is not just a guideline; it is a documented, universally accepted framework for performing tasks. In a manufacturing environment, for instance, the sequence and handling of assembled parts, the safe operation of machinery, and the precise placement of materials must be meticulously outlined and mutually agreed upon by both operators and management.

"By capturing these details for delivering a high-quality product in a safe, efficient workstation, team members are empowered to analyze metrics that gauge the reliability and repeatability of the process. This clarity opens doors to a wealth of opportunities for meaningful improvements.

"If you have a consistent measurement system, you can accurately assess 'where you are' and engage the team in identifying 'where you want to be.' If the process is not documented or leadership chooses to allow (or ignore) off-standard practices, it creates ambiguity and undermines metric integrity. This is not just a minor issue; I have observed that companies that allow deviations from documented standards are likely to tolerate similar slippage in other critical areas, including finance. This tolerance can lead to manipulating numbers merely to survive a quarterly review and, as we have seen in recent media reports, to catastrophic failures in profit and accounting reporting. This jeopardizes the retirement portfolios of dedicated employees and erodes community trust."

"I do not want to sugarcoat this," Molly asserts. "The lack of diligence around standards is a key reason many employees perceive that their employers only pay lip service to value their input. They have witnessed 'programs' come and go. They often fall into a relentless cycle of hope and disappointment, believing management is serious this time, only to see leadership fail to uphold the agreed approach. This breeds confusion and frustration among workers. In this chaos, improvements become, at best, fleeting and coincidental and, at worst, manipulated. We must honor our standards if we are to respect our people and their valuable ideas genuinely."

"Team, I recognize I have emphasized the importance of standards repeatedly, but I have a compelling object lesson to drive this point home. I need three volunteers to come up front—a woman and two big guys, please."

As the three volunteers step forward, Molly asks, "All right. What is your name, and what do you do?"

"Marci Collins," she replies. "I am a Child Care Supervisor for TLC."

"Excellent. Please stand over here while we learn about your partners, men?"

"I am Kalib Neen," he responds. "I am a physical therapist."

"Good. And you, sir?"

"You know me...I am Keith Milner, a skilled trades representative for HARDAWAY's manufacturing team."

"Of course. Now, men, I need you to grab one of Marci's feet and lift her carefully, so she stands approximately two feet taller than normal."

"Marci, hold on to the guys' shoulders to steady yourself."

Molly turns to the men and asks assertively, "Was that difficult at all?"

"Not at all!" Keith jokes. "We are studs...we can handle it!"

Molly then faces the audience and declares, "Starting any new program is just as straightforward, wouldn't you agree? A little balancing and some initial energy, and voilà...a program is launched!"

She turns back to the men, emphasizing, "I know you are both strong, but can you hold her up there for the next two hours? How manageable would that be? What about two years? Or even two days?"

"Well, we could probably manage it for a couple of hours," Kalib responds, "but I know it would get quite difficult eventually."

"Someone from the audience, please bring a chair up here!" Molly requests firmly. "Men, place Marci on the chair and spot her as she stands. Can you handle that?" Molly jokes as the female participant poses confidently.

"In this exercise, height symbolizes better quality, enhanced safety, higher profits, and more. Just as the chair firmly supports Marci while the men monitor her stance, a strong foundation of standards, paired with unwavering management support (akin to spotting), is essential for our two companies to excel. If our workforce relies on a weak foundation, just as Marci would if she depended on the two men to uphold her morale and innovative ideas, they will inevitably collapse. Ideas can only thrive and be sustained on a robust foundation of standards. This clearly illustrates why we sometimes experience dissatisfaction among our workers."

"As a crucial final thought, in an environment that prioritizes standards, floor-level employees are motivated to share their ideas because they trust management to enforce accountability in implementing these ideas. Employees need confidence that management will be decisive about the standards while also encouraging participation in the improvement process."

"We are committed to educating for advancement!"

Employees who have demonstrated their dedication and possess a voice within their departments must be allowed to showcase their capabilities. The next critical step in boosting productivity is to provide training on the latest technology, equipping them with the tools they need to contribute to the company's vision. Refer to the slide for more details."

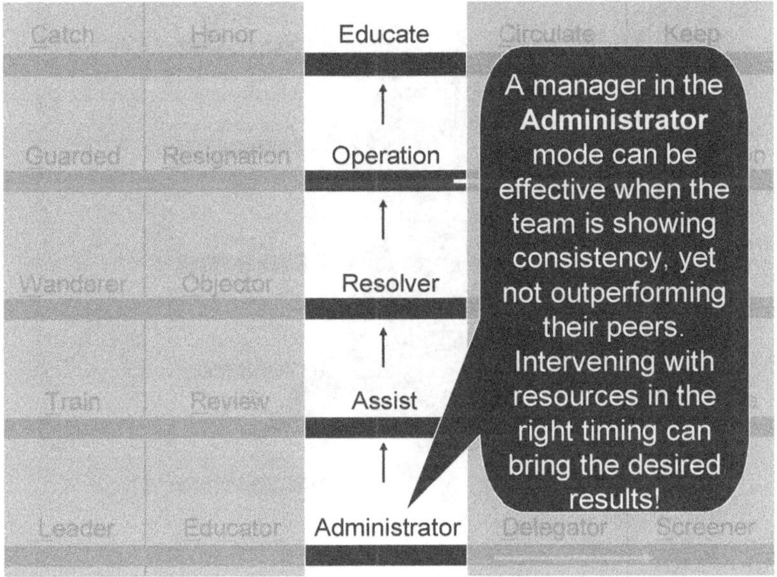

<u>C</u>irculating...*influence!*

"As a trained worker shows confidence in one area, they can be cross-trained in others. In this way, they will become more valuable/versatile. More often than not, an employee needs responsibilities to be responsible. A stretched winner can become a CEO! See the slide."

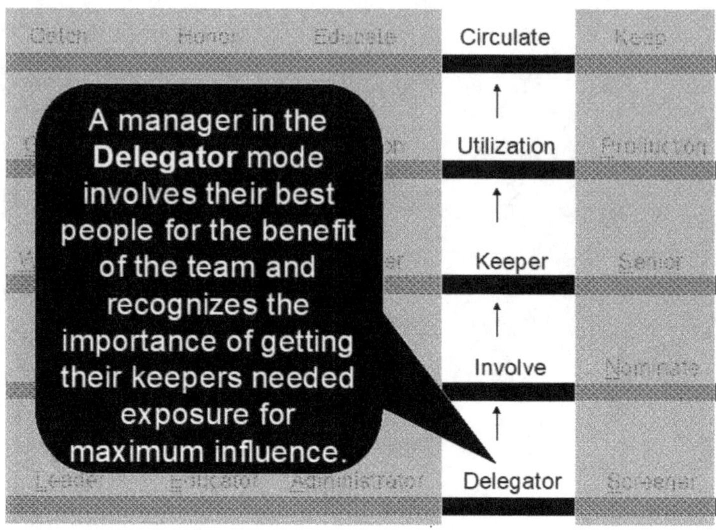

"And lastly…"

<u>K</u>eeping…*distractions to a minimum!*

"Remember, if everything is a priority, then nothing is. In an empowered environment, an effective leader removes obstacles that stifle or distract the group's ability to run the business. A competent manager can buffer unwanted roadblocks and ensure their team is working on the right things. Please see this next slide."

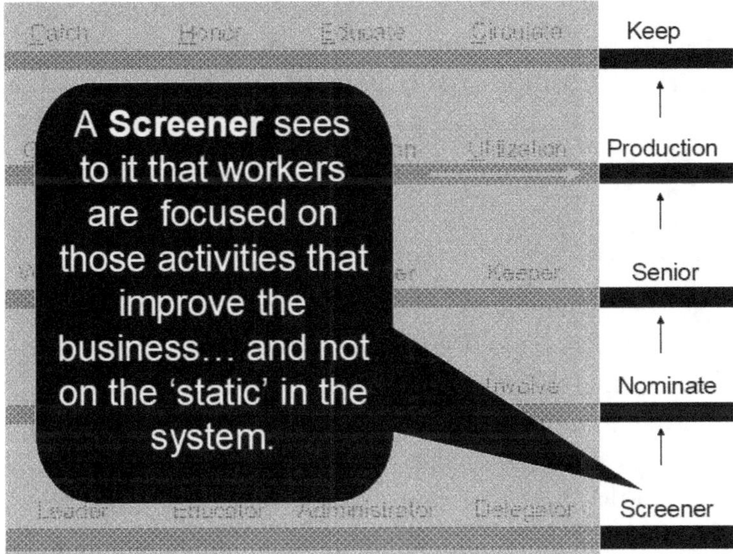

"We now have a few moments before we break," Molly announces with a warm smile. "So why don't we take this time to finalize your review notes? Any burning questions?"

"Yes, I have one," an audience member interjects. "Isn't that standard discussion unrealistic? What does this really mean for our day-to-day operations? How are we supposed to enforce this?"

"Make no mistake about it," Chad replies as he steps forward, exuding confidence. "Implementing standards requires dedication! While it may seem more convenient—at least, in the short term—to let various divisions and their management operate freely, the reality is that standards demand accountability from the very beginning along with ongoing, real-time monitoring."

"Let us consider the manufacturing landscape: Mass versus Lean. At first glance, mass production is often characterized by high inventory levels and a more authoritarian management style. Conversely, Lean typically indicates lower inventory levels. However, contrary to the common American interpretation of Japanese business philosophy, Lean does not invariably lead to participative leadership. While soliciting ideas, garnering support, and promoting continuous improvement are indeed the cornerstones of lean manufacturing, accomplished lean managers often adopt a more authoritarian approach when it comes to enforcing standards."

"The mindset is straightforward: you will adhere to the standard. Your colleagues will adhere to the standard. There will be no exceptions. Nonetheless, we will create a regular platform for you to discuss these practices. If a team member can persuade others that a new idea holds promise, we will initiate a trial period. This trial will be clearly defined, with set start and end dates and specific tracking metrics agreed upon in advance. Those involved in the trial will document their vision with the end goal in mind—an insight for success. Periodic check-ins from fellow team members will ensure we monitor our progress along the way."

"A concise final report will be presented to the decision-makers. If the practices demonstrated during the trial receive approval to be established as official policy, a comprehensive communication will be distributed to all stakeholders. This will not only foster initial awareness and understanding but will also serve as a foundation for ongoing coaching, compliance, and auditing processes over time."

"Okay, I am starting to grasp it a bit better," acknowledged the audience member. "But where do the soft skills fit into this scenario?"

"That is an excellent question," the speaker replied. "Throughout this continuous improvement cycle, management must actively listen to the insights from frontline employees. It is vital to gather input from the 'doers' within the organization on critical aspects such as process feasibility, sustainability, and consistent follow-through. We need to nurture an environment that encourages contributions. Remember, standards are merely the beginning; they lay the groundwork for further improvement."

"Managers drive progress and elevate processes when they honor the solid foundation of standards. This is because the valuable ideas from skilled individuals can be measured, effectively reducing subjectivity. Standards do not constrain creativity; they unleash potential!" Chad concludes passionately. "Does that clarify your question?"

"Yes, thank you," came the response.

"To ensure we are all on the same page, let me summarize," Chad said, wrapping up. "Rob and I expect everyone in this room to fully embrace the Leader and Educator approach when it comes to enforcing standards. We will adhere to our documented procedures and understand the underlying rationale behind them. Regarding floor-level suggestions, we anticipate that you will skillfully switch between the roles of Administrator, Delegator, and Screener. As you learned yesterday, focus on assisting, involving, and removing distractions so your teams can turn business improvement into a reality. Thank you all - enjoy your well-deserved break!"

Review Notes--Section: *__Performance__*

A discerning manager must first evaluate their management style and how they interact with employees. What are their strengths? How do they relate to their colleagues? As managers navigate the constant flow of people, processes, and practices, they should respond in one of five ways to drive performance. These responses are outlined in the STAMP template, which varies depending on the organization's stage of development. These interactions are dynamic and follow the C-H-E-C-K model.

For instance, an employee in the Guarded Stage requires recognition from an authority figure for their contributions. This acknowledgment often motivates employees who are praised for their efforts—essentially, "catching them doing something right."

Employees who feel respected are more likely to adhere to departmental standards agreed upon and may even suggest more efficient ways of working.

In the "Operation" Stage, where employees are effectively performing their tasks, a manager needs a training-oriented mindset. Often, reliable employees can feel stifled while performing repetitive jobs. A supervisor can enhance production and creativity (leading to better client service) by providing opportunities for "educating them for advancement." Leading companies prioritize ongoing professional development.

As individuals become empowered and find their best fit within the group (the Utilization Stage of group development), they still need to boost their productivity. This can happen by "circulating their influence." Granting them more responsibility presents new challenges. In many large corporations, talented individuals can get lost in the crowd. If you want someone to take responsibility, provide them with opportunities to do so.

Leaders will inevitably rise to the top, often embodying the labels assigned to them. The "power of expectations" resonates not only in the classroom but also within the business world.

However, reaching the final step in many organizations remains a rare achievement. This crucial step involves intricately linking individual and departmental goals to the organization's overarching objectives, all of which are rooted in the corporate vision or mission statement. In its purest form, the "Production" mode takes the values set at the highest levels and cascades them down through the ranks. When a company successfully attains this significant milestone, a manager's role becomes vital in inspiring individuals and teams to aim even higher—the secret lies in minimizing distractions to foster focus and determination.

In this environment, leaders lead, organizers organize, thinkers innovate, and visions transform into reality.

The performance phase is the pinnacle of the preceding stages and should guide every decision made within the organization. While technology will undoubtedly shape our future, no machine has ever negotiated an inspiring decision or landmark business deal. Every impactful move, every financial triumph, and every satisfied customer springs from a human being making a pivotal choice at just the right moment. Performance-driven employees recognize that if they fail to treat their customers with respect, someone else will.

*The most remarkable companies of the 21st century will be those that invest wholeheartedly in their people, leading to genuine organizational **success**. It appears to have recently worked at a pharmaceutical company as well.*

CASE STUDY FIVE
Performance

Background: "Quality issues ran rampant throughout operations – from raw materials that weren't consistent to manufacturing that varied too much. Research has shown that manufacturing and product quality problems caused 60% of drug shortages."

Intervention: The leaders introduced the scientific method of Define, Measure, Analyze, Improve, and Control. Operational excellence has evolved from a business target to a regulatory requirement.

Results: Link: https://biostrategenix.com/2025/09/16/how-a-pharma-giant-saved-12m-lean-six-sigma-case-study/ Saved $12 million in systematic improvements, cut product changeover times from 12 hours to 6 hours, and lot-to-lot changeovers dropped from 4.5 hours to 1.5 hours. These improvements boosted their production capacity by 28%. They produced between 200,000 and 750,000 more units each month while maintaining their quality standards.

Biostrategenix. (2025). Biostrategenix. https://biostrategenix.com/

2:00-2:15 Break

2:15-3:00 Behaviors, Pete O'Neil

"Thank you all for being here promptly," Pete O'Neil opens the final session. "As we approach the conclusion of this weekend, we are going to delve into the essential behaviors that leaders must embody to expedite the STAMP renewal. These behaviors fall into two distinct categories: result-driven behaviors, which relate to the objective aspects of our business, and people-driven behaviors, which, while often more elusive, are equal if not more crucial."

With a gesture toward the flip chart, Pete captures the group's attention. "Let us take a closer look at the specific behaviors in both categories. I encourage each of you to take a moment to rate yourself on a scale of 1 to 10 for each of these behaviors. Keep your scores close at hand, and when you return to your workplace, seek feedback from a peer to evaluate your performance. Comparing these scores will provide valuable insights, and I believe the average will serve as a powerful starting point for your growth and development.

Result-Driven Behaviors

Theory X

QUALITY MINDSET: Ensures consistent, world-class quality.
- *Meets customer expectations.*

1 - 2 - 3 - 4 - 5 - 6 - 7 - 8 - 9 - 10

CONTINGENCY PLANNING: Recognizes the ripple effect.
- *Calculates multiple long-term organizational reactions.*

1 - 2 - 3 - 4 - 5 - 6 - 7 - 8 - 9 - 10

CREATIVITY: Thinks outside traditional boundaries.
- *Links innovation to pragmatism.*

1 - 2 - 3 - 4 - 5 - 6 - 7 - 8 - 9 - 10

SYSTEM THINKING: Puts the puzzle together.
- *Calls "big picture" audibles when necessary.*

1 - 2 - 3 - 4 - 5 - 6 - 7 - 8 - 9 - 10

GLOBAL KNOWLEDGE: Understands business at the speed of thought.
- *Knows the times and trends as they relate to the industry.*

1 - 2 - 3 - 4 - 5 - 6 - 7 - 8 - 9 - 10

People-Driven Behaviors

Theory Y

HUMAN SERVICE: Looks to the interest of others.
- *Gets excited about other people's good ideas and gives due credit.*

1 - 2 - 3 - 4 - 5 - 6 - 7 - 8 - 9 - 10

CONSENSUS BUILDING: Collaborates with the team.
- *Harnesses diversity for company utilization purposes.*

1 - 2 - 3 - 4 - 5 - 6 - 7 - 8 - 9 - 10

COMMUNICATION: Speaks, writes and listens well.
- *Articulates complicated issues in a simple, persuasive manner.*

1 - 2 - 3 - 4 - 5 - 6 - 7 - 8 - 9 - 10

ENDURANCE: Perseveres under stress.
- *Has stood the test of time with strength.*

1 - 2 - 3 - 4 - 5 - 6 - 7 - 8 - 9 - 10

INTEGRITY: Does the honest thing
- *Can be trusted with financial and political resources.*

1 - 2 - 3 - 4 - 5 - 6 - 7 - 8 - 9 - 10

"We have taken the timeless Theory X versus Theory Y management debate and revitalized it for today's dynamic landscape. In the 1960s, Douglas McGregor insightfully defined these terms to contrast the authoritarian manager (Theory X) with the participative leader (Theory Y). Today, it is not a matter of choosing one over the other; it is about harmonizing both strategies. People drive success, and by weaving these diverse behaviors from the ground up, we can empower the flexible leadership we explored in the support section yesterday.

Embracing change is essential, and I understand it can be a daunting endeavor. It often requires a deep dive into ourselves, and that can be intimidating. The S-T-A-M-P sensitive manager and employee will face challenges like never before, but they are the ones who will guide organizations to lead in our ever-evolving world.

While it may seem that our discussion carries a touch of enthusiasm, I assure you, it is well-founded. By consistently embodying these ten behaviors, you can elevate your credibility and adaptability to new heights. The following slide showcases how these behaviors are sequenced along the S-T-A-M-P continuum, creating a seamless connection to the principles we have discussed. Remember, it is through the actions that we truly drive progress and create impact.

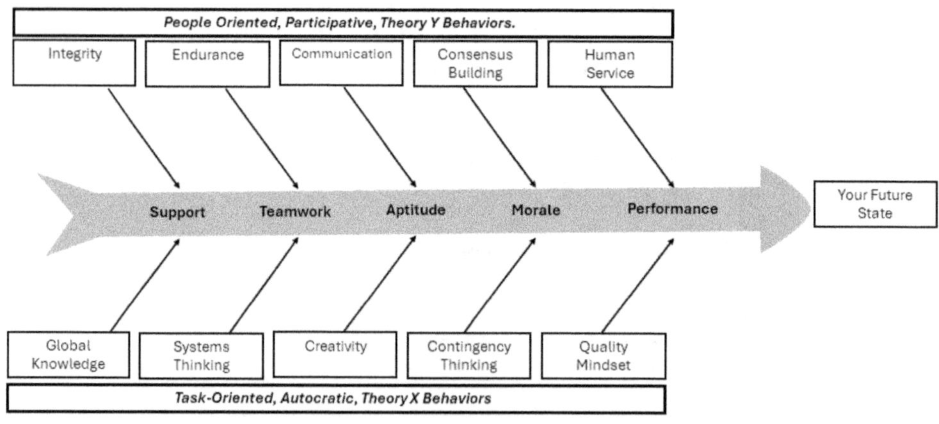

The two behaviors (in a tandem partnership) at each phase build upon one another, beginning with...

Set 1 - Management Intervention: To effectively demonstrate support during the leadership phase, a manager must have comprehensive knowledge of the industry they serve and the integrity to make ethical decisions. Knowing what to do and how to do it ethically forms the foundation of the STAMP renewal.

Set 2 - Human Resources: True teamwork is achieved when all participants have a clear understanding of the big picture and their role within it. Systems thinking, combined with the ability to persevere under stress, represents the next set of behaviors.

Set 3 - Individual Achievement: The ability to harness one's creativity and effectively communicate specific ideas demonstrates a strong commitment to achieving our business objectives.

Set 4 - Group Dynamics: Unexpected challenges are a regular part of business, making contingency planning a crucial component. Disagreements are also commonplace, so the ability to build consensus is critical. Developing 'Plan B' initiatives and obtaining buy-in from team members are key to maintaining momentum.

Set 5 - Continuous Improvement: Performance begins with a quality mindset and an ongoing desire to serve both fellow team members and society at large through positive human service.

Community service projects not only enhance a company's reputation," Pete concludes, "but they also provide employees with a healthy, balanced perspective. After all, no one on their deathbed says, 'I wish I spent more time at the office,' right?"

A question arises from the audience: "Pete, how do you objectively evaluate someone's integrity or serviceability? Aren't these behaviors somewhat nebulous and open to interpretation?"

"Sure, they are," a voice booms from the left side of the room. "Sorry for the interruption, Pete. There are no easy answers," Chad states in his straightforward manner. "Evaluating these qualities is challenging, but Rob and I are committed to assessing our people in this regard."

"I agree," Pete responds. "To directly answer your question, soft skills are harder to define. However, we cannot afford to ignore this approach. As we wrap up, I would like to invite Rob Lane to share a few words."

"Thank you, Pete," Rob begins. "You did a great job addressing the previous topic. In summary, the S-T-A-M-P of Approval mindset will help attract and retain employees who are well-balanced and can effectively accomplish their tasks. We are all imperfect human beings; at times, we may initially lack motivation, knowledge, or skills. However, we can make a meaningful impact in our organizations by adopting these ten behaviors. The key is to balance tasks, deadlines, and metrics with the diverse perspectives and opinions of multiple people."

"I want to express my sincere appreciation for everyone's participation this weekend," Rob concludes warmly. "Chad, would you like to share a few thoughts before we wrap up?"

"Absolutely. First, I want to extend a heartfelt thank you to the TLC team for graciously opening your facilities for our discussion," Chad responds. "This weekend has been truly enlightening, marking an exciting starting point for both organizations. I emphasize 'starting point' because it is only the beginning; we now have a clearer vision of the direction we want HARDAWAY Tools and TLC to take. While we have established the 'what,' we still need to explore the 'how.' We hope that your upcoming departmental meetings will illuminate that path. You can expect more details and initial discussion points in the weeks to come, and afterward, you will shape the agenda to reflect our collective vision."

"Before I finish, I want to touch on a theme we have explored extensively during our time together: alignment. We all must grasp our targets. I prefer the term 'targets' rather than 'goals.' Targets evoke the precision of marksmanship, requiring a keen alignment of vision and direction. Hitting the bull's-eye demands skill and intentionality; it does not happen by chance. Similarly, we have our work ahead of us, and with unwavering persistence and discipline, we just might hit that bull's-eye. As I drove here yesterday morning, I encountered a sign I have noticed many times before. However, this time it struck me in a new way. It read:"

**TARGET
ENFORCEMENT
AREA**

"It was a warning from the local police authorities that a ticket was forthcoming should you exceed the speed limit. Every time you see that sign, let it remind you that walking into your department is like entering your company's *Target Enforcement Area*. Each day, evaluate your behavior for consistency on those targets."

"I would like to invite Bob and Pete to come up front so we can honor them with this certificate. I never would have imagined your combined dissertations would breathe new life into both organizations. I am excited to see how these concepts will be applied. Let us give them a round of applause! Men, please come."

After the recognition, Molly then concluded, "Everyone, hard copies of the Teaming-Plus Self-Assessment Manual are available for you on the back table. Please take some time over the next few weeks to review it so that we are all on the same page as we continue our design and improvement campaign. Good night. Notice the cover sheet; it cleanly ties all the phases and steps together for Teaming-Plus."

Leadership Awareness
Support
L-E-A-D-S
Situational Agility
CI Attainment
Performance
C-H-E-C-K
Operational Excellence
Employee Alignment
Teamwork
T-R-A-I-N
Human Resources
TEAMING + PLUS
Teaming Alliances
Morale
G-R-O-U-P
Dynamic Interdependence
Self Actualization
Aptitude
W-O-R-K-S
Talent Development

CHAPTER 6 – THE RESULTS
A Hole in One

The four leaders met for breakfast and golf on the first Saturday morning of each month. They continued to update and strategize on contingency planning and adjustments to the S-T-A-M-P implementation. For example, six informational sessions were initially developed. These cross-functional, cascading meetings extended from the board of directors to the hourly employees on the floor. Here is a brief syllabus rundown...

- ✓ Part 1 was a no-holds-barred discussion. The participants were required to face the grim reality in their departments (the current state). These meetings utilized the 5-Table Exercise to define their issues and countermeasures.

- ✓ Part 2: **Support: Your Right** delineated for the members the company's unwavering commitment to people development, as well as individual and corporate expectations for *Leadership*.

- ✓ Part 3: **Teamwork: Your Role** focused on the benefits of proper employee diagnosis, training, and placement—the resulting benefits of the right people in the correct positions with the appropriate perspective -*Alignment*.

- ✓ Part 4: **Aptitude: Your Range** moved employees to new heights in productivity, while also identifying how their level of autonomy can result in a *Concerted Effort* for the good of the company.

- ✓ Part 5: **Morale: Your Resource** highlighted the interconnectedness between healthy group dynamics and the *Momentum* created.

✓ Part 6: **Performance - Your Responsibility:** Detailed company and departmental goals, challenging employees to evaluate their behavior and activities within those targets. The TARGET ENFORCEMENT AREA provided them the framework for *Success!*

For many departments, the first sessions focused on eliminating waste and inefficiency by utilizing the 5-Table problem-solving tool. Both organizations agreed that a clear definition of the problem was crucial to its solution. For example, at HARDAWAY, one outcome was a diagnosis of why mediocrity was so prevalent and why sub-standard behavior was not only tolerated but often supported. The team members broke down this subtle mentality into a logical flow. They developed the following slide to explain what they termed **the "Cycle of Mediocrity."**

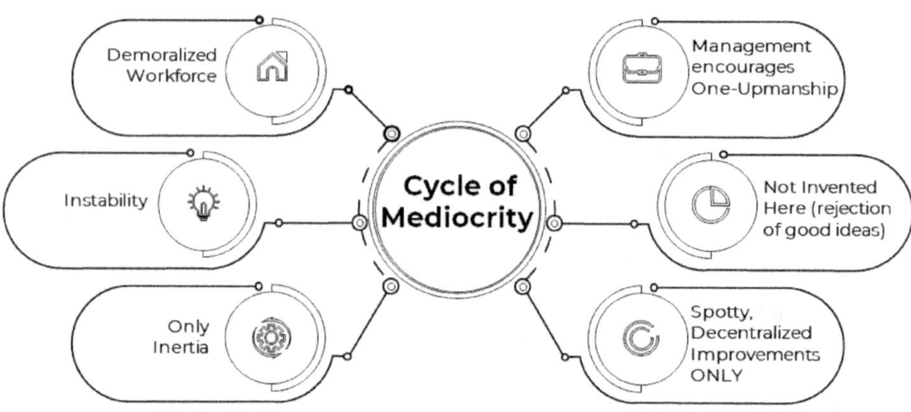

This negative input synopsis was accompanied by a letter from Lyle Smith, HARDAWAY's Manufacturing & Quality Vice President (on the next page).

HARDAWAY TOOLS

Leadership Team, After my first 5-Table exercise, I concluded that one of the reasons we have slipped in quality, cost, and timing of late has been my tolerance (no, my tacit endorsement) of four subtle yet harmful practices...which, as of today, will stop! I am taking full responsibility for what happened in the past and holding each of you accountable should it happen again.

Point #1 – **I did not honor standards or those who pushed them in the past.** Let us admit it: standards can be boring if left to their own devices. I now understand that they must be cultivated and regularly evaluated by the team. Therefore, when it came time for our advancement strategy (after being honest with myself), I generally looked for those "cowboys" who were unique, different from the next one. Anyone aspiring to promotion in their career knew this and worked to stand out to get upper management's attention. The reaction to the system was that most people harbored a disdain for other people's good ideas. The 'not-invented-here' attitude permeated our offices, and at times, we missed good ideas, and people were not given due credit for their accomplishments. System improvement was stalled!

Point #2—**The effect on our operations was that a few good ideas were implemented,** but only in pockets—nothing system-wide. This made it difficult to measure improvement, and the outcome on the floor was usually mere inertia, with many hardworking people doing their best day in and day out. However, due to _**my**_ lack of leadership and coordination, we did not get the expected holistic results.

Point #3 – The result was further complicated because **many new practices sponsored by the current leader often conflicted** with the prior administration's direction. Due to differences in loyalty, the new practice, despite its potential benefits, was not implemented with full global endorsement. This promoted both direct and indirect friction within departments and across functions.

Point #4 - We are always talking about stability, aren't we? Why is that? **Because we are unstable**, and we know it. Inertia, combined with friction, has hindered our ability to achieve true momentum. The ultimate result is instability in our processes, communications, and procedures. This has profoundly affected our people, who, at times, have become apathetic and sarcastic.

There is much truth in this letter, which, as you can imagine, was very hard for me to admit. I love this company and its people. I am learning that the key to our turnaround must begin with honesty, and I challenge every one of you to be more introspective every day, truly support our global best practices, and ensure they are replicated. Now, honoring and building on our standards will be the first criterion for promotion! I eagerly await your emails and opinions...

Sincerely,
Lyle Smith

Lyle Smith, Mfg. & Quality Executive Vice President
cc: Chad Gray & Robert Jiminez

TLC formally adopted the C-H-E-C-K model to supplement its Quality Assurance Department. One of the steps that gained traction was 'Educating for Advancement,' in which the agency committed the necessary resources to train the entire workforce as Yellow Belts - an industry-standard set of entry-level skills in continuous improvement. The goal was to provide more advanced training for 25 percent of the workforce, enabling them to earn a Green Belt, and for the remaining 5 percent to become highly advanced Black Belts. A series of initial training follow-up efforts (projects) showed progress in many areas, which enhanced their internal high-potential advancement programs.

Both groups also developed daily business reminders to reinforce their agreed-upon standards. Here are a few examples:

--We are about human development.

--Have no 'divisions' between departments. All hands on deck!

--Garnish everyone in the effort. Work at it!

--We own our barriers...

--Know your customers. The customer is the next process/group in the flow, and the supplier is the preceding process. We are in this together!

--People First! Collaboration is non-negotiable...

--Driven to perfection...

Other leadership principles reinforced included:

--Leadership equals...trust, commitment to helping those closest to the process, always honoring standards, and letting them see you through the hard times.

--Define the target, share the path to attain it, and invite people to take the journey together.

Next, HARDAWAY decided to streamline the number of management levels. This promoted greater autonomy in decision-making and broadened the leader's sphere of influence. A leaner approach, coupled with attractive buyout packages for employees with 30 years of seniority, enabled HARDAWAY to begin rehiring the laid-off residential employees.

TLC initiated, with the help of HARDAWAY's Staff Development Department, a user-friendly, effective employee training program. It utilized the T-R-A-I-N model, resulting in reduced staff turnover.

Both organizations developed a balanced people- and result-driven performance appraisal system. Individual expectations were reviewed quarterly, and management provided regular progress updates.

HARDAWAY also took other proactive steps for improvement. They eliminated unprofitable divisions and did not worry about Wall Street's initial perception. They sold off the small residential tools division and bought a chemical lawn and industrial landscaping service. This proved to be a good move.

TLC, as tricky as it was, discontinued its original temporary living outreach for people experiencing homelessness. Since they were not reimbursed for those services, Rob Lane made this decision after participating in an executive 5-table exercise.

The retreat sparked further energy through increased collaboration and partnership. HARDAWAY began to employ a group of the last homeless young men who had turned their lives around at TLC. The two also started a joint effort to provide childcare for HARDAWAY's employees, using TLC's skilled care staff. Also, some in HARDAWAY's HR ranks began weekend training sessions for TLC's new employees.

HARDAWAY consolidated design, product development, and manufacturing under a single umbrella to promote smoother hand-overs during launches. This reduction in the number of VPs ultimately resulted in cost savings. The 'all-hands-on-deck' theme minimized finger-pointing when problems occurred. Graphically, the following simple value stream arrow helped employees understand their roles and the connection between internal suppliers and customers.

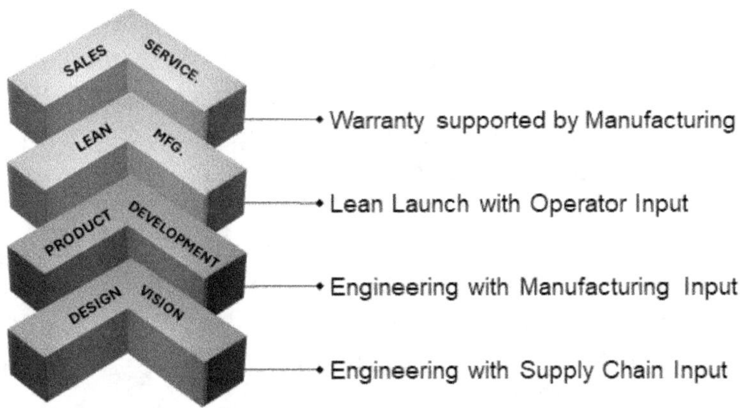

Concerning the **Boundaries + Behaviors = Culture** *(BBC Formula)*, Hardaway's manufacturing division narrowed their numerous, chaotic metrics into four unambiguous measurables that focused employees on what really **'COUNT$'**- that being:

1) Throughput,
2) Quality,
3) Operating expenses, and...
4) Leveled Inventory.

These metrics were displayed visually in an Obeya (big) strategy room, with a wall dedicated to each. This became production-central, where the leadership team developed their long-term organization plan using the L-E-A-D-S model as short-term day-to-day expectations.

One of the alignment outcomes was the institution of an awareness campaign built around floor-level support called **"OPERATOR, MAY I HELP YOU?"** This program required greater upfront operator involvement in designing the manufacturing process and leveraged an ongoing engineering presence throughout the initial launch months. The wall between product development and manufacturing engineers/production workers began falling. All salaried personnel were assigned roles and responsibilities within the program, and the yearly strategic (hoshin) planning was integrated through the OPERATOR campaign.

As the employees saw leadership enforcing this new approach, they began to trust and offer even more ideas for improvement. One zone constructed a safety awareness board with family pictures, area safety metrics, and countermeasures. They began tracking near-miss incidents rather than accidents. Using the 5-Whys, they taught other areas to realize that an accident is simply the effect of many near misses going undetected. With the new proactive emphasis on near misses and root-cause analysis, the team experienced a drastic drop in severity rates and lost-time numbers.

Another zone began using simple, hand-drawn value stream maps to track productivity opportunities. This practice has found merit and is expanding into the office areas.

Under Hardaway's supervision, the production operators saw firsthand how a business can improve the bottom line when all employees are engaged. They appreciated the pun and renewed attention to their ideas.

Before they knew it...

Summertime had crept up on them.

The season of...golf!

CHAPTER 7 – THE FUTURE
Playing Another Round

Bailey's Country Club was aglow for the 2nd Annual TLC Golf Tournament as the same four men approached Hole #1.

"Pete, didn't we win this last year?" Bob bragged after his tee shot.

"Well, here we go again, Chad. It looks like those bunker ball magnets are at it again for those two," Rob mused, watching Bob Jiminez's patented slice once more head toward the mid-way bunker.

"I am sure glad I am riding with you, Rob," Chad joked. "Who knows if Pete and Bob will even make it through the day?"

"It must be an HR thing," Rob laughed. "I really wish they would come up with some stamp of approval for golf lessons."

"Now there is an idea!" Pete shouted as the two sped off in their cart. "I think my wrists could use a little *support*!"

"Yeah... and if those heavy breathers show a little *teamwork*," Bob shouted, "and give us some pointers, maybe we would get better."

"After all," Pete said, "we have the *aptitude* for this, don't we?"

"That might be a stretch!" Bob quipped.

"Our *morale* is sinking," Pete joked. "LOL, I can feel it."

"Yeah, just like your ball," Bob responded. "I thought Bailey's outlawed quicksand in their bunkers this year. Go ahead, hit it, and do not let it affect your *performance*."

"Oh, that was weak... Zorro!" Pete shouts as he swings the sand wedge, drawing a Z in the air as if marking an enemy's shirt.

"But not as weak as that shot!" teases Bob.

Meanwhile, waiting at the number two tee, Chad comments to Rob, "Those boys are having fun, aren't they?"

"Yeah, but next year, let us leave them at home," laughs Rob. "Speaking of next year, what goals do we want to set for HARDA-WAY and TLC?"

"You know, I was thinking about that," Chad replies. "Why don't I have my training department assemble a self-directed workbook for each S-T-A-M-P component?"

"You mean like a Support Workbook, a Teamwork Workbook, and so on?" Rob questions.

"Yes, they could probably have the first one ready in a few months," Chad answers.

"That is a great idea," Rob compliments. "Why don't we package and sell them to other companies and non-profits that would like to connect, as we did?"

"That sounds like a smart financial decision for TLC, Rob," Chad acknowledges. "You are learning!"

"Well, thanks to you," Rob says. "And next year, let us market them at the tournament."

Finally, Pete and Bob drive up to the tee. "At this rate, we will be here until next year!" Chad comments.

"Well, Pete," jokes Bob, "do you think we have honors?"

"Very funny. Where is that HARDAWAY weed whacker when we need it?"

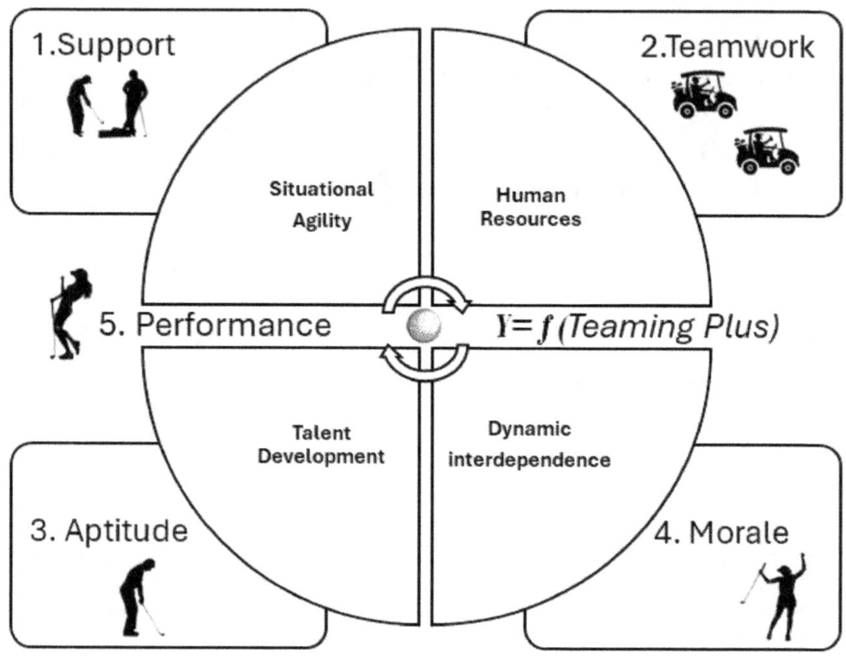

CONCLUSION – THE APPLICATION
Dawn Patrol

Thank you, Chief Executive Officers (and those who wish to follow in their footsteps), for joining us on the journey of our four leaders. In golf, those committed to their craft are often referred to as the "dawn patrol." They are up before dawn, brewing coffee and lacing up, pulling in the course parking lot even before light. Maybe even striking their first drive with no sun. If your home is on or near a golf course, you can see them, halfway down fairway one...with a flashlight in hand. They are committed!

In the same way, those newly devoted to the S-T-A-M-P of Approval framework and implementation must take the time to learn the five acronyms, understand what each step in each phase entails, and apply the inertia and friction mitigation strategies outlined in the pre-readings to move a step to the right. For each move right, leaders at all levels (strategic, operational, and tactical) can manage less and lead more, limit their current focus, and redirect their energy toward building a better future. This approach can reduce firefighting time, allowing them to focus more on monitoring progress toward the desired state. Are you ready to climb the steps? More importantly, are you ready to pull your team into the learning?

Leaders, leadership development, and human resources managers should be closely aligned on the design, priorities, and status of this future state, where more and more team leaders are moving to the right. *This will not happen by accident.* The forces of entropy and mediocrity are strong, yet they are no match for your focused attention. A Stephen Covey reminder, "we are not a product of our circumstances, we are a product of our decisions." So, pull your HR leaders into the discussion and take them with you out to Gemba!

Now what? Where should you begin?

Support - Conduct an *anonymous* leadership skills assessment whose results are visible only to the survey-takers. Ensure its anonymity! After each member understands the results, have them break down what percentage of the month they are Leaders, Educators, Administrators, Delegators, and Screeners (obviously, they will need to be trained on the terms' meaning). Discuss the breakdown and build development strategies to increase the percentages on the right. *As **situational agility** grows, so will your leaders' **awareness** of themselves, their people, and their departments.*

Teamwork: Give your HR leaders educational opportunities for adult learning. A good start - have them read Daniel Pink's book, *A Whole New Mind*, and Iain McGilchrist's *The Master and His Emissary*. Have the HR managers assess the strengths and weaknesses of their process and position succession planning approaches, as reported by supervisors and above, and how these lead to the monthly percentages of telling, reviewing, assisting, involving, and nominating their direct reports. *Investing in your **human resources** executives will lead to greater **employee alignment.*** PS: Run them through a 3-month operational stint (walk-in OPs moccasins).

Aptitude – Begin educating workers in the five stages of individual achievement. Link movement to the right to advancement opportunities and build clear paths for success. Employees need to understand that this path will not unfold as designed, but HR leaders should find examples of successful progressions to leverage and share to build confidence in the approach. Promotion is never guaranteed, but staying on the left side is certainly not fulfilling for team members in the long run. *All employees' desire **talent development.** It gives **self-actualization** a fighting chance.*

Morale – Teaming-Plus skill development is not a smooth process. Trial-and-error is the only way. Taking the safe way out and letting the business results, succession planning, and team dynamics run their course without leadership intervention is sure to lead to mediocrity. Give diverse style individuals opportunities to participate on teams, learn from those with whom they may not get along, and experience the feeling of group attainment in achieving goals. Interpersonal challenges build character. *Healthy **team interdependence** can lead to results* through **teaming alliances.**

Lastly. **Performance** – Catch your people doing things right. Be methodical with this! List all your direct reports, check them off as you recognize them, and work your way through the list. By year's end, you should be through the list. Require it from your direct reports, as well. Honor standards...SO YOU CAN...honor your people and their ideas. The C-H-E-C-K list is self-explanatory. *Make **continuous improvement** a habit so the team can attain **excellence.***

Final Word: As you reimagine traditional management paradigms, embrace situational agility, cultivate talent, and foster your team's interdependence; the S-T-A-M-P phases serve as a poignant and memorable reminder that leadership's true essence lies in the ability to inspire, adapt, and serve— transforming not just businesses but the lives of those who drive them forward.

The pursuit of excellence is forged by intentional action, steadfast commitment, and the courage to lead with purpose. The dawn patrol beckons—are you ready to take the first swing?

We are confident of your continued success!

T. Wiles Fowler, CEO, BusinessLeadership.com

PS: CEOs - also consider finding a not-for-profit executive to partner with on this S-T-A-M-P journey. How will you two mitigate resistance? Perhaps someone will also **write** a book about your partnership successes?

Change…for a…Dollar?

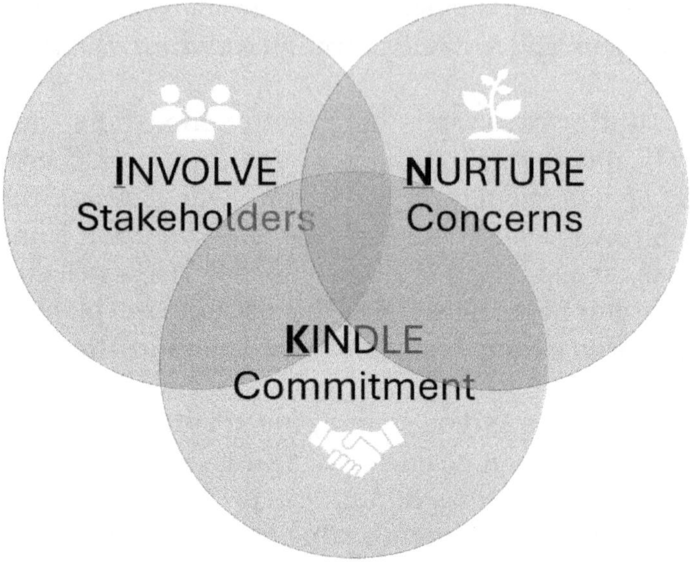

When the <u>ink</u> dries, resistance fades!

Summary

Dear Leaders,

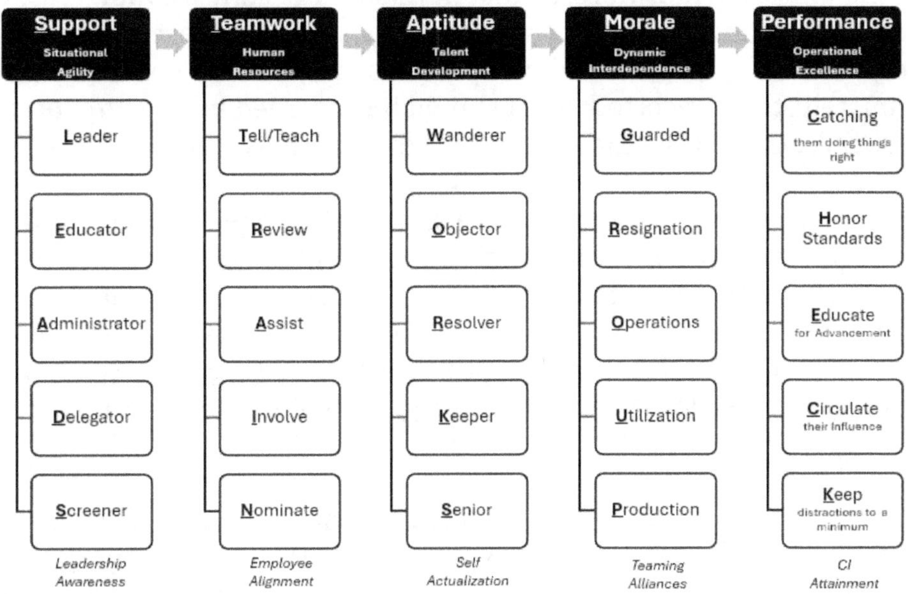

Let us dive into the concept of Teaming-Plus, starting with its cornerstone ... **Support**. This lays the groundwork for the entire framework. *Situational agility* in leading groups is pivotal in the new Teaming-Plus concept. It is essential to ensure team members are placed in positions where they can learn, grow, and contribute effectively. So, I call this the *CEO's S-T-A-M-P of Approval*, and it takes teamwork to the next level: Teaming-Plus.

S = Support. This is primarily flexible *leadership*. Are we leading with situational agility? Are we leading people according to their bent? Are we flexible in how we intervene with staff members? Are my C-suite direct reports adaptable as well? This is the foundation for Teaming-Plus.

Then, are we placing people appropriately and partnering with *human resources?* Are we equipping them with the necessary skills and acumen to make meaningful contributions? Are we *developing talent*? Are my people feeling a sense of self-actualization? If we place them in the correct positions where they can do their jobs, their aptitude and engagement improve, and they become eager to contribute. Furthermore, as that happens, it becomes contagious. It recognizes and leverages group dynamics, with respect for *interdependence*, to gain rounded perspectives and develop new skills. Ultimately, this concerted effort should be observed in *operational excellence*. Do you see the sequence? Let us amplify it for you.

1 - If people are supported as needed and placed in positions where they can grow, their aptitude and willingness to grow flourish. This ultimately affects the team and how members relate to one another, hopefully resulting in performance. In relation to situational agility, I use the acronym **L-E-A-D-S:** <u>L</u>eader, <u>E</u>ducator, <u>Ad</u><u>ministrator</u>, <u>D</u>elegator, and <u>S</u>creener ... moving from left/direct to right/indirect.

2 - When it comes to **T = Teamwork**, for human resources, I use the acronym **T-R-A-I-N**. So, I can <u>teach</u>, *do as I say*, <u>review</u>, *still do as I say; but here is why*. I then <u>assist</u> them where needed, <u>involve</u> them through delegation, and give them more responsibility. Finally, I <u>nominate</u> them and their projects for broader influence.

3 - Then, when it comes to **A = Aptitude**, we are looking at *Talent Development*. We recognize that individual workers undergo distinct phases, i.e., **W-O-R-K-S**. They start <u>wandering</u> around, wondering where they fit. Often, the next stage is the <u>O</u>bjection stage, where they complain that the work does not match the presentation made at orientation. However, if you can help them stick through and reach the **R** phase, they become a <u>Resolver</u> and start to operate within their comfort zone. If you can have a resolver consistently grow and contribute, they can evolve to a <u>**K**, a keeper</u>, like a gatekeeper, guarding the mission and vision of the organization. And then if the keeper maintains resiliency, they may advance to the

<u>Senior</u> stage for peak effectiveness. So that is the five stages of individual aptitude development.

4 - Then we move to **M = Morale** or the *Dynamic Interdependence* phase. The acronym is **G-R-O-U-P**. Initially, they are <u>Guarded</u> of one another. They do not know where they fit in, nor do they know their teams. Moreover, often when things go wrong, people start to <u>Resign</u> from the team due to frustration and conflict that result from storming. However, with facilitating guidance, if you can get them through that phase, they reach the O phase, which is <u>Operational</u>, and they start to do what they are asked.

They start working together as a group, and things begin to fall into place. If you are lucky, you reach the next phase, <u>Utilization</u>. Moreover, we have people placed in areas where they are the most effective. In baseball, a short, stocky guy might be a good catcher, but a sleek, fast person may be a better fit for center field or shortstop. Are the people placed appropriately so that they can utilize their strengths individually, creating a multiplying effect for the group? Effective utilization of each member's unique strengths is key to system momentum. And then, ultimately, they may reach **P,** <u>the production</u> step. Moreover, that is where things are humming. They understand and align with one another for maximum impact.

5 – Culminating in a chance to ... **Perform**—an opportunity to attain and sustain *continuous improvement.* The acronym is C-H-E-C-K (similar to quality control). It starts by <u>Catching</u> people doing things right, rather than things wrong. Next, we need to <u>Honor standards</u> as the baseline and <u>their</u> <u>ideas</u> to improve them. That helps stimulate performance if they are heard. We then aim to <u>Educate them for advancement</u>, enabling more responsibility, growth, and impact, which allows us to <u>Circulate their influence</u>. Lastly, **K,** we <u>keep distractions to a minimum</u> for more unfiltered opportunities. So, there it is - at a high level - the S-T-A-M-P of Approval framework. Five phases.

CEO PAUSE: Please take 5 minutes to initially review the template's sequential inputs and outputs below and begin self-assessing your company's gaps. *Which of the five domains are you or your direct reports struggling with? What is your initial reaction?*

	S-T-A-M-P of Approval				
Phase	Support	Teamwork	Aptitude	Morale	Performance
Cause | Input	Situational Agility	Human Resources	Talent Development	Dynamic Interdependence	Operational Excellence
	↓	↓	↓	↓	↓
Effect | Output	Leadership Awareness	Employee Alignment	Self Actualization	Teaming Alliances	CI Attainment

Opportunities for Improvement ______________________________

____

____

____

____

Signed ______________________________ Date _____/_____/_____

Appendices and References

Appendix A

Bob Jiminez's Final DSL Research Paper
Academic basis for the <u>S</u>upport & <u>T</u>eamwork portion.
Enhancing Leadership Development Through Human Resources

Pre-Reading / Table of Contents

Abstract
Enhancing Leadership Development Through 'Human' Resources
Overview of Leadership
Overview of Leadership's Interventions
      Give and/or Receive *Direction*
      Impart and/or Utilize *Information*
      Supply and/or Exploit *Resources*
      Award and/or Influence *Opportunity*
      Provide and/or Leverage *Overwatch*
Situational Agility Makes Leaders Aware!
Human Resources
      HR Introduction
      HR Considerations
      HR for Learning
      HR for Performance
      HR for Employee Stages
      Customer-Driven HR Culture
Tying HR to Leadership Development
Conclusion: Human Resources Enable Employee Alignment

Abstract

Leadership styles, leadership development, and human resources have each evolved as distinct disciplines over the decades; however, many chief executive officers (CEOs) spend their careers trying to align these areas. This paper will examine the relationship between situationally agile leaders and the essential resources required to enhance their flexibility and effectiveness. Aimed at the C-suite, this discussion explores the connections between situational agility, leadership awareness, human resources, and actual employee placement and alignment. Operational leadership and human resources share a symbiotic relationship that is sometimes fraught with conflict and confusion. We will address these challenges to build momentum. There are five levels of leadership development, each accompanied by resources designed to support that progression. Pragmatic executives have long anticipated an integrated solution that is both highly aligned and practical.

This paper delves into the intricate relationship (vital interplay) between leaders and the critical resources at their disposal to enhance this agility. This connection is dynamic, marked by both collaboration and occasional conflict. Our goal is to untangle this complexity and drive mission accomplishment. Leadership is essentially providing support to those being led. This involves five key tasks - providing directions, sharing information, helping, creating opportunities, and overseeing individuals throughout the process. Leadership development, however, involves a reciprocal relationship between those same elements of direction, information, assistance, opportunity, and oversight (top cover). When applied correctly, human resources can be a powerful enabler of leadership effectiveness through proper placement, clear roles/expectations, and employee retention and development, ultimately advancing members and the mission. These five distinct levels of leadership development will be supported by tailored resources that facilitate goal achievement and essential employee succession.

Enhancing Leadership Development Through 'Human' Resources

Today's business complexity forces organizations to design and develop agile leadership thought processes and practices (Schein, 1990; Zheng et al., 2010). This flexibility is evident in chain-of-command structures, personnel, communications, and marketing (Sushil, 2016). Compounded by multicultural idiosyncrasies, this makes for a fluid work environment (Pettinger, 2002). How does today's executive create a balancing act that allows individuals to blossom while ensuring corporate alignment on what matters most? These are complicated issues. The status quo, as well as classic Douglas McGregor's broad continuum, i.e., the Theory X versus Theory Y approach (1966), overlooks much of the necessary fidelity in countermeasures for informed decisions. The Flexible Leadership approach has started to mitigate some of this inertia (Yukl & Lepsinger, 2004). Today's executives must display adaptive leadership (Calarco & Gurvis, 2006) through modeling, shadowing subordinates, setting high behavioral expectations, and holding themselves and their teams accountable. This cannot be accomplished through a single annual personnel review. The partnership must be more regular, with interim expectations communicated along the way.

Human resource leaders can structure this cadence, require its participation, and record progress or degradation. Harvard (2018) notes that effective leaders are also committed followers. Managers who lead by understanding the dynamics of followership (Davis, 2017) recognize that subordinates are energized by their motivations (Kohlberg, 1981). They guide more effectively by considering their workers' perspectives on the stages of moral development: rewards/punishment, external rules, and internal principles – thus leading from an understanding of self-motivation and the tenets of effective followership. Military leader, COL Amelia Duran-Stanton, Army Chief, Ready and Resilient Integration (2021) agrees. She observes the importance of leaders who promote "a sense of responsibility of how to be a better follower in order to improve (their) leadership and management skills…they need to self-reflect on how they can improve on being a follower and how they can support their leaders and managers" (AUSA article). She posits that such competencies serve as the proving ground for promotion to leadership ranks.

Overview of Leadership

The Theory X (tasks) and Theory Y (people) management approach narrows its focus to extreme dichotomies and tendencies, emphasizing one over the other (McGregor, 1966). This reductionist approach lacks the practical flexibility to respond to the complexities of contemporary business environments. It often overlooks the subtle reality in the relationship between completing assignments and the interpersonal continuum. Charan (2024) acknowledges that developing digital-age leaders requires adaptability to the pace of change and the onslaught of information. Historically, decision-making often revolved around a binary choice between what was best for people … and what was best for the task at hand.

While McGregor's model was effective in the 1970s, the rapid pace of change today necessitates a more sophisticated methodology. Leaders must navigate a continuum of intervention styles, from autocratic to empowering, to enable subordinates to flourish. A critical question remains regarding whether the significant investments in leadership training have genuinely improved the human condition (Kellerman & Hoffman, 2018). Are leaders intervening at appropriate junctures, or does their reliance on McGregor's extremes shape their default (Arslan & Staub, 2013)? Is it sufficient to consider only the dichotomy of task versus people in leadership decisions? Must there not be a broader spectrum of interventions to facilitate effective team collaboration and goal achievement?

Furthermore, how can flexibility be harnessed to promote greater employee engagement and enhance communication? Can cultivating patience help mitigate the apprehension associated with failure? Edmondson (2012) emphasizes a continuum from leaders who impose structure to those who permit autonomy. Responsive leaders can draw upon a diverse range of strategies within this continuum to optimize their involvement, conceptualized through the new acronym L-E-A-D-S. *(Readers, in preparation for the upcoming retreat, please rate yourself below (on) the five levels of situational agility and engage in some reflective analysis of each type.)* We present the leadership style along the L-E-A-D-S continuum, a typical statement that captures the essence of the mode, a self-assessment scale, and some examples below:

__L__eader

(Brophy, 2010) *__Do__ as I say!* In extreme situations, such as when a fire breaks out in a theater, moviegoers want clear directions to the safest exit, regardless of whether the announcement is made by a bellman who is mean or loud. How can you provide direct guidance? Your personal score: 1-10?

1   2   3   4   5   6   7   8   9   10

Being a Leader: examples?

__E__ducator

(Winston, 2001) *Do as I say, but here is __why__.* Other leaders often need a rationale for a demanded action. Providing feedback solidifies learning through failure. Examples?

1   2   3   4   5   6   7   8   9   10

Adding insight to direction?

____

____

***A**dministrator*
(Dunn & Dunn, 1983): *You are close; have you considered…?* i.e., a baseball batting coach. The root word is "minister," meaning to assist coworkers when needed and to push for that final adjustment.

1   2   3   4   5   6   7   8   9   10

Success example when suggesting slight modifications?

____

____

***D**elegator*
(Pardey & ILM, 2007) *I do, you watch…you do, I watch…you do, and I watch elsewhere.* This refers to on-the-job training and the interim steps achieved toward solo leading.

1   2   3   4   5   6   7   8   9   10

Examples   of   autonomy   development?

____

____

***S**creener*
(Condolff Bevenour, 2015) *To major on the majors* - to buffer unwanted system noise so your leaders can lead.

1   2   3   4   5   6   7   8   9   10

Any similar interventions for smoother operations?

____

____

At times, along the L-E-A-D-S scale, aspiring managers have the unique opportunity to foster the growth of both the group and individual members. This transformative journey often follows a predictable path. At its core, leadership is about providing unwavering support to those being led (Berke et al., 2008). This crucial support encompasses offering clear direction, sharing valuable information, extending a helping hand, creating meaningful opportunities, and guiding and protecting individuals. Nevertheless, actual leadership *development* thrives on that same dynamic list, a reciprocal relationship that intertwines direction, information, assistance, opportunity, and oversight. In this context, leaders not only advocate passionately for those in their charge but also take the initiative to seek direction, information, assistance, and advancement opportunities that benefit themselves and the success of their functional direct reports (Silver & Franz, 2021). Together, we will explore these vital components in greater detail, starting with giving and receiving direction.

Overview of Leadership's Interventions

Direction

There are times when it is best to be direct (like herding people to the exit during a theater fire). The *Leader* Role involves understanding one's teams, motivating leads, and employing leadership/followership tactics suited for success (Yukl & Lepsinger, 2004). Based upon the situation, leaders provide clear direction, foster alignment, and require commitment (McCauley & Fick-Cooper, 2019).

Attuned leaders know how to think and plan strategically (Adair, 2010). They realize (at times) that, as in the theater scenario, groupthink (allowing everyone to have a say) might make some vocal individuals feel they have been heard. However, their action or inaction could result in the death of everyone in the room, including themselves. Now this is an extreme example, but is it any different than allowing teams to pool their ignorance? History is full of businesses that once thrived but are no longer in existence because thoughtless managers were given a say (Carroll & Mui, 2008). Who were the mid-level guys who were once convinced that newer, greased carriage spokes were the most innovative transportation thing their company could do (Stack Exchange, 2018)?

Leaders Give Direction

Briker et al. (2021) studied 60 autocratic supervisors and nearly 300 employees in a work environment. The results showed that employees (if there existed a connection with their supervisor) happily followed direct instructions. Stern directions were respected when the team knew their supervisor had their backs. If relationships and trust were present, the autocratic style worked. Badiru & Tourangeau (2023) compare leadership to specific areas of industrial engineering that follow scientific protocols. They view leadership as a predictable system (with rules and cadences) that includes scanning the environment, reflecting on what was seen, observed, and felt, processing the stimuli, determining intervention plans, and taking the necessary action. This autocratic formula is suitable when teams lack direction, information, and resources to make informed decisions. Lead, follow, or get out of the way is needed from time to time. Leaders will direct the team as necessary to utilize frameworks (tools, techniques, models, etc.) to move them forward.

Leaders Receive Direction

Feedback is the breakfast of champions (Blanchard, 2001). Authentic leaders recognize that they do not possess all the answers. Leadership consultant Damon Hayes-Milligan (2024) suggests that hiring managers bring on candidates who are smarter than the leaders running the departments. This gets at the essence of leaders benefiting from direction. They leverage it and multiply it for their own and the company's benefit.

Mulligan & Shaw (2020) challenge executives to hire for…purpose. They believe the best hires are those who address the company's significant priorities/gaps. They look to match the company's (mission) needs with the candidate's skills and abilities. The debate between hiring generalists versus specialists continues.

Information

The goal of all training programs is to harmonize knowledge into action in the workplace (Raelin, 2008). HR leaders utilize educational tools daily to support their work teams. Some ambitious HR leaders are even looking to strategically model and evaluate services from a financial and practical perspective (Director et al., 2013). The *educator*-style leadership role in HR aims to impart knowledge that benefits its workers and to analyze data into actionable insights for decision-making, alignment, and prioritization.

Educators Impart Information

Managers who convey necessary information - whether manual or digital - to team members facilitate excellence in organizations (Shapiro & Varian, 1999). Information is the lifeblood of existence, business, hopes, and dreams (Lan, 2005). Data transformed into information can provide leaders with the knowledge they need to make informed decisions. Datification is the science of this transformation of information (Elliott, 2013). Once an obscure term from the data modeling days of the 1980s, Datification has exploded into a quantum force in today's Information Technology (IT) landscape. With advancements in computation speed, internet use, automation, social media, and artificial intelligence, the range of communication and analysis has become increasingly data-driven. This trend now serves as a powerful catalyst for refining conceptualization, digitization, and market data, whether for personal enrichment or corporate growth.

This evolution has unveiled a captivating array of possibilities that are reshaping our world (FOWLER, 2015). Datification gives HR managers a competitive advantage. No longer a mere left-brain framework, it harnesses data in the dynamic marketplace. In an era where insights are the new currency, businesses that leverage this e-readiness have the potential to innovate.

Timo Elliott, a leading voice in the field, eloquently describes datification as "the process of taking previously invisible activities and transforming them into data" (Forbes, 2013, article). This enables HR leaders to track, monitor, and optimize their endeavors, paving the way for a future filled with innovative opportunities and fresh challenges (Askitas & Zimmermann, 2015; Waddill, 2018). It resonates with the concept of 'dark data' (information hidden, unknown, or overlooked), while also illuminating 'unknown activities' that are now exposed and can be harnessed for impactful insights.

In a world where data is growing at over 50% annually, with a $90 billion market (Big Data, 2025), datification employs a versatile, mixed-methods approach. Combining both qualitative and quantitative nuances, it assists personnel managers in defining, measuring, and elevating previously 'invisible' processes to extract actionable insights that empower better decision-making and ignite creativity (Luftman, 2015).

Datification seamlessly intertwines with various business management strategies, enhancing our understanding of workflows. For example, its principles echo deeply in lean manufacturing, championing transparency in metrics and fostering a culture of continuous improvement. Lean Six Sigma practitioners have leveraged measurable military logistics and precision (Pelly, 2022) to ensure clarity and communication during complex initiatives, such as wartime infantry operations (Optimization, 2025). That showcased datification's ability to drive accountability and facilitate the achievement of ambitious goals even in the most challenging environments (Fowler, 2015).

Educators Utilize Information

HR advocates who cultivate cross-sector partnerships for knowledge transfer are pivotal in driving value and transforming operations (Duberman & Sachs, 2019). In a world where knowledge is power, one potent tool at our disposal is the art of reframing (Bolman & Deal, 2014). Datification enables HR managers to stay ahead of trends, reframe their approach, and better support employees. Data is indispensable. It is not just a trend; it can reshape our perspectives and unveil a multitude of options.

Drawing on a diverse range of disciplines, including complexity theory, data warehousing, automation, and psychology, its allure is becoming increasingly practical. On networking platforms like LinkedIn Groups, a vibrant community of over one million members passionately engages in discussions about the transformative impact of datification and big data on business and everyday life, demonstrating their role as business enablers rather than mere concepts. Innovative technologies have unlocked a range of ways to 'digitize' or 'datify' our daily activities (Fowler, 2015).

Dr. Jonathan A. Jenkins (LinkedIn, 2025), a prominent big data blogger, encapsulates this notion: Platforms like X condense our fleeting thoughts into actionable data, Facebook transforms personal narratives into insightful stories, and LinkedIn turns professional interactions into quantifiable successes. He underscores the importance of honing our ability to express social and business exchanges as dynamic data formats, revealing profound insights into our interconnected global society. Reflecting on our reading habits further illustrates this transformation. Elliott also notes that devices like the Amazon Kindle do more than deliver compelling content—they track our engagement, providing invaluable insights into our reading speed and progress. This level of interactivity demonstrates how datification enriches our experiences and empowers us to make enlightened choices (Forbes, 2013, article).

As we delve deeper into the integration of datification into our lives, visionary human resource leaders who advocate for this data-driven approach will uncover extraordinary opportunities, setting their organizations apart in an increasingly complex and evolving landscape. In this thrilling new frontier, those who embrace datification will not only thrive but also redefine how we learn, perceive, and interact with data in our increasingly interconnected world (Kenon & Palsole, 2019).

Resources

Societal, demographic, cultural, and generational change (Cascio et al., 2011) are just a few of the fluid environmental factors HR leaders must address. Employees themselves can be overwhelmed by the various types of change. HR managers who focus on talent development (Axelrod & Coyle, 2011) give employees a better chance of navigating through the unpredictability. In the *Administrator* role, leaders proactively provide support to the teams as needed.

Administrators Supply Resources

Supplementing employees with the necessary resources to add value includes exposing them to relevant data (McDougall, 1999; Suresh et al., 2023), staffing positions to meet tactical timelines (Ammons & Roenigk, 2022), and providing capabilities through talent development (Sutton & Chatham, 2017). One excellent example of supporting employees in times of change is The Center for Creative Leadership's (2002) guidance for HR leaders on assisting employees in crises. Such advocacy is a worthy endeavor for personnel staff.

Administrators Exploit Resources

In the 1970s, author Robert Greenleaf echoed this sentiment about leaders who set the participative tone as servants. "Where there is no community, trust, respect, ethical behavior is difficult for the young to learn and for the old to maintain" (Robert K. Greenleaf Quotes, 2020: Greenleaf, 1977, Introduction; Paul Goodman in *Making Do*). Trust is the prerequisite for effective learning, growth, and supplying employees with resources.

Talent development occurs in both education (Horn, 2015) and business (Hamad et al., 2024), prompting team members to become more engaged, fostering holistic growth in individuals, which, in turn, benefits their organizations. Although effective, many of these approaches may overlook key elements essential to longevity and sustainability. These gaps in absence include limited (or missing) training in integrity (Tomić et al., 2024), reliance on narrow problem-solving techniques (Jong, 2016), a lack of appreciation for teamwork (Edmondson, 2013), and egocentric modalities (Ochnik, 2019). Let us unpack these opportunities.

The Fairfax County, Virginia, innovative and effective education-based initiative, Young Scholars (YS) talent development model (Horn, 2015), has been in place for years, improving talent specifically among lower-income students who rarely have the opportunity to be evaluated for advancement. The approach has proven successful, with a 565% increase in low-income student participation in the gifted program since 2003, resulting in over 75% of gifted students earning A's or B's. Additionally, there has been a 160% increase in typical teachers' learning of gifted students' assessments and interventions since 2012 (Horn, 2015).

YS's success is built on identifying and nurturing giftedness (Bernal, 2002; Elliott, 2003), in collaboration (Treffinger et al., 2004) with trained teachers assigned to every school through creative interventions (Paul & Elder, 2008) and the administration of non-traditional assessments that utilize the Shaklee (2002) Creative Behavior Ratings Scale. The targeted demographic often falls through the cracks due to low familial incomes and a lack of initiative (Smith et al., 1997). Nevertheless, over the last twenty years, several hundred of these students have benefited from this program. However, gaps do remain. There is limited training on integrity, sometimes relying on narrow problem-solving techniques, an under-appreciation for teamwork, and potential self-serving tendencies. Contemporary HR managers would benefit from incorporating the following modalities into their operations.

Integrity-Based Training. A formal review of the role of integrity in life and business provides students and employees with a strong foundation for self-actualization. Thoughts grounded in knowledge, reinforced by leaders, help mentees internalize virtues (Tomić et al., 2024) through real-life scenario learning and by imitating their mentors' modeled attitudes and behaviors. The virtues individuals collectively embody impact organizations (Williams et al., 2015), creating a virtuous atmosphere within a school or business. Integrity becomes contagious and often serves as a missing link in many talent development efforts. Fostering introspection, prioritizing service over self, and emphasizing internalized character and excellence can complement (broaden) a holistic talent curriculum (Ceberio et al., 2023).

Myopia Awareness. Both organizations and their team members can miss (due to myopia) the "complex, uncertain, ambiguous, and changeable" aspects of foresight and problem-solving (Catino, 2013, p. 3). Talent programs may fail to teach the intricate macro- and micro-level countermeasures needed to address today's challenges (Colvin et al., 2012). Just as human eyesight blurs at a distance due to myopia, workers without holistic problem-solving skills may miss obscure dangers. Mental myopia is a silent killer of innovation, limiting success and potential.

It also hinders individuals, students, employees, and companies from recognizing and capitalizing on opportunities. Catino (2013) argues that incorrect beliefs and practices increase the risk of missteps, similar to foresight failure (Turner & Pidgeon, 1997) and large-scale failures (Turner, 1967; Wilensky, 1967). Talent development practitioners must expand traditional, narrow-based problem-solving curricula to equip individuals better to address today's complex problems (Hallo, 2022).

Teamwork. Talent development is often an individual-based endeavor, when all of life and business are experienced in teams. From pre-school through Ph.D. programs, these are always conducted with groups of students. In business, all employees belong to a department. Why do many developmental modalities miss the group dynamic aspect?

Edmondson (2013) asks business leaders to challenge their mentees by introducing conflicting and/or contradictory ideas. She concludes that life is a paradox, yet a world of possibility. She contends that teams provide significant insight into addressing dilemmas. Cultures of playful discipline, encompassing a broad range of perspectives, can emerge within chaos and fluidity, opening the world to insightful epiphanies. Talent development programs are generally too introspective; nonetheless, focusing on growth through relationships and talent conversations will have a positive, rippling effect (Smith & Campbell, 2011).

Egocentric Modalities. Individual Development Plans, also referred to as IDPs (Warner, 2007), are a formal approach to helping employees develop their skills and abilities. Although the form's name may, by its nature, dictate (limit) that the employee primarily looks inward. An individual who focuses solely on personal development may overlook the benefits of peer review. Changes in employment (COVID-19, virtual technologies, a younger, more fluid workforce) have led to greater worker dependency and opportunities (Grant & Parker, 2009); if recognized and adapted to by workers (Ochnik, 2019), they will be supported by business decision-makers. In other words, deferring to and assisting others is a great way to advance one's career. Selfishness at work is a significant gap that many talent development curricula do not address, and we encourage them to shift from an egoistic to a more altruistic approach (Batson, 2011). A robust, targeted talent focus may increase employee integration into organizations and align them with their priorities (Sundari & Praseeda, 2019).

HR leaders should champion their employees, who in turn provide human capital (Culpepper, 2018). Every productive initiative, every business success, and every vision brought to life came from an individual with a good idea. HR managers who structure their talent development programs holistically can reap the benefits for decades. Leading in the Administrator role (root word: minister, to serve) in designing talent development programs, emphasizing integrity and teamwork, and avoiding myopia and egocentrism can yield the fruit of their labor for decades. Invest in people, and they will invest in the company (Dewald & Wilson, 2018).

Opportunity

HR leaders (in the *Delegator* role) should partner with operational leaders to free up time and provide mentees with opportunities to perform through structured transfer (Bloom, 2021). Opportunity comes in many ways. Edmondson (2012) challenges leaders to apply this type of ongoing "collective learning" (p. 27) through what she has coined *teaming,* a dynamic verb... a "mindset and practices (within) teamwork, not by the design and structures of effective teams" (p. 13). Teaming occasions are designed as proving grounds for development. How does this teaming approach differ from mere teams and teamwork? This acumen encompasses hard science skills, pragmatic interdependencies among group members, nimbleness, and speed in problem-solving (Magni & Caporarello, 2022).

Delegators Award Opportunity

Employment can bring weird, irrational, and incredible ways for humans to navigate the workplace (Sutter, 2023). Opportunities abound in the VUCA world (Mack et al., 2016). Keen HR managers listen to operations as to their essentials and begin to match high-potential workers to real-world needs presented by their functional counterparts. Edmondson's teaming (2012) approach facilitates this competency testing.

This mindset leverages groups in employment to unite efforts, spark new ideas, seek solutions, and address issues (Edmondson, 2012). It involves a complex, often temporary, interdependent learning model, coupled with interpersonal intelligence, to resolve conflict, facilitate communication, and achieve success. Typically, it is introduced to a group of individuals in response to a crisis or a specific industry need. The path is bumpy, often reverting to partial past solutions and tweaking them to address current needs.

It works best with fluid environments, such as areas requiring cross-shift coverage in multidisciplinary workspaces, where collaboration, complexity, and effective communication are needed (Edmondson et al., 2022). Another prerequisite for teaming is the willingness of team members to learn, both introspectively and interpersonally. Looking inward and applying your gifts and talents externally is the beginning of effective teaming. Further, how should we think as group members who excel at teaming? It often (Edmondson, 2012) relies on the following 'old-fashioned skills.'

~Blending independent and interdependent competencies,

~Clarifying roles as needed in real time,

~Working to establish trust amid chaos, and

~Determining the coordination of these variables (p.14).

Teaming comes from leveraging learning (Edmondson et al., 2002, pp. 128-146). Is there a model that can memorably summarize these enabling variables? Yes, Lencioni (2016) consolidated teaming into three key components. He challenges workers to be *humble*, *hungry*, and *smart* (p. 96). Employees and leaders who come to work humbly are more likely to garner support from their coworkers. World-renowned leadership guru Ken Blanchard reminds us that none of us is as smart as all of us (Dixon, 2007). Additionally, being hungry can lead to focusing on learning from others, and that success can stem from connecting with many people throughout one's career (Lapin, 2014). Lastly, being smart may involve specific cognitive skills, but Lencioni likens it more to interpersonal savviness and assessing teammates' skills. A wise person understands their strengths and weaknesses and recognizes what other team members bring to the table when facing work-related dilemmas. The key is to blend these three characteristics to spark greatness. How can teaming strategies respectfully move operations to sustainability and longevity? Leaders who perform the Delegator Role provide opportunities for team members to thrive, and teaming is a practical, tactical approach to accomplishing this.

Delegators Influence Opportunity

Great leaders not only bring out the best in others but also capture opportunities for themselves (Irwin & Tassopoulos, 2018). A healthcare example: Achieving positive patient outcomes is the goal of all healthcare systems. These results are not created in a vacuum—at least not the ones that lead to genuine healing. Edmondson (2012) proposes that the "verb" teaming be done "on the fly" and occurs in environments that lack stability (e.g., healthcare and military), which require staff consistency and nimbleness. She elaborates that it is accomplished in "fast-moving work environments (that) need people who know how to team (and) to act in moments of potential collaboration when and where they appear" (Edmondson, 2012, pp. 12-14).

Teaming can fix real-world problems. Nimble leaders can leverage it. In healthcare, poor teamwork can result in suboptimal patient outcomes. However, caregivers "often experience physical and emotional problems when teamwork is the exception rather than the rule and (the) lack of respect, the ecological norm" (Gordon et al., 2014, p. 47). When teaming capabilities are not present, errors occur. One real-world health-related concern is central line-associated bloodstream infections (CLABSI), or another example, leaving surgical instruments inside a patient. These preventable lapses in care, deemed "never events" (Gordon et al., 2014, p. 49), are of great concern to both patients and community stakeholders

(Hackman et al., 2024). Effective teaming's push for accountability breeds greater awareness (and follow-through) to reduce many of these inexcusable mishaps.

Another example of poor teaming and coordination of services in global healthcare involved the discharge care of frail and elderly patients. A Swedish care system found that poor coordination was a key factor in patient readmissions and declining health (Emilsson et al., 2022). The effectiveness of patient treatment plans, follow-up, and ongoing care was assessed in the patients studied. Their report concluded, "Collaboration is a prerequisite for the individual to get the support that meets...needs. Thus, it is also...necessary...to achieve good quality" (p. 322). Teaming affords the chance to make caregivers more effective.

Team robustness stems from individuals who understand their roles, strengths, and how they contribute to the group's overall effectiveness. Those who advance their teaming skills also understand this about their coworkers and multiply their efforts when coordinated. Buchbinder and Shanks (2017) highlight some leadership qualities and protocols that tie a nice bow to this short treatise on teaming. They encourage leaders to exhibit professionalism, "trust...passion, visibility, communication, openness in admitting fault, and balance" (p. 37). Teaming provides the necessary opportunities to demonstrate acumen and competencies, leading to better goal outcomes and a sense of joint accomplishment. How about having your team try it? Leaders should practice the delegator mode to allow members to exercise their teaming skills.

Overwatch

Overwatch - a military protection tactic. A small group of leaders position themselves to see the landscape where team members work. As a *screener*, they protect movement, foster long-range foresight, and remove obstacles (noise, risk, liabilities) so that members can perform as intended (Safire, 2007).

Screeners Provide Overwatch

There is a protective component to leadership. Kennedy International Chief Executive Officer, Laurence Kennedy (Noble, 2024, Capitol Times), speaking in the context of security, asserts, "Overwatch is preventing threats by empowering individuals and organizations to live and operate with confidence" (p. 45). This highlights a key outcome for leaders using Overwatch. It is the strategic imperative for team success. In today's fast-paced environment, the concept of Overwatch stands as a crucial strategy for effective team management and protection. Drawing on principles outlined by Safire (2007), Overwatch generally empowers teams to eliminate distractions and refocus their energy on core responsibilities. It is within the Screener mode that authentic protective leadership emerges, offering the vital oversight needed in a world steeped in uncertainty. Screeners are not just observers; they are strategic thinkers who seek clarity amidst ambiguity, helping navigate potential risks even before they escalate (Wetherbee, 2016).

Consider, for example, the role of overwatch personnel stationed at critical locations, such as the White House. Equipped with binoculars and drones, they maintain constant communication with organizations such as the FAA, ensuring a comprehensive view of the landscape and airspace (Baldwin, 2019). This level of vigilance not only safeguards the immediate environment but also fosters a culture of safety and preparedness among team members and visitors alike. Screeners play a key role in identifying potential threats, even those that may not yet be defined. Through proactive monitoring, they anticipate risks and communicate promptly to effectively implement pre-established protocols—all the skills needed within business circles.

Picture the watch commander orchestrating logistics while the team at ground level acts on constant updates—a well-oiled machine driven by the Overwatch philosophy. Strategic foresight is another critical aspect of Overwatch, employing predictive tools such as the Futures Wheel (Yondar, 2024) and STEEPLE analyses (Business Chronicler, 2022). These prognostic frameworks enable Screeners to anticipate future challenges and opportunities, and to craft contingencies to mitigate risks. By understanding where a threat might lead, teams can take decisive action beforehand, ensuring they remain one step ahead. In a dynamic world, effective Overwatch is not just an advantage; it is an imperative. By adopting this strategic approach, executives can cultivate resilience, enhance their operations, and ultimately ensure the safety of their personnel, customers, and missions. Embracing Overwatch means cultivating a proactive mindset to prepare us for the challenges ahead. Let us commit to this indispensable strategy for enhanced protection and performance.

Screeners Leverage Overwatch

As the world shrinks in size, drawing information to our fingertips, stress can accompany that data. Indeed, HR leaders can foster a culture of safety for their employees. However, workers need to learn to protect themselves and to utilize the resources at their disposal. Suri & Yadav (2019) stress the supportive culture as a sustainer of team members. How can HR foster self-preservation among employees (Martin et al., 2020)?

Workers can protect themselves through honesty, healthy introspection, and having a source/ally in transparency ready with helpful and protective feedback (Arneson, 2010). Blanchard calls this the breakfast of champions (Fields, 2009). It is where leaders meet the crucible of development, fortifying social and emotional intelligence (Hughes & Miller, 2011). This is often visualized as personality evenness, characterized by neither too many high highs nor too many low lows. Leadership author Mike Robbins (2022) acknowledges, "Patience is powerful. It can help us persevere, reduce stress, and overcome challenges" (Chapter 2).

Other overwatch principles that team members need on the ground for business should leverage include the protection offered by networking (Michaelides, 2020), partnering with laterals (Brindle & Mainiero, 2000), grasping power networking (Kramer, 1998), and the sharing of (and receiving) relevant information (Greek, 2014). Being aware of these resources can help prevent self-sabotage in the workplace (Potter, 2013).

Situational Agility Makes Leaders Aware

The L-E-A-D-S continuum of leadership intervention facilitates employee empowerment. Schneider (Case Center, 2015) highlights three hopes for every manager: that their people will demonstrate what he terms the three I's of initiative (i.e., imagination, inspiration, and independent thinking, pp. 49-52). Managers who foster "the ability (in their people) to work together toward a common vision; the ability to direct individual accomplishments toward organizational objectives" (Gould, 2018, p.4) – is the secret weapon.

Employees who look beyond themselves just enough to partner with others for mission accomplishment, make self-actualization a reality, align their energies for teaming, and help sustain business potential. How flexible are you and your people? Please consider the L-E-A-D-S path for their development through exploiting calculated human resources.

Human Resources

The six critical competencies for human resource (HR) leaders, as identified by Ulrich (2012), include understanding industry context, modeling trust, building team capability, leading change, honoring innovation, and applying the latest technologies (Waddill, 2018). Effective HR does not simply promote the latest fads or labels in the personnel field (such as HR 'Management' versus HR 'Development'); instead, it integrates benefits from all subsystems. HR development should not come at the expense of essential employee-forward services, such as insurance, retirement, and payroll, as well as in-between support throughout the hire-to-fire continuum, as needed (Anderson & Langley, 2017).

Ulrich's competencies provide a framework for navigating the complexities of the modern human resource world. Understanding industry context is not just about being aware of trends; it involves a deep comprehension of the nuances and dynamics within the specific industry. Modeling trust is essential for fostering a positive workplace culture. HR leaders must demonstrate integrity and reliability to create an environment where employees feel valued and supported. Trust is a foundational element that encourages open communication, collaboration, and engagement, all of which are crucial for a thriving organization (Shockley-Zalabak et al., 2010). "Trust is the glue of life. It is the most essential ingredient in effective communication - the foundational principle that holds all relationships" (Covey et al., 1994, p. 203).

Building team capability involves not only enhancing individual team members' skills and competencies but also cultivating a sense of collective efficacy (Ma et al., 2017). Leading change is another critical competency, particularly in an era where organizations must be agile and responsive to shifting market conditions. HR leaders understand that for change to occur, the pain of the same must outweigh the pain of the change (Robbins, 2016). Honoring innovation is vital in a rapidly evolving business landscape. HR professionals must foster a culture that encourages creativity and experimentation, recognizing that innovation can emerge from any level within an organization (Bloom, 2021). Ultimately, leveraging the latest technologies is crucial for refining HR practices and enhancing operational efficiency. Thus, personnel types should be adept at harnessing these advances to streamline processes, enhance the employee experience, and provide data-driven insights for informed decision-making (Davis et al., 2013). How can this be accomplished?

Human Resources (HR) Introduction

An examination of contemporary human resource textbooks (Carbery & Cross, 2015) reveals a critical need for clarity and standardization in HR terminology and practices. The wide range of terms reflects various, often conflicting, opinions expressed by practitioners over the years. Key questions demand answers: Is HR the broad umbrella process? Do Human Resource Management (HRM) practitioners overlook essential talent development? Is HR Development (HRD) narrowly focused on enhancing employee competencies? Furthermore, do these frameworks fail to encompass the organizational vision and mission planning that the Strategic Human Resources Management (SHRM) approach clearly emphasizes (Schuler & Jackson, 1999)? All relevant right-brain, comprehensive questions that beg clarity (Pink, 2006).

It is essential to determine which designation truly encapsulates the entire system rather than merely highlighting micro aspects. This debate is not just ongoing; it is critical. Carbery & Cross (2015) deserve commendation for their thorough review of the history of human resources. They effectively clarify pivotal concepts: the distinction between performance-enhancement training (Evans, 1992; Manpower Services Commission, 1981), development (Baum, 1995), formal and informal education (Garavan et al., 1995), and the fundamental nature of teaching/learning itself (Mankin, 2009). Understanding and leveraging these development nuances (shades) are vital tools for HR managers.

HR is fundamentally about empowering an organization's workforce, fostering a robust understanding of the business (Gerber & Lankshear, 2000), and clarifying each employee's critical role within the organization (UN, 2001). This triad understanding lays the groundwork for stability in future operations (Das Gupta, 2020). A striking example of HRD's effectiveness occurred in Abuja, Nigeria:

When Fowler (2025) represented the U.S. State Department's mission to equip West Africa leaders with vital project management skills, this experience underscored a significant reality: some cultures de-prioritize immediate concerns, often postponing for future considerations—an urgent challenge when instilling the importance of deadlines.

HRD must thoughtfully integrate cultural values into its teaching methodologies (Ardichvili & Jondle, 2009). It is imperative that HRD fully embrace and respect global and cultural differences in its interventions to maximize effectiveness (Li, 2019).

HR Considerations

The world has become increasingly interconnected, yet significant business and cultural disparities remain, highlighting the urgent need for effective knowledge transfer (Bartlett & Ghoshal, 1998). Within a single organization, the demand for data can span multiple cultural boundaries in just a single day. Thus, HR practitioners must establish a strong partnership with IT to develop seamless systems for transmitting and receiving vital information that employees can easily access (Crumpton, 2015).

In many ways, the transactional has evolved into the transnational. This expansion can render local policies insufficient and possibly obsolete, as they often lack the comprehensive scope necessary to navigate diverse functions, geographic regions, and cultures. HR leaders must adopt a wider vision (Mutsuddi, 2012). If they neglect to do so, they can rest assured that their competitors are already capitalizing on this opportunity. Do conventional HR leaders fully understand the intricacies of adult learning in their knowledge transfer processes (Bean, 2023)? How can attracting and retaining a global workforce bolster this endeavor? Moreover, how can we more effectively engage and inspire younger workers (Lawler & Hundley, 2008)? These are not just abstract questions;

they are indispensable considerations for any forward-thinking HR strategy. What about the needed pivotal nature of flexibility in HR practices (Schwartz, 2023)? Is agility understood, honored, and practiced? How can we quantify its business value (Rupp, 2024)?

While pursuing higher revenues and lower costs remains paramount, any aspect that lacks a direct correlation to these metrics tends to be undervalued—and this is precisely the essence of agility. Agility empowers organizations to increase revenue, reduce costs, or mitigate risks when faced with unforeseen challenges (Schwartz, 2023, LinkedIn). Is hiring an employee to fill a role sufficient in today's dynamic landscape? Are specialists a sustainable long-term solution? Or does cultivating flexibility within HR systems and among new hires themselves create a more resilient foundation for organizational success and employee succession over time (Colvin et al., 2012)? The answers to these intricate questions hold the key to unlocking potential in an ever-evolving business environment. Will your HR managers adapt? The debate continues (Wang & Murnighan, 2013).

HR For Learning

As the world becomes increasingly interconnected, how can human resource managers effectively foster learning across diverse cultural and regional landscapes? Leaders should adopt a macro perspective (Boyd, 2001) rather than get bogged down in micro details. Let us start by examining the terminology we use. Labels can be constraining; indeed, language itself can stifle our thinking. Cultural psychiatrist Iain McGilchrist (2019) posits that while words serve as valuable tools for reference, they often become thought-limiting forces that direct our thinking rather than grounding it. Does this limitation detract from the field of human resources? Does it confine the thinking, expression, policies, expectations, and vision of HR leaders?

Take, for instance, the distinction between 'HR Development' and 'HR Management.' Is the term developing inherently superior to managing? I would argue that these labels often reflect a marketing strategy rather than a meaningful difference, neither good nor bad. Can individual development truly flourish without established policies, payroll processes, and other essential HR functions? Is one not dependent upon the other? Leaders in the personnel realm tend to unlock their full potential when they grasp both the nuances of processes and the richness of language, thereby enhancing their ability to connect with a diverse audience.

Another compelling example of a false dichotomy is the often-cited differentiation between leadership and management. Are these concepts truly distinct (Rohatgi, 2013), or do they intertwine in a complementary dance? Biblical scripture implies that they are inseparable. An example: Consider the Hebrew character of Moses: he expanded his leadership prowess by integrating effective management techniques, appointing elders to handle the numerous requests from the children of Israel as they navigated the harsh wilderness on their way to the Promised Land (NIV, 1978/2011, Deuteronomy 1:9-18). Similarly, today's HR leaders can match pragmatic management skills with visionary leadership qualities to navigate the perplexities of our modern world. It is not a matter of choosing one over the other. Just as Moses sought counsel from his father-in-law, demonstrating remarkable human resource management through his humility, today's leaders can learn to blend these essential skills to thrive.

HR For Performance

How can HR facilitate high performance within organizations? One practical approach is to adopt design thinking, as highlighted by Riana et al. (2020). This methodology is essential not only for problem-solving but also for fostering an innovative culture that promotes continuous improvement. However, a key challenge leaders often face is avoiding exploring new possibilities. This reluctance may stem from a misalignment in how the current state of operations is measured or from getting caught in a cycle of ineffective processes—that is, chasing their tail without moving forward.

It is critical to recognize that achieving high performance goes beyond the purview of human resources alone. There is an underlying (operational) thought process that must be leveraged to pave the way for meaningful performance improvement. Productivity figures such as Henry Ford (1926) and Taiichi Ohno, founder of the Toyota Production System, have emphasized that without standardization, there can be no lasting improvement (Katō & Smalley, 2011). Standardizing processes provides the framework for performance enhancement by creating a baseline against which progress can be measured. Standards are the ruler for gauging and scaling improvement. Will HR see this benefit (Zirar et al., 2021)?

Another key insight that many leaders overlook is the importance of understanding their current state. This appreciation serves as the foundation for establishing a baseline against which one can gauge the desired 'to-be' state. Without this clarity, it is not easy to plan for or achieve advancement. The adage 'what gets measured gets improved' rings especially true here. HR is instrumental in this process, providing the tools, data analytics, and insights necessary to benchmark performance, identify areas for improvement, and drive growth. To illustrate this point, I recall an insightful experience (Fowler, 2015) from his deep-level tour of Toyota's Georgetown, Kentucky facility, during which several executives from Ford Motor accompanied him. He elaborates,

> During our tour, we were immersed in Toyota's daily production routines, in which they employ both visual and audio cues to monitor operations. For instance, specific, familiar songs resonate through the facility whenever a production line halts, helping teams identify the source area and

rapidly address issues. At one pivotal moment, a senior-level Ford executive observed the situation and remarked to a young Toyota group leader, "You all are really messed up today." The young man, who was actively managing his team's efforts during a critical moment, paused. He looked up at the taller executive and replied with unexpected confidence, "Yeah, but at least we know it!"

This moment was revealing and indicative of a crucial difference in mindset. The ability to openly acknowledge one's own difficulties, as demonstrated by this group leader, reflects a fundamental understanding of one's operational reality. This transparency fosters an environment where continuous improvement is not only possible but also embraced as a necessity. So, why do many business leaders struggle to gain a clear understanding of their current 'as-is' state? This ambiguity prevents them from effectively envisioning the 'to-be' state, creating path barriers to strategic planning and innovation (MacLennan & Markides, 2021). Additionally, in today's fast-paced business environment, what risks does the 'tyranny of the urgent' pose? When leaders prioritize immediate concerns over long-term strategy, they may inadvertently neglect the essential groundwork needed for sustained improvement. The pressure to deliver quick results can lead to reactive decision-making, stifling creativity, and preventing organizations from fully realizing their potential.

In summary, fostering high performance requires a comprehensive understanding of current processes, a commitment to standardization, and an environment that encourages continuous improvement, regardless of the idea-submitter's level. HR can play a pivotal role in guiding operations through this journey, equipping leaders with the insights and tools necessary to measure, analyze root cause and opportunity, and improve performance (HCM, 2007). By addressing these foundational elements, organizations can move beyond mere survival to prosper in an increasingly complex business landscape.

HR For Employee Stages

Human resources deal with humans. When individuals are involved in business scenarios, unpredictability can arise. HR managers must understand that workers go through five general phases in their development. From being new and idealistic, through some storming and complaining, to possible engagement, with the goal of consistent and improvable productivity. What can HR managers do to smooth out an employee's predictable career path - from reliance to independence?

From an HR perspective, two vital processes require attention: 1) Employee Onboarding and 2) Placement. Sensitive onboarding serves as the foundation for talent development (Davila & Pina-Ramirez, 2023). It makes it possible. It considers both the present and the future, initiates engagement, shortens the new employee orientation period, and fosters a learning environment. Savvy HR managers use best practices, job aids, templates, and checklists. Strong onboarding nurtures longevity.

Next, enablers for better employee placement include decision support for linking roles to the organizational mission (Widianta et al., 2018), leading to informed selection, talent strategies, and placement to optimize performance (Ikhsanuddin et al., 2024). Placement is the first decision made after a new employee starts. Ikhsanuddin observes that placement considers four key factors: worker education, work knowledge, work skills, and work experience. Effective employee placement enhances the team's macro skill set (Luecke, 2004). As workers are linked with one another, teaming possibilities increase. People can then recognize their interdependence with others (force multiplication) and collaborate to find solutions (Edmondson, 2012).

The human resources office should be more than just a punitive function where records are kept in files and used as evidence for employee discipline. Wouldn't it change a worker's perspective if HR were considered helpful to workers? One way to achieve this effectively is to provide accurate personality and strength assessments (Rath, 2007) to enhance workers' self-awareness and foster a sense of connectedness with others, thereby promoting the potential for robust teaming.

Human resources personnel's priority is to meet employees where they are in their development. There are (up to) five milestones that workers go through. Some make it to five; many do not. The first of five stops along the way includes being *new and idealistic.* Then, many become disappointed with the culture when *reality differs* from what was presented during their orientation. If an employee's concerns are addressed at this time and they work through the frustration without seeking *greener pastures*, companies have a real shot at seeing a positive *impact.* If those impactful workers remain with the organization for an extended period, their *longevity* can significantly contribute to productivity in the real world. What is HR's responsibility as workers move through each of these milestones? We will review them.

New and Idealistic

Getting new employees up to speed (Bradt & Vonnegut, 2009) typically involves providing consistent *direction*, including onboarding, placement, reporting cadences, and adherence to the chain of command. Employees want to understand their new environment quickly. HR leaders can help operational leaders streamline the orientation process and enhance comfort levels.

Reality is Different

HR and operational leaders, in tandem, provide relevant *information* through coaching during this time. Shadowing (DiMattia, 1996), also known as on-the-job (OJT) training, pairs new employees with more experienced ones to learn responsibilities and skills and help them overcome new-worker frustrations. OJT training (Barron et al., 1997) offers adults practical, informal learning. Developmental educator Dr. Lawrence O. Richards (Sell, 1992) advocates moving beyond cognitive dumping (i.e., orientation classes, PowerPoint presentations, and mere wide-aisle area tours) by relating what is taught in class to real-time, day-to-day operations. This is accomplished through review, repetition, learning, and gathering information…while on the job. The resolution of most worker complaints can move them to the next level.

Greener Pastures

Staff turnover (Allen & Vardaman, 2021) and quiet quitting (Serenko, 2023) hurt morale, efficiency, and effectiveness. What should HR leaders do to mitigate the Great Resignation (Matuson, 2024)? How do organizations retain high-performing individuals and mitigate premature exits due to dissatisfaction? HR leaders can *assist* skeptical employees by offering a structured career development path and by monitoring job satisfaction (Martin, 2022). Levit & Booksx (2008) suggest frontloading better selection, thorough background checks, supportive probation periods, and iterative, accessible learning throughout a worker's career. Most employees want to contribute with a sense of belonging. Executives would do well to understand the power of partnering with their HR leaders (Mariscotti, 2020).

Impact

Leadership training (Russell & ATD, 2015) may be the linchpin for employee retention and development. Once workers have (in their minds) resolved that their place of employment is not perfect, further leader development can provide them with insights into personal growth and productivity. HR managers can offer additional *opportunities* for ambitious workers. Utilization management techniques (Gray & Field, 1989) have traditionally been applied to processes such as cost reduction and energy realignment, which can now also be applied to employee development and growth. Have we placed them in the best position to thrive, contribute, and safeguard the company's mission and vision? If the answer is yes, and they stay committed, companies can leverage the final stage.

Longevity

Senior workers can make the most significant impact when their managers provide overwatch—protecting them from noise and distraction. Doyle & Doyle referred to Gain Management (1992) as a thought process aimed at fostering teamwork, productivity, and profitability. This can be accomplished by giving your senior leaders the flexibility to shadow younger, less experienced workers. In essence, this becomes a non-formal retention and development program. HR executives help operational leaders lead! Sounds easy, but it is not. A few strategically placed winners are a force multiplier for improvement and for speed (Stack, 2018).

In conclusion, we study leadership and human resources because they bring value to organizations and individuals. Decisions move life forward. There is great worth in considering leadership (Alvesson & Spicer, 2012) for three primary reasons: Globalization (Adler & Bartholomew, 1992), Self-Actualization (Visiontemenos, 2012), and Impact (Weiss, 1999). How so?

1) Globalization: Leaders who push (and achieve) for results must recognize and appreciate the business, cultural, and political nuances worldwide. This includes understanding the technologies, tastes, work ethic, work style, national expectations, and trends through real-time adaptation (Northouse, 2013).

2) Self-Actualization: When life's basic needs are fulfilled, humanity can then start to transform technology for the greater good. Leadership acumen is what drives this progress for the individual, their contributions to their community, and society at large.

3) Impact: Leadership is the key ingredient to move from a myopic worldview to a purpose-driven life (Craig & Snook, 2014).

Leadership, technology, and human resources, when aligned and intertwined, become a cord of three strands that is not easily broken (Bositkhanova & Dadaboyev, 2025).

Customer-Driven HR Culture (T-R-A-I-N)

Understanding the complex dimensions of culture is essential for human resource managers as these serve as both outputs and inputs within organizational systems. This cyclical interaction profoundly influences not only teams and companies but also extends to national contexts. An inquiry into leadership qualities is crucial to determine whether organizational leaders are architects of their internal culture or succumb to harmful prevailing norms.

Structure emerges as a pivotal element that drives behavior (Eckelman & Nasiri, 2011), which in turn delineates organizational culture (Cihon & Mattaini, 2020). Schein (2004) offers a comprehensive analysis of the multifaceted nature of organizational and business cultures. He believes this encompasses a few core elements:

1) Structural Stability – that being culture, the stalwart of group identity, often exists under the conscious awareness of team players, which dictates patterns of behavior that define 'how things are done,' often requiring no explicit explanation. The omnipresence of culture ensures that its influence permeates every function and activity across the organizational landscape, establishing a comprehensive framework within which organizational behaviors manifest. "Culture eats strategy for breakfast!" – Peter Drucker (Tallman et al., 2023).

2) Patterning - Culture fosters coherence among group behaviors, values, and rituals. Structural definitions encapsulate social norms within an organization, as illustrated by job descriptions, regular meeting schedules, routines, formal agendas, and both spoken (and silent) leadership expectations. These documented structures, encompassing policies and standard operating procedures

(SOPs), provide clear guidance for acceptable and unacceptable behaviors, thereby setting distinct boundaries (Malin, 2000).

Additionally, the philosophy underlying lean manufacturing provides insight into organizational culture. It emphasizes three integral behaviors that catalyze organizational growth and maturity: respect for people, continuous improvement, and learning, along with a process-and results-driven approach. (Michigan.gov, 2004; Team, 2021). Further illuminating this discourse, the Global Leadership and Organizational Behavior Effectiveness (GLOBE) Project, a comprehensive study, scrutinized the behaviors of 17,000 managers across more than 950 organizations, spanning 62 distinct cultural contexts (McCauley, 2017; Northouse, 2016, p. 431). This extensive research cataloged both desirable and undesirable leadership traits:

Desirable Attributes include trustworthiness, foresight, positivity, confidence-building, intelligence, win-win problem-solving, administrative skills, an orientation to excellence and justice, proactive planning, dynamism, motivational capacity, decisiveness, communicativeness, coordination skills, honesty, encouragement, motive arousal, effective bargaining, being well-informed, and team-building proficiency. Quite the list!

Undesirable Attributes include isolation tendencies, irritability, ruthlessness, asocial behavior, non-explicit communication, dictatorial tendencies, non-cooperativeness, and egocentrism (Northouse, 2007). The implementation of organizational outcomes cultural assessments, as espoused by Hutcherson (2014), enables companies to identify weaknesses proactively. It is imperative, especially under the stress of contemporary budgetary constraints:

> Organizational Optimization (OO) is the new approach to evaluating your organization, examining its current health, and maximizing its future potential. Its purpose is to

strategically align the organization, optimize the execution of its strategy, and culturally set the stage for growth and prosperity. The OO Assessment can be applied to any organization, whether an international conglomerate, a federal agency, a city, a professional sports team, or an entrepreneurial organization looking to upgrade operations (Hutcherson, 2014).

In today's ever-changing workplace, a holistic approach to Human Resources (HR) can be transformative. Imagine a unified framework (directing inertia into momentum) by combining Human Resource Management (HRM), Human Resource Development (HRD), Strategic Human Resource Management (SHRM), and other pertinent services into a single, cohesive system. By doing so, we create a more elegant and practical process that embodies the philosophy of T-R-A-I-N, centralizing our efforts around the benefit of the workforce. Below are the five specific tactics (competencies) HR executives should weigh.

1) TELL/TEACH: Communication is the foundation of successful onboarding and employee engagement (Janson, 2025). By articulating the organization's values, expectations, and culture, we can provide new hires with the clarity and understanding needed today. Seminars, orientation sessions, and mentoring can serve as platforms for sharing critical instruction, thereby fostering a sense of belonging from the outset (Davis, 2011; Sims, 2002). *In essence, provide DIRECTION!*

2) REVIEW: Continuous feedback is essential for growth. By engaging in regular reviews with employees, we can partner with them on their journey towards job self-actualization (Huang, 2012). This involves creating structured opportunities for workers to discuss their development, identify areas for improvement, and explore professional avenues (Smith, 2018). The review process not

only enhances performance but also strengthens the employer-employee relationship by demonstrating a commitment to member success and well-being. *In essence, share <u>INFORMATION!</u>*

3) ASSIST: A relevant HR system should model employee support. Assisting them as needed (through coaching, counseling, resources, or training) can give them a sense of value and help them overcome challenges related to roles and responsibilities (Hawley, 2004). This support primarily works during transitions, when change occurs, or when employees encounter specific career obstacles (Stone, 2007). *In essence, <u>MINISTER!</u>*

4) INVOLVE: Employee involvement in performance applications and succession planning is crucial for fostering a sense of ownership (Wolfe, 1996). By engaging employees in discussions about performance goals, future opportunities, and the criteria for success, we not only empower them but also cultivate a culture of transparency and mutual respect (McCredie, 2018). This collaborative approach can lead to greater job satisfaction and retention, as employees feel that they have a say in their career trajectory. *In essence, provide <u>OPPORTUNITIES!</u>*

5) NOMINATE: Recognizing talent from within is a requirement of an effective HR strategy (Chikungwa & Chamisa, 2013). Nominating employees for advancement when they demonstrate competence shows an organization's commitment to rewarding hard work and potential (Fisher, 2008). Retention and morale are multiplied.

By integrating these five principles into a single, holistic HR framework, organizations can create a thriving workforce that can navigate the complex scenarios of the modern work environment. The T-R-A-I-N model not only emphasizes workforce development but also underscores the idea that effective HR practices foster a culture of growth, support, and shared success. Ultimately, this approach positions HR as a central pillar of strategic organizational development, paving the way for long-term sustainability and effective succession planning for both workers and the agency. *In essence, <u>PROMOTE</u>!*

Tying HR to Leadership Development

HR teams have the unique opportunity to directly influence several dozen executive leaders throughout their careers. The value of employee engagement cannot be overstated, both for individuals and for the company as a whole (Films of Australia, 2015). HR leaders have control over many motivators for employees, including incentives (Adler, 2013), survey administration, findings, and action planning (Folkman, 1998), while formalizing Employee Resource Support initiatives (Rodriguez, 2022). The age-old adage applies here: priorities are determined by two things (pocketbooks and calendars). Do not be fooled! How companies allocate their time and resources to employees determines the level of priority assigned to them.

Will executives invest in the competencies and outreach of employee resource groups (ERGs), or will mere inertia determine career outcomes? Each CEO will determine that. If groups of workers are provided with clear directions, accurate information, assistance, and opportunities, organizations can position themselves to be protected and prosper through the principles of overwatch. Human resources help develop leaders, and leaders, in turn, help provide resources (Lawler et al., 2018). It is a reciprocal win-win!

In short, we encourage a few final tactical considerations for CEOs, including iteratively and anonymously measuring employee engagement (Phillips et al., 2016), formalizing an employee reward system (Armstrong, 2007), aligning lower-level metrics with the broader company's strategic objectives and key results (Niven & Lamonte, 2016), and investing in a knowledgeable Organization Development lead (Singh & Ananthanarayanan, 2013). These thoughtful Hoshin interaction models provide the infrastructure for personal growth, enabling the C-Suite (strategy) to align their future success with others (tactical) (Kesterson, 2015).

Conclusion: Human Resources Enable Employee Alignment

Broad, fair, and equitable talent development necessitates a level playing field where we see foundational leaders apply situational agility (Dearlove, 2023) and combine mission with individual focus. Leadership awareness creates a force multiplier that empowers workers to achieve self-actualization, measured alongside other contributions that are interconnected and work in tandem. Leaders who know their people place them in positions that align with those of other team members. Like a sailboat Captain, they orchestrate the level of effort among multiple shipmates, adjusting the sails to take the most direct course for speed. Human resource leaders align individuals' varied skills to maximize their impact (Beyerlein et al., 2003).

Flexible HR leaders move organizations toward excellence by aligning worker placement in the correct positions at the right time (Pawłowska, 2023). Improvement guru Mark Graban (2016) lists organizational alignment as the first pillar of the infrastructure needed for continuous improvement. One of the world's best hospitals, the Cleveland Clinic (CCIM Model, 2019), also incorporates visual management (not hiding data), structured problem-solving, and adherence to standard work to complement its systems approach. HR managers play a crucial role in employee placement, creating awareness and providing training, thereby aligning individual efforts with company objectives (Panchadsaram, 2019). Leadership (support) coupled with employee (alignment) positions agile companies to better navigate in the world of volatility, uncertainty, complexity, and ambiguity (Nandram & Bindlish, 2017), and human resource managers are the key enablers and organizational glue.

Succession planning and talent engagement are more than just human resources functions; they also involve dialogue with the organization's leadership (Rothwell, 2022). For far too long, these two processes have been discrete; often created in vacuums. Operations executives tend to handpick their own candidates for promotion, while HR runs their typical personnel management functions.

Human resource and operational leaders should work in combination to develop team members, not only for those deemed for near-future promotion, but for all employees to some degree (UKG, 2025). Direction, information, resources, opportunities, and oversight support the leader's intervention for team and individual development. Evidence of HR's effective input is observed in stable employee placement, fulfilled roles, retention, and engagement, as well as in individual development and impactful actions (Eigenhuis & Dijk, 2008).

In concert, this aligned HR/OPs dyad support system fosters a unified front for employees and provides linkages to advance them in the following ways (Kenton, 2005).

1) Employees who receive direct guidance from their superiors, coupled with a suitable fit placement from HR, tend to adjust quickly. Nittrouer et al. (2022) found that leadership partnering with human resources in advocacy strategies promoted career stability and advancement.
    →So, ***start them well and point them*** in the right direction.

2) Employees who are provided consistent information develop a better understanding of organizational expectations, their roles within that system, and start to contribute more quickly. Dollard et al. (2019) found that a social safety environment increases workers' comfort level and productivity.
    →So, ***guide them and align them.***

3) Employees resourced adequately (knowledge, time, attention, money, and supplies) tend to advance. NATO employment leaders (2012) found that "financial incentives, flexible forms of service and employment status, compatibility of

career and family, career planning, professional development (and) training (suitability)" increased retention and empowerment (p. ES - 1).

→ So, ***support them to keep them***.

4) Employees allowed to be responsible need to take on responsibilities (Richardson, 2015). He found that identity clarity, values, adaptability, relationships, operational thinking, and co-creation enabled responsibility.

→ So, ***challenge them and watch them*** through opportunity.

5) And lastly, protected employees who feel (and know) a sense of mutual trust (Shea, 1984) are more likely to be promoted. Basini (2012) challenges executives who want to build trust to be more human, more serious, and more ambitious in aligning metrics with their mission (p. 158). Employees require vulnerability and threat intelligence (Haber & Hibbert, 2018).

→ Therefore, ***set them free, but keep an eye on them.***
See Figure 1 on page 154.

Applied together, these five principles lay the foundation for employee development, one that acknowledges the necessity of partnership between functional leaders and HR professionals. When organizations invest in clear communication, appropriate placement, holistic resourcing, meaningful responsibility, and trust-building, they cultivate a workforce that is not only capable but also engaged and resilient in the face of change. This distinction should not be underestimated; it underpins organizational agility, succession continuity, and sustained talent engagement. Both leaders and HR professionals (dyad) must share ownership of employee growth pathways, identify and address gaps, and ensure that every team member has access to advancement.

Cliff Notes: Executive officers are not concerned with the labels given to functions. They want results, regardless of the name. In summary, the mission is to integrate HR, HRD, HRM, and SHRM into a unified system in which ongoing attention to resources aligns with employee needs (Simms, 2002). This often follows a predictable path:

1) TELL/TEACH: hire and orient new employees better (Davis, 2011),

2) REVIEW: partner with employees in their on-the-job (O-T-J) journey to self-actualization (Smith, 2018),

3) ASSIST employees as needed (Hawley, 2004)

4) INVOLVE employees in performance and succession planning (McCredie, 2018), and

5) NOMINATE them for promotion when ready (Fisher, 2008). T-R-A-I-N is a memorable HR acronym. Ultimately, the measure of success lies not only in metrics such as retention and promotion rates, but also in the sense of belonging and purpose that employees experience.

> ***"Success in HR is not just about managing resources. It is about inspiring and unleashing the full potential of individuals."***
>
> *- Dr. Dieter Veldsman, Chief HR Scientist, at AIHR (2025).*

Figure 1

Leadership Development through Human Resources

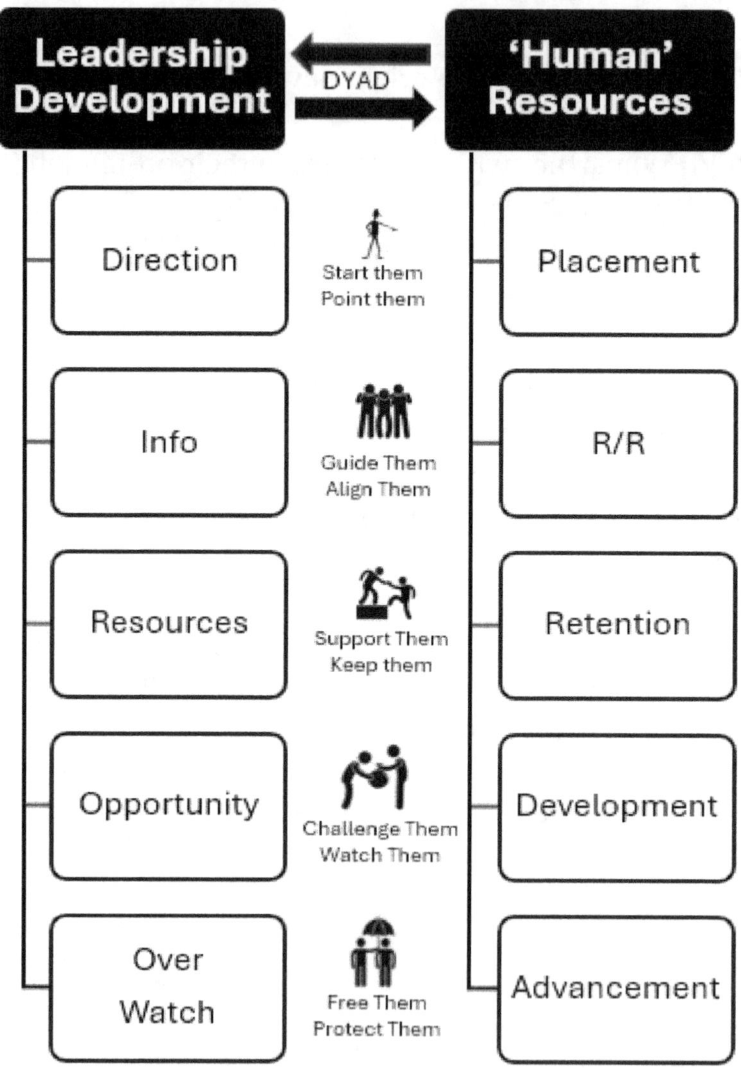

Appendix A References

50+ Incredible Big Data Statistics for 2024: Facts, Market Size & Industry Growth. (2025). Big Data Analytics News. https://bigdataanalyticsnews.com/big-data-statistics/

Adair, J. E. (2010). *Strategic leadership: How to think and plan strategically and provide direction* (1st ed.). Kogan Page.

Adler, J. (2013). *Examining contributions to a corporate microblog as a basis for an employee incentive system* (1st ed.). Anchor Academic Pub.

Adler, N. J., & Bartholomew, S. (1992). Managing globally competent people. Academy of

Management Executive, 6, 52–65.

Allen, D. G., & Vardaman, J. M. (Eds.). (2021). *Global talent retention : understanding employee turnover around the world*. Emerald Publishing Limited.

Alvesson M, Spicer A (2012). Critical leadership studies: The case for critical performativity.

Human Relations 65: 367–390.

Ammons, D. N., & Roenigk, D. J. (2022). Staffing factor calculation: Projections for uninterruptible services. In *Tools for Decision Making* (3rd ed., Vol. 1, pp. 180–186). Routledge. https://doi.org/10.4324/9781003129431-17

Anderson, J., & Langley, A. (2017). *Employee reward structures* (Sixth edition). Spiramus.

Ardichvili, A., & Jondle, D. (2009). Ethical Business Cultures: A Literature Review and Implications for HRD. *Human Resource Development Review*, *8*(2), 223-https://doi.org/10.1177/1534484309334098Links to an external site.

Armstrong, M. (2007). *A handbook of employee reward management and practice* (2nd ed.). Kogan Page.

Arneson, S. (2010). *Bootstrap leadership : 50 ways to break out, take charge, and move up* (1st ed.). Berrett-Koehler Publishers.

Arslan, A., & Staub, S. (2013). Theory X and Theory Y Type Leadership Behavior and Its Impact on Organizational Performance: Small Business Owners in the Şishane Lighting and Chandelier District. *Procedia, Social and Behavioral Sciences*, *75*, 102–111. https://doi.org/10.1016/j.sbspro.2013.04.012

Askitas, N., & Zimmermann, K. F. (Eds.). (2015). *Using internet activity data to analyze human resources issues* (1st ed.). Emerald.

Axelrod, W., & Coyle, J. (2011). *Make talent your business : how exceptional managers develop people while getting results* (1st ed.). Berrett-Koehler Publishers.

Badiru, A. B., & Tourangeau, M. L. (2023). *Leadership matters : industrial engineering framework for developing and sustaining industry* (First edition.). CRC Press. https://doi.org/10.1201/9781003311348

Baldwin, P. E. (2019). *Issues facing the United States Secret Service* (P. E. Baldwin, Ed.). SNova.

Bartlett, C. A., & Ghoshal, S. (1998). *Managing across borders : the transnational solution* (2nd ed.). Harvard Business School Press. https://search.ebscohost.com/login.aspx?direct=true&scope=site&db=nlebk&db=nlabk&AN=35053

Barron, J. M., Berger, M. C., & Black, D. A. (1997). On-the-job training. W.E. Upjohn Institute for Employment Research. https://search.ebscohost.com/login.aspx?direct=true&scope=site&db=nlebk&db=nlabk&AN=28072

Basini, J. (2012). *Why should anyone buy from you? Earn customer trust to drive business success* (First edition.). Financial Times Prentice Hall is an imprint of Pearson.

Batson, C. D. (2011). Altruism in Humans. New York: Oxford University Press.

Baum, T. (1995). *Managing Human Resources In the European Tourism and Hospitality Industry: A Strategic Approach.* Chapman and Hall.

Bean, C. (2023). *The Accidental Instructional Designer : Learning Design for the Digital Age* (Second edition). ATD Press.

Berger, L. A., & Berger, D. R. (Eds.). (2011). *The talent management handbook : creating a sustainable competitive advantage by selecting, developing, and promoting the best people* (Second edition). McGraw-Hill.

Berke, D., Kossler, M. E., & Wakefield, M. (2008). *Developing leadership talent* (1st edition). Pfeiffer.

Bernal, E. M. (2002). Three ways to achieve a more equitable representation of culturally and linguistically different students in GT programs. Roeper Review, 24(2), 82-88. doi:10.1080/02783190209554134

Beyerlein, M. M., Johnson, D. A., & Beyerlein, S. T. (2003). *Team-based organizing.* Emerald. https://www.emerald.com/insight/publication/doi/10.1016/S1572-0977(2003)9

Blanchard, K. H. (2001). *High five! The magic of working together* (First edition.). Morrow.

Bloom, D. (2021). *Employee empowerment : the prime component of sustainable change management* (1st ed.). Routledge.

Bolman, L. G., & Deal, T. E. (2014). *How great leaders think : the art of reframing* (1st edition): Jossey-Bass, A Wiley Brand.

Bositkhanova, N., & Dadaboyev, S. M. U. (2025). Revolutionizing workforce planning: the strategic role of AI in HR strategy. *DISCOVER GLOBAL SOCIETY, 3*(1), Article 100. https://doi.org/10.1007/s44282-025-00252-y

Boyd, D. W. (2001). *Systems analysis and modeling: a macro-to-micro approach with multidisciplinary applications.* Academic Press.

Bradt, G. B., & Vonnegut, M. (2009). Onboarding : How to get your new employees up to speed in half the time (1st edition). Wiley.

Briker, R., Walter, F., & Cole, M. S. (2021). *Hurry up! The role of supervisors' time urgency and self-perceived status for autocratic leadership and subordinates' well-being.* Personnel Psychology, 74(1), 55–76. https://doi.org/10.1111/peps.12400

Brindle, M., & Mainiero, L. A. (2000). *Managing power through lateral networking.* Quorum. https://search.ebscohost.com/login.aspx?direct=true&scope=site&db=nlebk&db=nlabk&AN=62727

Brophy, J. R., & American Academy of Orthopedic Surgeons. (2010). *Leadership essentials for emergency medical services.* Jones & Bartlett Publishers.

Buchbinder, S. & Shanks, N. (2017). *Introduction to health care management, 3rd Ed,* (Chapter 1 - 4, pp. xvii–106) (4 hours).

Calarco, A., & Gurvis, J. (2006). Leadership in Action: Flexible Flyers: A Leader's Framework for Developing Adaptability. Center for Creative Leadership.

Carbery, R., & Cross, C. (2015). *Human resource development: A concise introduction.* New York: Palgrave Macmillan Ltd, ISBN: 978-1-137-36009-0

Carroll, P., & Mui, C. (2008). *Billion-dollar lessons : what you can learn from the most inexcusable business failures of the last 25 years.* Portfolio.

Cascio, W. F., Boudreau, J., Russo, D., Davis, A., & Shannon, J. (2011). *HR strategies for employee engagement.* (Second edition.) FT Press.

Chapter 6: The Three 'I's of Initiative - The Case Centre. (2015). The Case Centre. https://www.thecasecentre.org/products/view?id=134206

Catino, M. (2013). *Organizational myopia : problems of rationality and foresight in organizations* (1st ed.). Cambridge University Press.

Ceberio, M., Kosheleva, O., Kreinovich, V., Ernest, N., Bede, B., & Cohen, K. (2023). Integrity First, Service Before Self, and Excellence: Core Values of the US Air Force Naturally Follow from Decision Theory. In *Fuzzy Information Processing 2023* (Vol. 751, pp. 320–324). Springer Nature Switzerland. https://doi.org/10.1007/978-3-031-46778-3_30

Charan, R. (2024). *The Leadership Pipeline : Developing Leaders in the Digital Age* (Third edition). John Wiley & Sons, Inc

Chikungwa, T., & Chamisa, S. F. (2013). An Evaluation of Recognition on Performance as a Motivator: A Case of Eastern Cape Higher Education Institution. *Mediterranean Journal of Social Sciences.* https://doi.org/10.5901/mjss.2013.v4n14p219

Cihon, T. M., & Mattaini, M. A. (Eds.). (2020). *Behavior science perspectives on culture and community* (1st ed. 2020). Springer. https://doi.org/10.1007/978-3-030-45421-0

Cleveland Clinic. (2019). *Continuous Improvement | Cleveland Clinic.* Cleveland Clinic. https://my.clevelandclinic.org/departments/patient-experience/depts/continuous-improvement

Colvin, H. M., Taylor, R. M., & Institute of Medicine. Planning Committee on Workforce Resiliency Programs. (2012). *Building a resilient workforce :*

opportunities for the Department of Homeland Security, workshop summary* (1st ed.). National Academies Press.

Condolff Bevenour, C. V. (2015). Career Evolution: Building Your Leadership Legacy. In *Unleashing Your Inner Leader* (pp. 163–182). John Wiley & Sons, Inc. https://doi.org/10.1002/9781118936689.ch10

Cook, M. F., & American Management Association. (1992). *The AMA handbook for employee recruitment and retention.* American Management Association.

Covey, S. R., Merrill, A. R., & Merrill, R. R. (1994). *First things first : to live, to love, to learn, to leave a legacy.* Simon & Schuster.

Craig, N., & Snook, S. (18 August 2014). From Purpose to Impact. Harvard Business Review.
https://hbr.org/2014/05/from-purpose-to-impact

Crumpton, M. A. (2015). *Strategic human resource planning for academic libraries : information, technology, and organization* (1st edition). Chandos Publishing.

Culpepper, P. D. (2018). *Creating Cooperation : How States Develop Human Capital in Europe.* Cornell University Press.
https://doi.org/10.7591/9781501723629

Das Gupta, A. (2020). *Strategic human resource management : formulating and implementing HR strategies for a competitive advantage* (1st ed.). Routledge.
Routledge. https://doi.org/10.4324/9780203455746Links to an external site.

Davila, N., & Pina-Ramirez, W. (2023). *Effective onboarding* (1st edition). Association for Talent Development.

Davis, C. J. (Ed.). (2017). *Servant Leadership and Followership : Examining the Impact on Workplace Behavior* (1st ed. 2017). Springer International Publishing. https://doi.org/10.1007/978-3-319-59366-1

Davis, A. (Alison B., & Shannon, J., 2011). *Set new hires up for success with the proper orientation program* (1st edition). FT Press Delivers.

Davis, A., Shannon, J., Cascio, W., Boudreau, J., Sesil, J., Waber, B., Biswas, B., & Director, S. (2013). *The Definitive Guide to HR Management Tools (Collection)* (1st edition). Pearson.

Dearlove, D. (Ed.). (2023). *Particular uncertainty : leading with agility and resilience in an unpredictable world.* John Wiley & Sons, Inc.

Dewald, J., & Wilson, W. B. (2018). *Achieving Longevity : How Great Firms Prosper Through Entrepreneurial Thinking.* University of Toronto Press.
https://doi.org/10.3138/9781442622739

Dieter Veldsman. (2025). AIHR. https://www.aihr.com/blog/author/dieter-veldsman/

DiMattia, S. S. (1996). [Rev. of *Workplace issues -- Structured On-the-Job Training: Unleashing Employee Expertise in the Workplace by Ronald L. Jacobs and Michael J. Jones*]. *Library Journal (1976)*, *121*(5), 39.

Director, S., Cascio, W., & Boudreau, J. (2013). *Key Tools for Human Resource Management (Collection)* (1st edition). Pearson.

Dixon, M. L. (2007). *Leadership styles, diversity in work groups, work group effectiveness, and turnover intention.* ProQuest Dissertations & Theses.

Dollard, M. F., Dormann, C., & Awang Idris, Mohd. (Eds.). (2019). *Psychosocial Safety Climate : A New Work Stress Theory* (1st ed., 2019). Springer International Publishing. https://doi.org/10.1007/978-3-030-20319-1

Doyle, R. J., & Doyle, P. I. (1992). Gain Management : a process for building teamwork, productivity, and profitability throughout your organization. AMACOM.

Duberman, T. L., & Sachs, R. (2019). *From competition to collaboration : how leaders cultivate cross-sector partnerships to drive value and transform health* (1st ed.). HAP.

Dunn, K. J., & Dunn, R. (1983). *Situational leadership for principals : the school administrator in action.* Prentice-Hall.

Duran-Stanton, A., & Masson, A. (18 May 2021). *Lessons in Followership: Good Leaders Are Not Always Out Front.* Association of the United States Army. https://www.ausa.org/articles/lessons-followership-good-leaders-arent-always-out-front

Eckelman, M. J., & Nasiri, F. (2011). Thinking in Systems by Donella H. Meadows. *Journal of Industrial Ecology*, *15*(1), 156–157. https://doi.org/10.1111/j.1530-9290.2010.00314.x

Economic and Social Commission for Asia and the Pacific. (2001). *HRD for the empowerment of people with disabilities : seven innovative approaches submitted for the 2000 ESCAP HRD award.* United Nations.

Edmonson, A. P. (2002). "The Local and Variegated 1nature of Learning in Organizations: A Group-Level Perspective," Organization Science 13, no. 2: 128–146.

Edmondson, A. C. (2012). *Teaming: how organizations learn, innovate, and compete in the knowledge economy* (1st ed.). Jossey-Bass.

Edmondson, A. C. (2013). *Teaming to innovate* (1st ed.). Jossey-Bass.

Edmondson, A., Marianne Lewis, & Wendy Smith. (2022). *Both/And Thinking.* Harvard Business Review Press.

Eigenhuis, A., & Dijk, R. van. (2008). *HR strategy for the high-performing business : inspiring success through effective human resource management.* Kogan Page. https://search.ebscohost.com/login.aspx?direct=true&scope=site&db=nlebk&db=nlabk&AN=262749

Elliott, J. (2003). Dynamic Assessment in Educational Settings: Realizing Potential. Educational Review, 55, 15-32

Elliott, T. (24 July 2013). The Datification Of Daily Life. *Forbes.* https://www.forbes.com/sites/sap/2013/07/24/the-datification-of-daily-life/

Emilsson, M. U., Strid, A.-L., & Söderberg, M. (2022). Lack of Coordination between Health Care and Social Care in Multi-Professional Teamwork - the Obstacle for Coherent Care of Older People Suffering from Multi-

Morbidity. *Journal of Population Ageing, 15*(2), 319–335. https://doi.org/10.1007/s12062-020-09300-8

Evans, B. (1992). *The politics of the training market : from Manpower Services Commission to training and enterprise councils*. Routledge. https://doi.org/10.4324/9780203039984

Evans, C. (2003). *Managing for knowledge: HR's strategic role* (1st ed.). Butterworth-Heinemann.

Factors Affecting Attraction, Recruitment & Retention of NATO Military Medical Professionals. (2012). NATO Science & Technology Organization.

Fields, K. L. (2009). Feedback: The Breakfast of Champions. *American Agent & Broker, 81*(2), 22.

Fisher, J. G. (2008). *How to run successful employee incentive schemes: creating effective programs for improved performance* (3rd ed.). Kogan Page.

Folkman, J. (1998). *Employee surveys that make a difference using customized feedback tools to transform your organization*. Novation's Group. https://search.ebscohost.com/login.aspx?direct=true&scope=site&db=nlebk&db=nlabk&AN=6752

Ford, H., & Crowther, S. (1926). Today and tomorrow. Associated Bookbuyers' company.

FOWLER, T. W. (21 December 2015). *CEO's Love #Integration: How #Datification Saved #Lean! There once was a Fortune 500 company CEO who had his manufacturing division floor-level supervisors and operators trained in "lean." The consulting company he hired taught the typical lean tools, such as 5-Why, 5S, Kanban, error-proofing, and value*. Linkedin.com. https://www.linkedin.com/pulse/ceos-love-integration-how-datification-saved-lean-timothy-fowler/?trackingId=BeR51L4lS9ai6dZ5o2SxUg%3D%3D

FOWLER, T. (2025). *Right-Brain Problem Solving In A Left-Brain Business World*. SlideShare; Slideshare. https://www.slideshare.net/slideshow/right-brain-problem-solving-in-a-left-brain-business-world/7487230 (Also searchable on the archived InternetMedicine website).

Futures Wheel – Yondar. (2024). Yondar.org. https://yondar.org/toolkit/the-futures-wheel/

Garavan, T. N., Costine, P., & Heraty, N. (1995). The emergence of strategic human resource development. *Journal of European Industrial Training, 19*(10), 4–10. https://doi.org/10.1108/03090599510095816Links to an external site.

Garman, A. & Dye, C. (2009). *The healthcare c-suite: Leadership development at the top (Ache Management)*, (Part 1, xi - 52) (2 hours).

Gerber, R., & Lankshear, C. (2000). *Training for a competent workforce* (1st ed.).

Gordon, S., Feldman, D. L., & Leonard, M. (Eds.). (2014). *Collaborative caring : stories and reflections on teamwork in health care* (1st ed.). ILR Press. https://doi.org/10.7591/9780801454639

Gould, N. (2018). FROM THE PRESIDENT. *Manitoba Teacher, 97*(3), 4-.

Graban, M. (19 January 2016). *Cleveland Clinic Improvement Model, Part 1: Alignment & Visual Management*. Lean Blog. https://www.leanblog.org/2016/01/the-cleveland-clinic-improvement-model-part-1/

Grammarly. (2025). *Grammarly*. Grammarly.com. https://app.grammarly.com/

Greenleaf, R. K. (1977). *Servant leadership: a journey into the nature of legitimate power and greatness*.

Grant, A. M., & Parker, S. (2009). Redesigning work design theories: The Rise of relational and proactive perspectives. *The Academy of Management Annals*, 31(1), 317–375.

Gray, B. H., & Field, M. J. (1989). Controlling costs and changing patient care? The role of utilization management (1st ed.). *National Academy Press*.

Greek, J. (2014). *Social Network-Powered Information Sharing* (First Edition). Rosen Publishing.

Haber, M. J., & Hibbert, B. (2018). *Asset Attack Vectors : Building Effective Vulnerability Management Strategies to Protect Organizations* (1st ed., 2018). Apress. https://doi.org/10.1007/978-1-4842-3627-7

Hackman, D. C., Pollack, J., & Baker, M. (2024). Individual perceptions of complex projects: A window into project team and stakeholder mental models. *International Journal of Project Management*, 42(4), Article 102603. https://doi.org/10.1016/j.ijproman.2024.102603

Hallo, L. (2022). Holistic view of intuition and analysis in leadership decision-making and problem-solving. *Administrative Sciences*, 12(1), 1–25. https://doi.org/10.3390/admsci12010004

Hamad, N. M. A., Adewusi, O. E., Unachukwu, C. C., Osawaru, B., & Chisom, O. N. (2024). HUMAN RESOURCES STRATEGIES FOR TALENT DEVELOPMENT IN YOUNG STEM ENTHUSIASTS. *Malaysian Journal Of Human Resources Management*, 1(2), 105–110. https://doi.org/10.26480/mjhrm.02.2024.105.110

Haneberg, L. (2015). Coaching training (1st edition). ATD Press.

Hannah, S. T., & Avolio, B. J. (2011). Leader character, ethos, and virtue: Individual and collective considerations. *The Leadership Quarterly*, 22(5), 989–994. https://doi.org/10.1016/j.leaqua.2011.07.018

Harvard Business Review (2018). https://hbr.org/2018/08/research-to-be-a-good-leader-start-by-being-a-good-follower.

Hawley, C. F. (2004). *201 ways to turn any employee into a star performer*. McGraw-Hill.

Hayes-Milligan, D. (12 August 2024). Council Post: To Be A Strong Leader, Hire People Smarter Than You. *Forbes*.

(HCM). The Role of HR in HCM. (2007). In *Human Capital Management*.

Horn, C. V. (2015). Young Scholars: A Talent Development Model for Finding and Nurturing Potential in Underserved Populations. *Gifted Child Today Magazine*, 38(1), 19–31. https://doi.org/10.1177/1076217514556532

Huang, J.-T. (2012). Be Proactive as Empowered? The Role of Trust in One's Supervisor in Psychological Empowerment, Feedback Seeking, and Job Performance. *Journal of Applied Social Psychology, 42*(S1), E103–E127. https://doi.org/10.1111/j.1559-1816.2012.01019.x

Hughes, M., & Miller, A. (2011). *Developing emotional and social intelligence : exercises for leaders, individuals, and teams* (1st edition). Pfeiffer.

Hutcherson, R. (2014). Organizational Optimization. Https://Www.Https://Optimize-Consulting.Biz. https://optimize-consulting.biz/the-book/

Ikhsanuddin, Abd. Majid, M. S., & Sofyan. (2024). The Influence of Selection, Talent Management, and Employee Placement on Employee Performance and Its Impact on the Performance of PT Pupuk Iskandar Muda Aceh. International Journal of Scientific Research and Management (IJSRM), 12(3), 6014–6024. https://doi.org/10.18535/ijsrm/v12i03.em07

Irwin, T., & Tassopoulos, T. (2018). *Extraordinary influence : how great leaders bring out the best in others* (1st edition).

Janson, S. (2025). *Onboarding - New in Job: Incl. Bonus – Recognize bad employers when you apply, deal with your boss & colleagues, change & restart with communication, teamwork & team spirit, and integrate as an employee* (7th ed.). Best of HR – Berufebilder.de.

Jong, J. de. (2016). *Dealing with Dysfunction : Innovative Problem Solving in the Public Sector.* Brookings Institution Press.

Katō, I., & Smalley, A. (2011). *Toyota kaizen methods : six steps to improvement.* CRC Press.

Kellerman, B., & Hoffman, M. (2018). *Professionalizing Leadership* [Broadcast]. Tantor Media, Inc.

Kennedy International – Logistics and Security Services. (2025). Kennedyint.com. https://kennedyint.com/

Kenon, V. H., & Palsole, S. V. (Eds.). (2019). *The Wiley handbook of global workplace learning* (1st ed.). Wiley Blackwell.

Kenton, B. (2005). *HR-- the business partner : shaping a new direction.* Elsevier. https://doi.org/10.4324/9780080478395

Kesterson, R. K. (2015). *The basics of Hoshin Kanri* (1st edition). CRC Press.

Kohlberg, L. (1981). *The philosophy of moral development : moral stages and the idea of justice* (First edition.). Harper & Row.

Kramer, M. (1998). *Power networking : using the contacts you do not even know you have to succeed in the job you want.* VGM Career Horizons. https://search.ebscohost.com/login.aspx?direct=true&scope=site&db=nlebk&db=nlabk&AN=13397

Lan, Y. (2005). *Global information society : operating information systems in a dynamic global business environment.* Idea Group Publishing. https://doi.org/10.4018/978-1-59140-306-7

Lapin, D. (Daniel E.). (2014). *Business Secrets from the bible : Spiritual Success Strategies for Financial Abundance* (1st edition). John Wiley & Sons, Inc.

Lawler, J. J., & Hundley, G. (2008). *The global diffusion of human resource practices institutional and cultural limits* (1st ed.). Emerald JAI.

https://www.emerald.com/insight/publication/doi/10.1016/S1571-5027(2008)21

Lencioni, P. (2016). *The ideal team player : how to recognize and cultivate the three essential virtues : a leadership fable* (1st ed.). Jossey-Bass, a John Wiley & Sons, Inc. imprint.

Levit, A., & Booksx, I. (2008). Success for Hire : Simple Strategies to Find and Keep Outstanding Employees (1st edition). ASTD Press.

Li, J. (2019). Frame your research in the field of HRD and with cultural sensitivity: important considerations for publications in HRDI. *Human Resource Development International, 22*(2), 113–115. https://doi.org/10.1080/13678868.2019.1572242

LinkedIn. (2025). *LinkedIn*. LinkedIn. https://www.linkedin.com.

Luecke, R. (2004). *Creating teams with an edge : the complete skill set to build powerful and influential teams.* Harvard Business School Press.

Luftman, J. N. (2011). *Managing IT human resources : considerations for organizations and personnel* (1st ed.). Business Science Reference. https://doi.org/10.4018/978-1-60960-535-3

Ma, Z., Long, L., Zhang, Y., Zhang, J., & Lam, C. K. (2017). Why do high-performance human resource practices matter for team creativity? The mediating role of collective efficacy and knowledge sharing. *Asia Pacific Journal of Management, 34*(3), 565–586. https://doi.org/10.1007/s10490-017-9508-1

Mack, O., Khare, A., Krämer, A., & Burgartz, Thomas. (Eds.). (2016). *Managing in a VUCA World* (1st ed., 2016). Springer International Publishing. **https://doi.org/10.1007/978-3-319-16889-0**

MacLennan, A. F., & Markides, C. C. (2021). Causal Mapping for Strategy Execution: Pitfalls and Applications. *California Management Review, 63*(4), 89–122. https://doi.org/10.1177/00081256211019799

Magni, M., & Caporarello, L. (2022). *Team Management : Creating and Managing Flexible and Resilient Teams.* (1st ed.). EGEA Spa - Bocconi University Press.

Malin, N. (2000). *Professionalism, boundaries and the workplace.* Routledge. https://search.ebscohost.com/login.aspx?direct=true&scope=site&db=nlebk&db=nlabk&AN=61024

Mankin, D. (2009). *Human Resource development.* Oxford University Press.

Manpower Services Commission. (1981). *Review of services for the unemployed:* MSC.

Mariscotti, E. E. (2020). *Corporate risks and leadership : what every executive should know about risks, ethics, compliance, and human resources* (1st ed.). Routledge, Taylor & Francis Group.

Martin, E. M., Myers, K., & Brickman, K. (2020). Self-Preservation in the Workplace: The Importance of Well-Being for Social Work Practitioners and Field Supervisors. *Social Work (New York), 65*(1), 74–81. https://doi.org/10.1093/sw/swz040

Martin, Q. (Ed.). (2022). Career development and job satisfaction. Nova Science Publishers.

Matuson, R. (16 December 2024). The Great Resignation Returns: 2025 Exodus. *Forbes.* https://www.forbes.com/sites/robertamatuson/2024/12/16/great-resignation-2025-worker-exodus/

McCauley, C. D., & Fick-Cooper, L. (2019). *Direction, Alignment, Commitment.* (1st ed.). Center for Creative Leadership.

McCauley, P. (2017). Essentials of engineering leadership and innovation. In CRC Press eBooks. https://doi.org/10.1201/9781315374796

McCredie, H. (2018). *Improving managerial talent : practical psychology for human resourcing and learning and development professionals* (1st). Routledge. https://doi.org/10.4324/9780203713006

McDougall, R. (1999). *Resource management* (1st edition). Sun Microsystems /and/ Suresh, A., Ramkumar, J., Baskar, M., & Bashir, A. K. (2023). *Resource Management in Advanced Wireless Networks.* (1st ed.). John Wiley & Sons, Incorporated.

McGilchrist, I. (2019). *The Master and His Emissary : The Divided Brain and the Making of the Western World* (New Expanded Edition). Yale University Press. https://doi.org/10.12987/9780300247459Links to an external site.

McGregor, D., Bennis, W. G., Schein, E. H., & McGregor, C. (1966). Leadership and motivation : Essays of Douglas McGregor. M.I.T. Press

Michaelides, N. (2020). *The Power of Networking*

Michigan.gov. (2004). Ford Motor Company Lean Behavior Survey. Michigan.Gov. https://www.michigan.gov/documents/cis_wsh_lb_survey_134162_7.pdf

Mulligan, D., & Shaw, G. (2020). *Hire purpose : how smart companies can close the skills gap.* Louisiana State University Press. https://doi.org/10.7312/mull17948

Mutsuddi, I. (2012). *Managing human resources in the global context* (1st ed.). New Age International.

Nandram, S. S., & Bindlish, P. K. (Eds.). (2017). *Managing VUCA Through Integrative Self-Management : How to Cope with Volatility, Uncertainty, Complexity and Ambiguity in Organizational Behavior* (1st ed. 2017). Springer International Publishing. https://doi.org/10.1007/978-3-319-52231-9

New International Version: Holy Bible. (2011). BibleGateway.com.

Nittrouer, C. L., Dean, E. E., Shogren, K. A., Hurley-Hanson, A. E., & Giannantonio, C. M. (2022). Career Progression: Strategies Used by Self-Advocates with ASD and Their Allies. In *Generation A* (pp. 45–63). Emerald Publishing Limited. https://doi.org/10.1108/978-1-80262-263-820220003

Niven, P. R., & Lamonte, B. (2016). *Objectives and key results : driving focus, alignment, and engagement with OKRs* (1st ed.). John Wiley & Sons, Incorporated.

Noble, B. (25 September 2024). *Capitol Times Magazine Issue 14|Paperback*. Barnes & Noble. https://www.barnesandnoble.com/w/capitol-times-magazine-issue-14-capitol-times-magazine/1146367097

Northouse, P. G. (2007). Leadership: Theory and Practice. 4th ed. Thousand Oaks, CA: Sage Publications, 2007, pp. 322-3

Northouse, P. G. (2013). Leadership Theory and Practice (7th Edition). SAGE Publishing. 428.

Northouse, P. G. (2016). *Leadership : theory and practice : [pbk.]* (7th ed., international student ed). SAGE.

Ochnik, D. (2019). *Selflessness in business* (Dominika Ochnik, Ed.). Vernon Press.

O'Neil, P. (2025). Paper [Unpublished] School of Business and Leadership. Regent University.

The Optimization Books - Optimize Consulting LLC. (2025, August 11). Optimize Consulting LLC. https://optimize-consulting.biz/the-book/

Panchadsaram, R. (2019). *What is an OKR? Definition and examples*. Whatmatters.com. https://www.whatmatters.com/faqs/okr-meaning-definition-example

Pardey, D., & Institute of Leadership & Management. (2007). *Organizing and delegating* (5th ed.). Elsevier/Pergamon Flexible Learning.

Paul, R., & Elder, L. (2008). The miniature guide to critical thinking. Tomales, CA: Foundation for Critical Thinking Press.

Pawłowska, A. (2023). *Flexible human resource management and vocational behaviour : the employability market orientation model*. Routledge.

Pelly, R. D. M. (2022). How Can Lean Six Sigma Foster Organizational Entrepreneurship in a Military Bureaucracy? *Dyskursy o Kulturze (Łódź. 2014), 16*(1), 55–80. https://doi.org/10.36145/DoC2021.09

Pettinger, R. (2002). *Managing the flexible workforce*. Capstone Pub.

Phillips, P. P., Phillips, J. J., & Ray, R. (2016). *Measuring the success of employee engagement : a step-by-step guide for measuring impact and calculating ROI* (1st edition). ATD Press.

Pink, D. H. (2006). *A whole new mind : why right-brainers will rule the future* (First Riverhead Books paperback edition). Riverhead Books.

Potter, B. (2013). *Elements of self-destruction (First edition.). Karnac.* https://doi.org/10.4324/9780429474156

Question of Leadership: How Can Leaders Best Support Employees who Are Experiencing a Crisis away from Work, such as a Death or Serious Illness in the Family, Yet also Continue to Meet the Needs of the Organization? (2002). Center for Creative Leadership.

Quotlr.com Team. (15 July 2024). 146 Mouth-watering Trust Issues Quotes (I have trust issues, I got trust issues, family trust issues). Quotlr - Famous Motivational Quotes. https://quotlr.com/quotes-about-trust-issues/

Raelin, J. A. (2008). *Work-based learning : bridging knowledge and action in the workplace* (New and rev. ed.). Jossey-Bass.

Rath, T. (2007). *StrengthsFinder 2.0*. Gallup Press.

Riana, I. G., Suparna, G., I Gusti, M. S., Kot, S., & Rajiani, I. (2020). Human resource management plays a crucial role in promoting innovation and organizational performance. *Problems and Perspectives in Management, 18*(1), 107-118.

Richardson, T. (2015). *The Responsible Leader: Developing a Culture of Responsibility in an Uncertain World*. Kogan Page.

Robbins, T. (2016). *Tony Robbins - the official website of Tony Robbins*. Tonyrobbins.com. https://www.tonyrobbins.com/

(Robert K. Greenleaf Quotes (Author of Servant Leadership). (2020). Retrieved 28 November 2020, from https://www.goodreads.com/author/quotes/105978.Robert_K_Greenleaf).

Rodriguez, R. (2022). *Employee resource group excellence : Grow high-performing ERGs to enhance diversity, equality, belonging, and business impact*. Wiley.

Rohatgi, V. K. (2013). *Statistical Inference.* (1st ed.). Dover Publications.

Rothwell, W. J. (2022). *Effective succession planning: Ensuring leadership continuity and building talent from within* (6th ed.). AMACOM.

Rupp, C. "Gary." (2024). *The Lean-Agile Way : Unleash Business Results in the Digital Era with Value Stream Management* (First edition.). Packt Publishing.

Russell, L., & Association for Talent Development. (2015). Leadership training (2nd edition). ATD Press.

Safire, W. (14 October 2007). "On Language - Overwatch". *New York Times*. Retrieved 21 November 2015.

Schein, E. H. (1990). Organizational culture. American Psychology, 45(2), 109–119.

Schein, E. (2004). *Organizational Culture and Leadership*. San Francisco: Jossey-Bass. Retrieved from https://web.archive.org/web/20190321170635/http://www.untag-smd.ac.id/files/Perpustakaan_Digital_2/ORGANIZATIONAL%20CULTURE%20Organizational%20Culture%20and%20Leadership,%203rd%20Edition.pdf (Links to an external site.)Links to an external site.

Schuler, R. S., & Jackson, S. E. (1999). *Strategic human resource management*. Blackwell Publishers. United Nations.

Schwartz, M. (29 August 2023). *Assume with me that the digital world is a world of fast change. Organizations need to excel at responding quickly to those changes - that is what we call agility or nimbleness.* Linkedin.com. https://www.linkedin.com/pulse/agile-enterprise-mark-schwartz

Seijts, G., Espinoza, J. A., & Carswell, J. (2020). Utility analysis of character assessment in employee placement. *Leadership & Organization*

Development Journal, 41(5), 703–720. https://doi.org/10.1108/LODJ-07-2019-0314

Self-actualization and the art of leadership. (2012). Www.visiontemenos.com. Retrieved August
23, 2023, from https://www.visiontemenos.com/blog/self-actualisation-and-the-art-of-Links to an external site.leadership

Sell, P. W. (1992). *An analysis of the comprehensiveness and coherence of Lawrence O. Richards' philosophy of Christian education.* ProQuest Dissertations & Theses.

Serenko, A. (2023). The Great Resignation: the great knowledge exodus or the onset of the Great Knowledge Revolution? *Journal of Knowledge Management, 27*(4), 1042–1055. https://doi.org/10.1108/JKM-12-2021-0920

Seven Dimensions Films is a production company based in Australia. (2015). *The Value of Employee Ownership* [Video recording]. Seven Dimensions Films of Australia.

Shaklee, B. D. (1992). Identification of young gifted students. Journal for the Education of the Gifted, 15, 134–144.

Shapiro, C., & Varian, H. R. (1999). *Information rules : a strategic guide to the network economy.* Harvard Business Review Press.

Shea, G. F. (1984). *Building trust in the workplace.* AMA Membership Publications Division, American Management Association.

Shockley-Zalabak, P., Morreale, S. P., & Hackman, M. Z. (2010). *Building the high-trust organization : strategies for supporting five key dimensions of trust* (1st ed.). Jossey-Bass.

Silver, S. R., & Franz, T. M. (2021). *Meaningful partnership at work : how the workplace covenant ensures mutual accountability and success between leaders and teams* (1st ed.). Routledge.
https://doi.org/10.4324/9781003181477

Sims, R. R. (2002). *Organizational success through effective human resources management.* Praeger. https://doi.org/10.5040/9798400693953

Singh, G., & Ananthanarayanan, R. (2013). *Organizational development and alignment : the Tensegrity mandala framework.* SAGE.

Smith, P. (2018). *Learning while working : structuring your on-the-job training* (1st edition). American Society for Training & Development.

Smith, J. R., Brooks-Gunn, J., & Klebanov, P. K. (1997). *Consequences of living in poverty for young children's cognitive and verbal ability and early school achievement.* In G. J. Duncan & J. Brooks-Gunn (Eds.), Consequences of growing up poor (pp. 132–138). New York, NY: Russell Sage Foundation.

Smith, R., & Campbell, M. (2011). *Talent conversations : what they are, why they are crucial, and how to do them right* (1st edition)—Center for Creative Leadership.

Stack, L. (2018). *Faster together : accelerating your team's productivity (1st edition).* Berrett-Koehler Publishers, Inc.

Stack Exchange. (2018). *History Stack Exchange*. History Stack Exchange. https://history.stackexchange.com/questions/46866/did-any-carriage-manufacturers-make-the-transition-to-automobile-building

STEEPLE Analysis Explained - Business Chronicler. (10 December 2022). https://businesschronicler.com/business-strategy/steeple-analysis-explained/

Stern, T.V. (2024). *Lean Six Sigma : International Standards and Global Guidelines* (Third edition.). Routledge. https://doi.org/10.4324/9781003397649

Stone, F. M. (2007). *Coaching, counseling & mentoring: How to choose & use the right technique to boost employee performance* (2nd ed.). American Management Association. https://search.ebscohost.com/login.aspx?direct=true&scope=site&db=nlebk&db=nlabk&AN=181411

Sundari, Ms. V. M., & Praseeda, Dr. C. (2019). Career Development Conundrum of Educational Institutions – An Introspection of Student Talent Management. *International Journal of Recent Technology and Engineering*, *8*(4), 897–901. https://doi.org/10.35940/ijrte.D7507.118419

Suresh, A., Ramkumar, J., Baskar, M., & Bashir, A. K. (2023). *Resource Management in Advanced Wireless Networks.* (1st ed.). John Wiley & Sons, Incorporated. https://doi.org/10.1002/9781119827603

Suri, P. K., & Yadav, R. (2019). Transforming Organizations Through Flexible Systems Management. In *Flexible Systems Management*. Springer Nature. https://doi.org/10.1007/978-981-13-9640-3 Transformation Monia Verna Chapter 10 (p. 177, 178)

Sushil (2016). Theory of flexible systems management. In Sushil et al. (Eds.), Flexible work organizations, Flexible Systems Management (pp. 3–20), India: Springer.

Sutter, M. (2023). *Behavioral economics for leaders : Research-driven insights on the weird, Irwin, T., & Tassopoulos, T. (2018). Extraordinary influence : how great leaders bring out the best in others (1st edition). Irrational and incredible ways humans navigate the workplace.* John Wiley & Sons, Inc.

Sutton, B., & Chatham, R. (2017). *Building a winning team : technical leadership capabilities* (1st edition). BCS Learning & Development.

Tallman, S., Shenkar, O., & Wu, J. (2023). "Culture Eats Strategy for Breakfast": Use and Abuse of Culture in International Strategy Research. *Strategic Management Review (Norwell, Mass.)*, *4*(2), 193–229. https://doi.org/10.1561/111.00000057

Team, G. E. (14 September 2021). *Ford implemented lean manufacturing in its production system*. George Business Review. https://www.george-business-review.com/ford-implemented-lean-manufacturing-in-production-system/

The Power of Patience | Mike Robbins. (11 July 2022). The Power of Patience | author and speaker Mike Robbins

Tomić, V., Buljan, I., & Marušić, A. (2024). Developing consensus on essential virtues for ethics and research integrity training using a modified Delphi approach. *Accountability in Research: Policies & Quality Assurance, 31*(4), 327–350. https://doi.org/10.1080/08989621.2022.2128340

Treffinger, D. J., Young, G. C, Nassab, C. A, & Wittig, C. V. (2004). Enhancing and Expanding Gifted Programs: The Levels-of-Service Approach. Waco, TX: Prufrock Press.

Turner, B. A. (1976). The Organizational and Interorganizational Development of Disasters. *Administrative Science Quarterly, 21*(3), 378–397. https://doi.org/10.2307/2391850

Turner, B. & Pidgeon, N.F. (1997). Man-made Disasters, Second Edition, Oxford, Butterworth-Heinemann.

Ulrich, D., Younger, J., Brockbank, W., & Ulrich, M. (2012). *HR from the Outside In: Six Competencies for the Future of Human Resources* (Vol. 34, no. 12 (3 parts), part 1 (December 2012)). McGraw-Hill.

(UKG). *How to Align HR and Operations for Stronger Business Success | UKG.* (2025, October 8). UKG. https://www.ukg.com/blog/hr-leaders/how-align-hr-and-operations-stronger-business-successVogelsang, J. (Ed.). (2013). *Handbook for strategic HR. Section 5, Employee engagement : best practices in organizational development from the OD network.* AMACOM.

Warner, J. C. (2007). *Career Planning and Development* (2nd ed.). Worldwide Center for Organizational Development.

Waddill, D. D. (2018). *Digital HR : a guide to technology-enabled human resources.* Society for Human Resource Management.

Wang, L., & Keith Murnighan, J. (2013). The generalist bias. *Organizational Behavior and Human Decision Processes, 120*(1), 47–61. https://doi.org/10.1016/j.obhdp.2012.09.001

Weiss, D. S. (1999). *High-impact HR : transforming human resources for competitive advantage.* Wiley.

Wetherbee, J. (2016). *Controlling Risk in a Dangerous World : 30 Techniques for Operating Excellence.* (1st ed.). Morgan James Publishing.

Widianta, M. M. D., Rizaldi, T., Setyohadi, D. P. S., & Riskiawan, H. Y. (2018). Comparison of Multi-Criteria Decision Support Methods (AHP, TOPSIS, SAW & PROMETHEE) for Employee Placement. *Journal of Physics. Conference Series, 953*(1), 12116-. https://doi.org/10.1088/1742-6596/953/1/012116

Wilensky, H. L. (1967). *Organizational intelligence.* Basic Books.

Winston, R. B. (2001). *The professional student affairs administrator is a multifaceted role that encompasses educator, leader, and manager.* Brunner-Routledge. https://doi.org/10.4324/9780203782606

Williams, G., Haarhoff, D., Fox, P., & Villiers, M. de. (2015). *The virtuosa organization : the importance of virtues for a successful business* (1st ed.). Knowres Publishing.

Wolfe, R. L. (1996). *Systematic succession planning : building leadership from within*. Crisp Publications.

Yukl, G. A., & Lepsinger, R. (2004). *Flexible leadership : creating value by balancing multiple challenges and choices*. Jossey-Bass.

Zheng, W., Yang, B., & McLean, G. N. (2010). Linking organizational culture, structure, strategy, and organizational effectiveness: Mediating role of knowledge management. Journal of Business Research, 63(7), 763–771.

Zirar, A., Trusson, C., & Choudhary, A. (2021). Towards a high-performance HR bundle process for lean service operations. *The International Journal of Quality & Reliability Management, 38*(1), 25–45. https://doi.org/10.1108/IJQRM-10-2019-0330

Zenoff, D. B. (2013). *The Soul of the Organization : How to Ignite Employee Engagement and Productivity at Every Level* (1st ed. 2013). Apress. https://doi.org/10.1007/978-1-4302-4966-5

Zulfikar, I. V., Joeliaty, J., & Sartika, D. (2024). The Influence of Work Environment and Employee Placement on Job Satisfaction and Its Impact on Intention to Quit. *Kontigensi, 12*(2), 971–994. https://doi.org/10.56457/jimk.v12i2.629

Appendix B
Pete O'Neil's Final DSL Research Paper
Academic basis for the <u>A</u>ptitude, <u>M</u>orale & <u>P</u>erformance sections.
Talent Development & Teaming-Plus for Performance

Education for Advancement (Empowerment)
Circulate Their Influence (Expansion)
Keep Distraction to a Minimum (Filter
Performance Self-Assessment Workbook
Conclusion

Abstract

Individual talent and its development are often enhanced through teamwork and collective success; however, these essential elements are often isolated efforts. Many Chief Executive Officers (CEOs) dedicate their careers to bridging this divide. This raises the timeless question: 'How do I inspire my people to unite toward a shared vision?' In this paper, we will examine the complex relationship between talent development and the dynamic interdependence that fuels operational excellence. Crafted for the C-Suite, this discussion explores ways to increase worker autonomy, foster self-actualized decision-making, and promote micro-independence, which in turn produces macro-interdependence, building strong alliances around a CEO's vision, mission, and expectations. Every employee is part of a team at some point in their career journey. So, how can C-suite leaders create a coalition that drives ongoing system improvement? We will address these challenges directly and aim to generate lasting momentum. We will identify five distinct levels of individual development, each reinforced and amplified by five group dynamics that lead to processes that are not only improved but also more efficient and globally cost-effective. Visionary leaders have long sought solutions that are both strategically aligned and practically feasible. This paper will highlight the collaborative relationship between individuals and the teams they work in, demonstrating how this partnership acts as a powerful catalyst for cross-functional and intra-functional success. Our ultimate goal is to leverage this coaction to achieve a unified organizational vision. Let us embark on this journey together, where each level of talent development is deeply supported by teaming enablers that inspire genuine systemic improvement. We will introduce a new concept called Teaming-Plus. It will be built upon the scholarly and practical work of Edmondson (2012). All aboard!

Talent Development and Teaming-Plus for Performance

C-suite leaders are looking for momentum in growing their businesses, which is evidenced in their leadership candidates, and helps them reach their executive vision. The smart ones know they cannot do this alone. They need help; they need team members to step up. Often, they experience mere inertia, characterized by siloed agendas, friction between strong personalities, and (process) entropy that infects their operations. What can be done to stall this phenomenon?

It begins with aligning team leaders with the CEO's vision. This consists of three components, presented sequentially. The steps must be followed in this order; skipping disconnects progress. First, high-potentials must be prioritized, with aptitude development (Carter, 2010) fostered through targeted assessments and skill gap findings to enhance performance (Wingard & Farrugia, 2021). The up-and-comers must be understood and provided an opportunity to grow. Talent development can be both ambiguous and predictable.

Secondly, as individuals develop, they become valued assets for exponential and applicable group dynamics (Edmondson, 2012). Force multiplication occurs when team members align on an issue. One ox can pull 8,000 pounds, while two in tandem can move over 26,000. This (mathematical) example of achievement occurs when the right people coordinate, using close, on-hand resources to reach company objectives – think the speed of NASCAR pit stops versus Walmart's two-hour tire shop change process.

Step three revolves around performance – how executive leaders can stimulate it in their direct reports, instruct them to do the same for their team leaders, and ensure its expansion reaches the shop floor, medical unit, or anywhere customers reside. This paper will detail the individual, group, customer, and performance paths – all mission-critical!

History of Talent Development

From the dawn of man, people have been working on projects of one sort or another. Thus, the need for talent development was born—combining the Greek words "daimon" and "talanton" (Li, 2019). From early Chinese cultural training to the African states of Makuria and Aksum, which fought for independence against their European invaders in 642 AD, both were engaged in training warfighters. In addition to military talent, they excelled in diplomatic, economic, and technological capabilities, bolstering a strong cultural identity from the diversity of talent (Munro-Hay, 1991; Welsby, 2002). On to the invention and perfection of Henry Ford's conveyor assembly line, worker training has been at the forefront of innovation. History continues to show that most new ideas require talent development to bring them to life (Writer, 2025).

How best can talent development influence, and even enhance operational success? First and foremost, it must take priority in the minds of CEOs, in tandem with their Chief Operating Officers (and those responsible for managing other functional affairs). Jack Welch, the former, newly appointed (at the time) head of General Electric, spent time, resources, and energy on his HR talent development efforts through the Crotonville site and growth programs (Durett, 2006), situated in the scenic country hills of New York, which provided these up-and-comers the opportunity to learn, apply, and even challenge GE's business model. It was a marvelous concept that was brought "to life" (as the memorable GE tagline denoted) for its executive training. However, all good things have a shelf life (WSJ, 2024). It was sold to a group looking to outsource the area and facilities for conferences and the like. "It is a snapshot ... in time how companies used to motivate and reward shining stars," noted Bridget Gibbons, Director of Economic Development (2025) in Westchester County, where Crotonville resides.

This raises the question: Has COVID-19 changed talent development approaches for good? Why are Boeing, 3M, and others shredding (or planning to) their massive talent development centers? Is a separate site for this becoming obsolete? Is face-to-face training a thing of the past? Is that a good thing or a bad thing? The verdict is still out on this one.

Part of the rationale is bringing the training closer to where the process is happening. The Japanese concept of GEMBA (Petruska, 2012) is gaining traction. Learning occurs most effectively in the context where the work is done. A study of 232 patients' cycle time from the emergency department to the Intensive Care Unit (turnaround time) was reduced by over 80%, and the quality rate/sigma level increased from 2.25 to 2.82 through lean process attention/Gemba (Nikita & Singh, 2025).

With the sale of these staff development facilities, will content transfer suffer? Several subsequent studies will ask this question. Perhaps a hybrid might be best? How do executives ensure that workers learn and apply the needed skills?

When it comes to talent development, get organized (Biech, 2021). Developing a leadership plan is a two-fold process: one for the leader and one for facilitating it in others. As a basis for enriching leaders more generally, we will elaborate on Dalton & Hollenbeck's (1996) six-step guide to strategic and tactical milestones. Their plan is tailored to strengthen future executives and provides a comprehensive, step-by-step glide path for leader development.

Step one involves designing diverse interventions organized over time, including training, on-the-job support, and iterative check-ins. Their point ensures more than a snapshot-in-time event; instead, it is an ongoing partnership. Step two aligns senior and lateral involvement, ensuring no one works in isolation and that the process is directly tied to the organization's objectives and the work plan to improve relevant business metrics. To set the candidate up for success, the strategy focuses on leveraging the business work and behaviors the mentees are already performing. Blanchard sums up step three, "feedback is the breakfast of champions" (Appraisal, 2006, Description). The result supports relevant, timely on-the-job and after-the-fact scenario guidance for maximum impact. The authors highlight that the feedback (content) should supplement and reinforce the subject's documented plan. Step four captures the critical role the candidate plays within the organization. Executives support the strategy, i.e., formally leveraging the annual human resources development plan by "making development real, providing...experiences...support and feedback, and accessing organizational resources" (Dalton & Hollenbeck, 1996, step 4). Step five provides comprehensive support to the employee, including the scope of the effort, roles, responsibilities, and metric targets. The authors acknowledge that not all plan details may be used entirely, yet they encourage clear organization and expectations for the subject's development. Capturing the written micro-augmentation enhances clarity and increases program success. Lastly, step six asks, "Is the program being followed as laid out—are (their) plans active and are participants themselves developing?" (Dalton & Hollenbeck, 1996, step 6). In summary, verified success is observed in the subject's future behaviors, interactions, and outcomes. This path is measurable.

Stages of Talent Development (W-O-R-K-S)

How many organizations let the 'big one get away?' How many CEOs are kicking themselves, after the fact, for losing a top-tier employee? Especially to their competition. It was a complete surprise when the all-time great Green Bay Packer quarterback joined the interdivision rival Minnesota Vikings after a few twists and turns. There, he swept his old team in 2009 and led the purple-colored competitor to the NFC Championship Game. How many corporate Bret Favre's have gotten away? He was not the first.

Lee Iacocca left Ford Motor Company and went on to build the highly successful Chrysler brand, transforming it from near extinction to profitability by 1982. Did the milkshake mixer company leadership, which once employed McDonald's founder Ray Kroc, fail to see his talent and miss the opportunity of a lifetime? Did Google CEO Marissa Mayer's former employers regret the one that got away? Were their talent approaches blind to her potential? What about the CEOs of multiple information technology companies who failed to leverage Michael Dell before he founded his most successful computer company? Did certain news industry executives in the early 1980s overlook Oprah's potential? They had a fantastic talent right under their noses. What causes the lack of focus in some senior leaders? What supervisor who knew or worked closely with Richard Branson at the Student Magazine missed his potential? Do some insiders still have regrets? What school administrator missed the potential of Alibaba founder Jack Ma when he worked for them? How did they let him get away?

History is replete with executives who failed to see the talent in the office down the hall (Kaye & Jordan-Evans, 2014). What can today's CEOs do differently not to have regrets and say, 'You know, famous-so-and-so, used to work for me.' Individual development leads to predictability in performance, which in turn fosters comfort. Comfort, combined with inspiring challenges, tends to promote longevity, which in turn refines loyalty (Zenoff, 2013). Why do many senior leaders miss this progressive continuum and let talent walk out the door, or worse yet, send them packing?

The secret may lie between your employees' ears. How do they see themselves? What is the picture they paint through interactions with co-workers, supervisors, and the attention (or lack of) from senior leaders? Building on the brilliant discourse from a fellow doctoral student, DSL (Regent University, 2025), Robert Jiminez (2025), we may begin to gain insight. The spark may come to life when workers and supervisors (together) strive to develop skills (Carter, 2010) by proactively addressing the (agreed-upon) gaps in an employee's performance (Wingard & Farrugia, 2021). Perhaps not a complete rewrite, but a refocus, a tweak, or a better understanding of the ripple effect from action or inaction – would be prudent.

The first foundational enabler is the pursuit of personal excellence (Manz & Neck, 1999), coupled with clear expectations communicated by senior leaders to new hires. This pinpoints talent management (Mattone & Xavier, 2012) through orientation in four ways: aligning the near-future state with position needs, thoroughly testing candidates, matching candidate attributes to mission needs, and scaling or repeating this linkage diagonally throughout the organization. Kouzes & Posner (1999) challenge executives to reward and recognize the smooth transitions of new team members, aligning both the heart and mind to encourage commitment. This all starts when workers wander around, wondering where and how they fit. This marks the beginning of the talent development stages. We will define the stage for the employee in the W-O-R-K-S acronym, who they are in each stage, and what external motivations can be used to advance them to the next level, to become an independent employee, and then, if need be, to be a competent interdependent partner with others, blending strategic acumen for tactical group accomplishment. This evolution begins with:

The Wanderer (New & Idealistic)

Define Them. As a new, idealistic employee (Jiminez, 2025) starts in a company, many questions arise in their mind. So many that they can cloud one's understanding of a new role and/or their supervisor's expectations. Thus, the initial worker title, Wanderer Stage, commences. Others have described this period as "drinking from a fire hose" (Staff, 2023, online).

Learning procedures, processes, people, and places, and navigating propositions, possibilities, and priorities, all within the first two months, can put undue pressure on new employees at any level within an organization. However, the deeper (lower) within an organization, the more intense these perplexities become. Often, overload can be the day-to-day reality.

In-tune managers should pace (meter) the flow of information and expectations, much as gradual strength workouts followed by rest build muscle over time. This approach also fosters an understanding of the environment among new employees and awareness of their roles (Thompson, 2025). This stage is critical for potential competency and advancement. A manager's intervention cannot be overstated. Before joining TLC, I had six bosses in my first four years at my previous employer. It was a very unpleasant and turbulent work environment. I left as soon as I could. Now, what can operational leaders and human resources do/be for the wanderers in your organization?

Enhance Them. A well-planned orientation during the induction process can help sustain these new, idealistic workers (El-Shamy, 2003). New customer-focused employee strategies dilute confusion (Hickman & ASTD, 1999). They answer several questions that are most often not verbalized. What do these documented roles and responsibilities mean for me on a day-to-day basis? Is my reporting structure clear? How do I best relate to laterals? Who is considered trustworthy? How much can I share with my superiors? Will they perceive several questions as a weakness? Do I have to pull myself up with my own bootstraps?

How does a supervisor assess a new worker's soft skills (Tulgan, 2015)? Do they put them in situations to test them? Are they ready to be tested? The initial training sequence should be predetermined, at the very least, with a glide path that allows for flexibility (Hampel & Lamont, 2011). Does the organization have a formal talent development program (Biech & ATD, 2018)? When does it officially kick in? Orientation (Lawson, 2016) should address most of these questions before a new employee starts. The more precise the new employees' maturity path is from personnel and operational supervisors, the quicker new workers will catch on (think NFL scouting rigor). PDCA (Realyvásquez et al., 2023), with relevant new-employee measurement (Wealleans, 2017), emphasizes and leverages the planning (P) stage. What is the plan for success? Each function can partner with the human resources department to develop tailored approaches that meet specific needs (Jiminez, 2025). This sets the stage for success. Leveraging HR to enhance employee engagement is an effective strategy. They can be more than the group that merely put letters in employee jackets (Claxton, 2014). Other needed enablers focus on new employee comfort levels and safety (Burt, 2015), as well as a relevant, accessible, and referable employee handbook (Guerin & DelPo, 2005). These are just a few of the non-negotiables HR chiefs should implement for new members. Do things get better or worse at the next stage?

The Objector (Reality is Different)

Define Them. Objectors often realize that reality is far different from what they learned in orientation (Jiminez, 2025). Companies put their best foot forward to give new employees a fighting chance of staying and ultimately contributing. However, whether through inadvertent circumstances or orchestrated by company leaders, new employees often have to navigate conflicts, whether personal (Kaye, 1994) or occupational (Papke, 2016). Learning firsthand that *this place is not as it was displayed during my initial training* can build resilience if the new employee endures. It also provides leaders with an opportunity to see how their newer employees handle adversity. Navigating the Objector stage is no fun, but it provides decision-makers with valuable insights that require wisdom and a delicate approach at times. Managers' patience is needed. How can companies leverage these scenarios to enhance employee learning and sustainability amid frustration and turnover (Allen & Vardaman, 2021)?

Enhance Them. The ancient wise one, Solomon, said, as iron sharpens iron, conflict and friction, too, can sharpen one's skills, to help them prepare for even greater battles going forward (Proverbs 27:17). Workers who navigate internal, social, and/or relational conflicts learn to prioritize...to major on the majors and minor on the minors (Thorpe, 2018). In other words, measure the reaction percentage based on the level of impact or priority (to learn how to differentiate between the truly important and the tyranny of the urgent).

Providing clarity on roles and responsibilities, including supplier-customer linkages within and across functions, can mitigate potential conflicts (Kaye & Evans, 2003). When clarity is absent, and processes are left to chance (you would be surprised how prevalent this is), confusion sets in. As uncertainty grows, quiet quitting increases (Detert, 2023), decreasing productivity. Structured employee training in conflict management (*IJCM*, 1990), available employee relations management techniques (Singh & Kumar, 2010), and reframing resolution skills (Saundry et al., 2016) also provide workers with additional tools for problem-solving and conflict reduction. One such training course called Alternative Dispute Resolution (ADR) "examines the extent to which conflict management (can be) treated as a strategic issue and discusses the development of mediation (skills) and its impact on employment relations culture, the experiences of participants in mediation, and the relationship between ADR (Saundry et al., 2016; VA Office, 2020, online) and workplace justice" (Preface). Conflict can be leveraged both for employee growth (as an asset) and to help the company achieve its goals. Conflict: Do not run from it. Davila & Pina-Ramirez (2023) encourage HR executives to leverage the industry's onboarding best practices, pragmatic job aids, standard templates, and employee checklists. Even with these mitigation tools, workforce disillusionment may occur (Little et al., 2024). It can be a double-edged sword. When leaders closely monitor it, leverage it for problem-solving, and help workers process through it, the employee's sword (i.e., Solomon) can become very sharp. When wielded for critical mission purposes, stars are born. How can leaders help their teams get there?

The Resolver (Greener Pastures)

Define Them. Workers who navigate interpersonal and/or process problems and display emotional intelligence (Singh, 2006) when faced with adversity provide stability, enhance productivity, and improve employment retention (Garber, 2007). Employers who have done their diligence when hiring skilled workers, are clear on position needs, show orientation support, partner through difficulty, and understand employee motivation will reap organizational consistency.

The Resolver's satisfaction, impact, and retention are tied to improved employee performance (Amir et al., 2024) and are less likely to reduce effort (Detert, 2023) or seek 'greener pastures' (Jiminez, 2025). Employee loyalty is fostered by meeting individual and organizational needs (Cook & AMA, 1992). What can an employer do to make this the norm?

Enhance Them. Driving employee engagement and retention (Branham, 2000) involves utilizing a give-and-take approach with winners, measuring and communicating metrics (vision) to achieve goals, and taking the time to follow the PDCA process, with an emphasis on planning, i.e., getting the right people in place from the outset. Talent Retention (Phillips & Edwards, 2009) involves learning from and leveraging employment data, respecting cultural differences, conducting exit interviews, matching solutions to employee needs, recognizing interim successes, and keeping return on investment (ROI) at the forefront of the team (Allen & Vardaman, 2021). Leaders who strike a balance between support and accountability tend to experience improved retention (Phillips & Connell, 2003).

Retaining good workers (Cheema, 2010) comes from paying attention to their needs. A study of over 13,000 U.S.-based employees found that 64% sought better pay and benefits, 61% desired a work-life balance, and 58% preferred job responsibilities that aligned with their strengths (Hailey, 2022). Workers leaving US companies account for over $11 billion in lost expenses, so it pays to keep them. 30% attributed their departure to a toxic culture, 60% to interpersonal conflict with management, and more than 65% to a lack of appreciation (Science of People, 2025). Have you experienced such negatives?

Leaders can ensure accountability by reflecting on key questions with their HR staff. How accurate are our job profiles compared to actual day-to-day responsibilities? Do our education efforts effectively enhance employee acumen? Is onboarding refreshing for new workers? Are we in sync with achieving a work-life balance?

Two final points: 1) Change is inevitable, so leaders must ensure workers are prepared for it (Larkin & Larkin, 1994). 2) Perceived organizational support occurs through reciprocal employee actions (Eisenberger & Stinglhamber, 2011). Workers feel obligated to go the extra mile when they experience (sense) systemic support. Leaders know they have won hearts and minds when employees embody their employer's values. Resolvers are a valuable asset to any business, and much of the probability of success lies in the leader's attention to detail. Also, the fear of change is diluted with authentic organizational support (Keegan, 2015). Would more executives follow through here? What is the next individual advancement?

The Keeper (Impact)

Define Them. 'He is a keeper!' the soon-to-be mother-in-law tells her daughter. This young man has passed the loyalty test, bringing value to relationships and looking to become a family member for years to come. The same is true for employees categorized as **Keepers.** They have a record of partnering with their operational leadership over time in various scenarios that enhance individual and corporate performance (Vogelsang, 2013).

Burchell & Robin (2011) define a "great workplace as one where people trust the people they work for, take pride in what they do, and enjoy the people they work with" (p.17). This describes the essence and environment when keepers walk the halls. Keeper types delineate five characteristics. These include "credibility, respect, fairness, pride, and camaraderie" (p.18).

Do keepers have an impact on the bottom line? Absolutely! Alex Edmans (2010) demonstrated that the ripple effect of workers with high levels of commitment and satisfaction yields financial dividends. An exhaustive 8-year study found that over 100 companies with these types of workers saw their stock market gains double over the same period. Keepers are keepers. What can leaders do to magnify their influence?

Enhance Them. Two-way loyalty develops as workers and organizations collaborate to achieve shared objectives. Leaders create an environment conducive to growth (Hetrick, 2023) that builds bonds over time. Keepers guard the organization's mission and vision. They take their supervisor's goals and desires personally. No wonder they are so valuable to C-suiters. Organizations grow leaders into keepers in three Ways (Calarco et al., 2006). 1) They focus on training (both the formal and on-the-job domains) for worker cognitive flexibility: the ability to use a variety of thinking strategies and mental frameworks. 2) Emotional flexibility, where keepers can vary approaches in dealing with their own emotions, those of others, and the dynamics created between the parties, and 3) Dispositional flexibility (or personality-based acumen), showing the ability to remain optimistic, yet realistic at the same time. Leaders educate (invest in) their keepers (Calarco et al., 2006).

Other tactical interventions include supporting and leveraging peer-to-peer development groups (Rodriguez, 2022), facilitating high-performance sessions for workers (Daniels, 2000), and motivating and retaining key personnel to enhance organizational performance (Suswati, 2021). A work pattern study in high-stress environments (Suswati, 2021) revealed that employees utilize cognitive and emotional encouragement to enhance performance and increase task completion rates. High internal motivation was observed to help foster consistent improvement. This study also found that employee placement, when matched to the mission's needs, proved successful. One key lesson learned emphasizes the importance of considering the employee's strengths, skills, and knowledge in placement (Suswati, 2021). The better the match…the better the results (Hidayat et al., 2018). Company leaders who leverage business indicators to build an educated workforce will be impactful in achieving goals (Sternberg & Turnage, 2017) by driving the necessary innovations to attain them (Brown, 2022). Can things even get better here? Yes, they can!

The Senior (Longevity)

Define Them. Keepers with longevity (may graduate to the Senior role) continue to learn and grow each year as they contribute their expertise. Edmondson (2013) challenges the C-suite to be proactive in developing plans for (and with) their most committed and competent workers. This can yield exponential dividends in safety, quality, and cost (Stamatis, 2016). Edmondson continues to ask executives to challenge their senior-level team members by introducing conflicting and/or confounding ideas. Inter-department system function problems can be complex and have hidden contributing causes. Edmondson (2012) concludes that life is a paradox, yet a world of possibility. She contends that senior-level workers, through their teaming skills, can provide significant insight to address life and business dilemmas (Jiminez, 2025).

"Cultures of playful discipline, broad swath perspectives, within chaos and fluidity, can open up the world for insightful epiphanies. Talent development programs are often too introspective" (p. 126). As workers are linked with one another, teaming possibilities increase. People leverage interdependence and cooperation to find solutions (Edmondson, 2012).

Senior-level workers view HR positively and collaborate with personnel leaders to provide mentorship opportunities. They see the human resources office as more than a punitive function. Wouldn't it change a worker's perspective if HR were considered helpful (Jiminez, 2025)? Seeing respected co-workers interact positively with human resources managers can help alleviate some employee fears and open the door for HR to provide multidisciplinary support. One way HR can facilitate operations is by providing accurate personality and strengths assessments (Rath, 2007) to help workers gain better self-awareness and a greater sense of connectedness with others, thereby fostering robust teaming. How well do you know yourself and the potential strengths and gaps in your team members? What are some tactical interventions to harness the best from your seniors?

Enhance Them. Keeping your best people satisfied over time is ever on the minds of keen decision makers (Walker, 2022). Senior individuals want to learn and contribute (De Grip & Sauermann, 2012), and often, through their efforts, win new business for the companies that employ them (Welch, 2018). They are transforming organizations through flexible management approaches (Suri et al., 2020). How can we maintain that momentum?

Accessible succession planning, as outlined by Berger & Berger (2011), is a good starting point. Innovative HR departments are focusing on character development (Hannah & Avolio, 2011). "Character is an indispensable component of sustainable leadership performance" (p. 979; Furlong & Crossan, 2021, p. 235).

Liborius (2017) noted that humility and character correlated with (workers') perceptions of their manager's credibility for following. Nevertheless, Hannah and Avolio (2011) observe "most current theories ... do not include an in-depth discussion of character or other focus (to) drive such leadership" (p. 980; 身份中台, 2025).

Academia is urging industry leaders to address gaps in character emphasis and its importance in business (Wright & Quick, 2011). Senior-level workers should prioritize integrity. Interest in character growth (Seijts et al., 2020) and organizational success through effective human resources management (Sims, 2002) are also critical enablers here. As senior leaders mentor younger, less-experienced co-workers, they must understand the impact of recruitment, selection, and placement on employee performance. Meeting organizational needs with individual skills and desire appears to be the right approach (Suwarto & Subyantoro, 2019).

Kouzes & Posner (2017) pose five high-level questions for aspiring senior-level workers, presented as practices, along with additional subset questions. They include:

✓ Practice 1 – Are you *Modeling The Way* as an individual and for the organization you serve? Do your teams understand the primary values? Do you display them? How are you aligning corporate values cross-functionally and enterprise-wide? Is there evidence that more leaders are living the organization's shared values? Is there evidence that leaders give their time and attention to these values? To the mission of the organization? Are you leading by example and teaching others to replicate these values?

✓ Practice 2 – Are you *Inspiring the Shared Vision* by painting a welcoming future? For you and your employees? Moreover, are you supporting your superiors, laterals, and subordinates in this pursuit? Do you have ambitious goals for yourself and aspirations for those under your care? Do team members tend to see the glass as half-full?

✓ Practice 3 – Are you *challenging the Process* or just following the status quo? Are you honoring standards and trying to improve them? Do you challenge others to be innovative? Do you take risks and support your team when they do?

✓ Practice 4 – Do you *Enable Others to act* by supporting and recognizing team members for trying new processes? Are your people hungry? Does your team trust you?

✓ Lastly, Practice 5 – Do you *Encourage the Heart* in your people? Is there evidence of positive emotion and energy in your department? Are you afraid of conflict or harness it for joint success (Heffernan, 2012)? Discerning executives leverage their senior leaders to accomplish the mission.

Result: Self-Actualization

Self-actualization in work is a process (Lurie, 2009). As an employee onboards, learns their role, navigates conflict and adversity, and makes an impact through longevity, they are seeking self-actualization (SA) along the way. Am I making a difference? Am I fulfilled? Will I leave anything on this earth that outlives me? Behavioral expert Maslow (Johnson, 1986) defined SA "as self-realization or self-cultivation (and) … as the complete realization of one's potential as manifest in peak experiences which involve the full development of one's abilities and appreciation for life" (Maslow, 1962; Perera, 2024, online).

Another key support for self-actualization is the opinions of those they report to, e.g., as in the looking-glass-self theory (Leslie University, 2019). Am I impacting bottom-line results? Does my boss think highly of me (Canfield, 1990)? Do I have a record of accomplishments? These questions often stem from the divine, the dignity of human worth, and the honor of their work (Larue, 2023). The Japanese work culture, as exemplified in lean manufacturing principles and practices, has been popularized by the Toyota Motor Company; however, these operational learnings are also being adopted by several international companies. One of the pillars of this thinking is the importance of collaboration. How do I relate to others? To teams I am a part of? Do I contribute value to the group's goals? Am I loyal to the group (Reichheld & Teal, 1996)?

Much of talent development these days is so inward-focused (Jiminez, 2025). The individual piece of the Individual Performance Reviews (IPRs). Why do we neglect the 'we' in assessing employee acumen and potential? Where does this myopic personnel approach evolve? Could it be the way schools educate children today? When they arrive, many are so eager to learn, but the first instruction they often hear is, 'go sit down and shut up.' They then spend twelve years afraid to make mistakes, taking tests individually, seeking only one correct answer, avoiding problem-solving, and rarely engaging in group brainstorming. No wonder American achievement is so egocentric. What would it look like if children at school and employees at work were graded on their ability to interact with, or even lead, groups of people? How would they perceive themselves? Some foundational considerations must be examined.

Ross (2015) notes, "What is critical to making the self-leadership development process dynamic and forward moving (toward becoming a self-leader) are the experiences the individual goes through, and those …pushing the individual outside their comfort zone increase their chances of succeeding" (p. 12). Perceptive instructors challenge students to achieve this understanding. Self-concept and experience intermingle throughout life and evolve (or devolve) over time. In his groundbreaking work, *The Master and His Emissary* (2019), psychiatrist Iain McGilchrist challenges traditional learning modalities and the left-hemisphere dominance of modern education, which, he argues, thinks it knows everything yet knows less. It needs certainty and to be right. The right hemisphere, however, enables the simultaneous consideration of multiple ambiguous possibilities without prematurely closing in on any one outcome (Elizaphanian, 2023). How many potential Teslas have been stifled? Do formal grades accurately predict potential?

Ross (2014) continues, "Serendipitous experiences arise from situations...the individual finds themselves with little to no control over the circumstances. (They) only control...how to respond" (pp. 299-323). These experiences, in the simplest terms, are the unknown good, bad, and ugly situations one finds themselves in. An individual's reaction fosters the development and/or degradation of their cognitive and social abilities.

Aptitude Self-Assessment Workbook

Aptitude Enhancement: As workers are assigned to self-actualization roles (Psych & Ed Films, 1968) and are reinforced with positive feedback (Daniels, 2000), their potential for impact is enhanced. The improvement becomes exponential when coupled with other workers. Individual teaming competencies, such as humility, hunger, and social intelligence (Lencioni, 2016), can be observed in business systems that effectively meet customer needs through clear communication (Nemeth, 2008). For example, health caregivers who actively listen to their patients more effectively communicate their needs to clinical providers, who, at times, are on the move to attend to the next patient. Attentive nurses serve as a stopgap to get the provider's focus. This, coupled with providers who consider more than their next patient, can facilitate additional communication about patient needs. For example, the Cleveland Clinic

Foundation (Graban, 2016) conducts plan-of-care sessions with all medical stakeholders, who contribute to the patient's health during an in-person sit-down. These "huddles" offer multidisciplinary treatment perspectives and demonstrate to patients that they are supported and heard. Patients describe it as a powerful experience.

The H.E.A.R.T. Program is one such Cleveland Clinic effort in tandem with the healthcare customer survey group Press Ganey (2019). Teaming skills are listed around the HEART acronym as follows:

-- "**H**ear the concern
-- **E**mpathize with the way the person is feeling
-- **A**pologize for the experience the person is having
-- **R**espond with action to the problem
-- **T**hank the person for allowing you to make things right" (Cleveland Clinic, 2020, online).

How are your institution's leaders at listening?
Poor 1   2   3   4   5   6   7   8   9   10   *Skilled*
In what ways are they empathetic?

____

____

And lastly, give examples of your team's responsiveness to customer/patient needs.

____

____

Teams, Teamwork & Teaming

Now we turn our attention to how individual development can enhance team performance (Katzenbach, 1998). As workers develop more confidence and skills, they become more comfortable within their teams, with their results, and in their relationships (Shaw, 2017). However, at times, the terms team, teamwork, and teaming are used interchangeably, but they are not the same thing. To level set, let us delineate the differences. "A team is a group of people with a high degree of interdependence, geared toward achieving a goal or completing a task. In other words, they agree on a goal and agree that the only way to achieve the goal is to work together" (Parker, 2008, chapter 2; Kropp Jr. & Parker, 1992).

The practical definition of teams has been applied in all walks of life. Historical wisdom, such as Christ's twelve disciples being sent out two by two, has been an ongoing endeavor that continues to this day in the guidance of today's business gurus on team management. Hall of Fame football coach of the Green Bay Packers, Vince Lombardi, reflected many years ago, "Individual commitment to a group effort; that is what makes a team work, a company work, a society work, (and) a civilization work" (Forbes, 2019; quote). He captured the wide essence of teams. Nothing can stop the power of complementary and impactful forces.

The concept of 'we the people' in the formation of the United States is a testament to the collaborative efforts of its citizens, in essence, teams. Senge (2006) adds more color to the term team in supporting the power of looking forward by cheering, "The practice of shared vision involves the skills of unearthing ... 'pictures of the future' that foster genuine commitment and enrollment rather than compliance. In mastering this discipline, leaders learn the counter-productiveness of trying to dictate a vision, no matter how heartfelt" (Senge, 2006, p.9; Turnbull et al., 1996). Teams form and are sustained with common visions of the future (Jones, 2025).

Why leverage Teams? Because flexibility in a company, particularly in product, process, and/or service, contributes to longevity, coupled with relationships, knowledge (tribal) transfer, and cohesive teams, holds the group together (Ferris, 2000). Nimble organizations are providing the wiggle room for teams to be effective (Harbott, 2021). Hierarchical structures may stifle creativity. The "traditional mechanistic assumptions about organizations (that) underlie (many) of today's human resource management practices (Stewart & Carson, 1997); (need to) shift to organic organizational structures – (this is) critically important" (Ferris, 2000, p.54).

Teamwork, on the other hand, is "done by several associates with each doing a part but all subordinating personal prominence to the efficiency of the whole" (Merriam-Webster, 2021, online). Teamwork is used in business, sports, and countries, and is now even recognized in the name of a collaboration software from Microsoft, called TEAMS (Oksanen, 2025). Many industries logged on during and after the COVID-19 outbreak to facilitate communication—indeed, a vital resource for team members.

Teamwork has been around since the dawn of man. In early human history, groups of hunters flanked each other for protection. The Old Testament says, "In the way man might prevail against one who is alone, two will withstand him, and a threefold cord is not quickly broken" (ESV, 2001, Ecclesiastes 4:12; Currid & Chapman, 2017). This is a perfect illustration of the importance of teamwork. It provides force multiplication to tackle any issue, regardless of the industry. It works for hunting (and not being hunted), it works in sports (constant passing in basketball increases the percentage of a 'good shot'), and it works in the boardroom. It occurs when competencies, solutions, and skills are developed through members executing task plans, employing participative teaching methods, and sharing relevancy (Snell et al., 2005). Teamwork is born when people come together:

...in a collaborative style, (when) positive interdependence exists among members, who agree both to pool and partition their resources and responsibilities and to operate from a foundation of shared values. Team-generated goals determine the purpose of working together, and ground rules guide the team's operations. Collaboration is a voluntary relationship. (Hernandez, 2013, pp. 480-498; Hunt et al., 2003; Lencioni, 2002; Tuckman, 1965).

This collaboration (Friend & Cook, 2007) is "a style for direct interaction between at least two coequal parties voluntarily engaged in shared decision making as they work toward a common goal" (p.7). It is a matter of interaction, not just an activity. Balance is needed, along with mutual contribution. It involves a type of parity valued by the group members, characterized by shared leadership, accountability, and responsibility. Leaders facilitate participation by soliciting and responding to others' input (Schleien et al., 2014).

Collaboration is based on mutual goals. Joint decision-making may include each member completing an assignment, yet the group collectively determines the next steps. Each member brings the needed supplies to complete the task. "Individual members do not take credit for team success or blame others for team failures. When teams take time to celebrate their successes, they are also celebrating their cohesion" (King-Sears et al., 2015, p. 30).

Although teamwork is not a panacea, here is an example in which groups tasked with working together perceived it differently (Fowler, 2024). He explains:

I received a call from the US Department of State, requesting that a monitoring and evaluation specialist be assigned to an organization similar to the United Nations, specifically the Economic Community of West Africa States (ECOWAS) (Jaye et al., 2011). My first introduction to this organization came through a meeting at the Department of State in Washington, D.C. I was both excited and disappointed.

I quickly noticed that the State Department team representatives were often short-tempered, impatient, and sometimes rude to their African counterparts. This initially troubled me, and I did not understand why. The purpose of the US representatives was to support the economic development of West African nation-states through an initiative led by President Obama (at the time). This was my introductory meeting to get to know the customers and to prepare for my two-year trip to live in Abuja, Nigeria. I was tasked with providing leadership lessons and liaison services to the ECOWAS early-warning system director. This included executive shadowing and mentoring, as well as training the staff on the scientific method and program management discipline. At the time, I did not understand the term 'African time' or 'Nigerian time.' Their culture minimized the importance of deadlines, thereby diluting the power of teams and their input. They were more concerned with (present) life than (future) business, which made it challenging to teach project management and the importance of deadlines. I expected patience and professionalism from the Department of State team members, but at times I did not observe them. However, I soon learned that their patience had run out because the client was unable to meet program timelines. I did not like what I saw at first, but I later learned to understand it.

Cultural time orientation (Thoms, 2004) is a critical enabler for team assignment completion. The African team members were overly polite in all personal interactions, especially in written forms of communication (such as letters and emails), but tended to delay getting down to business. I expected the African clients to learn the scientific method and the concept of program management, including meeting deadlines. Many were slow in this expectation.

In this example, various teams were working against one another, which stalled progress.

Teaming, on the other hand, takes teams and teamwork to a new level. Building on both practices, Harvard professor Amy Edmondson (2012) elaborates on the concept of teaming:

Why (do we) call it *teaming*, rather than simply the creation of an effective team? Innovation is a dynamic process that unfolds in uncertain ways. This means that it is not always possible to know in advance exactly what skills you will need on a team or how long you will need them, making it difficult to plan and build a stable, well-designed team before the job gets underway. In a typical hospital emergency room, for example, patient outcomes depend upon seamless coordination and superb communication among diverse clinicians who may not even know each other's names at the outset of the encounter. That is teaming. High-quality teaming blends getting to know people quickly—their knowledge, skills, and goals—with listening to other points of view, coordinating actions, and making shared decisions (b-okk.cc). Effective teaming happens when everyone remains highly aware of others' needs, roles, and perspectives. Business leaders must understand and nurture the teaming process to foster innovation and ensure future success (Edmondson, 2012, pp. 12 ff; & 2013).

Teaming itself helps solve deep, intricate problems. To illustrate, Edmondson reflects:

The problems facing organizations and society...are increasingly complex and multifaceted, (requiring) multidisciplinary approaches. Consider what it takes to design, build, or maintain high-tech infrastructure projects, intelligent buildings, avionics systems, mobile telephone networks, or banking communication systems. Even products such as shoes that appear simple can become tremendously complex: for example, 50 biomechanical engineers, industrial designers, and electromechanical experts teamed up to make asymmetrical spikes for Olympic gold medalist Jeremy Wariner (Dionne & Carlile, 2016). In healthcare, organizations ... that vary in professionals' perspectives must be considered alongside patients' perspectives to produce successful innovation. In short, dealing with today's complex products and systems requires solving dozens, sometimes even hundreds, of interconnected problems. Thus...today's organizations must (leverage) deep specialized knowledge and manage integration across these domains of expertise (simultaneously). These two opposing challenges necessitate that organizations master extreme teaming — one that brings together diverse areas of expertise to solve particularly challenging problems (Edmondson & Harvey, 2017; Edmondson & Chesbrough, 2017).

In healthcare settings, for example, teaming begins with respect and openness to sharing, especially within a (hierarchical) interlevel, where joint care planning (involving patients, families, and the care team) leverages best practices, clinical protocols, and industry knowledge, while differentiating confrontation (team accountability) from insubordination (Gordon et al., 2014). In groups where teaming is practiced and understood, any member, regardless of their position or grade level, can raise a concern and confront superiors. This may be an unpleasant, yet necessary, collaboration skill (Snell et al., 2005). Even church leaders leverage teaming for mission success (Crosby, 2012).

Leadership for Teaming-Plus

Framing, an important teaming skill, aligns team members' focus to avoid scope-creep (Harrin, 2013). The critical nature of the problem or task at hand necessitates teaming.

If the work is not important, you probably do not have a team. However, framing the importance of the work is also critical in generating enthusiasm and engagement. After all, the work may be important, but unless the team sees it that way, it becomes functionally unimportant. This is a critical distinction. You can—and should—appeal to prospective team members in various ways to communicate the importance of the work. Making such connections can go a long way toward fostering interest in the task at hand (Bellomo, 2021, ATD, online blog).

Clarity of team player roles and member leadership expectations (Parker, 2008) rounds out the other prerequisites for robust teaming. Parker defines four primary roles: communicator, collaborator, contributor, and challenger. Regardless of the role a team member plays, teaming acumen requires a certain level of personal introspection. Outstanding leadership can take on an ego persona, where prominent personalities overwhelm situations and followers. "The word leader itself conjures up visions of a striking figure on a rearing white horse, crying, Follow me! The leader is the one who has power, authority, or charisma enough to command others" (Manz & Sims, 2001, p. 18; Treat, 2004). However, the Bible offers a more profound and broader perspective on leadership. The first-century missionary, Apostle Paul, said, "Do nothing out of selfish ambition or vain conceit. Instead, in humility, value others above yourselves, not looking to only your interests but also to the interests of others" (NIV, 1973, Philippians 2:3,4). Selflessness and discipleship carry biblical leadership.

How should this teaming leadership apply today? Manz & Sims (2001) acknowledge that technological advancements necessitate what they call 'super-leadership' (pp. 11-15), which enables others to lead while leveraging personal self-examination and understanding multiple team members' values, models, and interpersonal structures. They link this line of thinking to organizational culture. Humphrey (2018) identifies three contemporary realities that necessitate this type of leadership: 1) The flattening of organizations pushes all levels to display leadership qualities, 2) technology distributes roles and responsibilities, and 3) the intelligent communication software requires answers on the spot. This competency discourages the delay, 'I will get back to you' (Humphrey, 2018). No more will the status quo suffice.

In teaming practice, leaders amplify their influence by developing other leaders (Benson, 2022). This brings us to the critical nature of followership. It is incumbent to include it in the discussion of teaming-enabled leadership. Society cannot have one or the other; it is a package deal (Carsten et al., 2016). The study and comprehension of followership principles are productive on many levels. To illustrate, no coach would solely work with the quarterback position (in American football) and ignore the contribution of the other ten players on the field who follow when they hear the word 'hike!' Similarly, excluding the followership discussion from a leadership study would never result in a touchdown (Hurwitz & Koonce, 2016).

Burns (1978) rejects the authoritarian dichotomy between leaders and followers (that leaders are inherently higher, better, and more important than followers). He sees a joint relationship between values and motivations for the collective good. He contrasts dominance with authentic leadership (p.18). It is conveyed through relationships between people (Hollander, 1992). Followers come in all shapes and sizes - Riggio et al. (2008), note five different kinds: 1) the *sheep* who rely on the leadership for wisdom and direction,

2) the *yes-people* who are generally positive and supportive of the leader yet not very questioning, 3) the *alienated* who find multiple reasons to buck the system, 4) the fence sitting *pragmatists*, waving their recently wetted finger in the air and checking on the wind before moving; and lastly, 5) the *supporting star* followers unafraid to question the leader's counsel. Internalized teaming acumen involves understanding oneself, one's team members, and the kinetics between them (Offermann et al., 2004). Fowler (2024) adds further insight into followership with a real-life example. Back to his experience in Africa. He prompts, "My initial ECOWAS experience did not recognize followership." At first, he did not fully understand:

> Nigerian business culture is hierarchical. People generally defer to those who are older than they are or who occupy a higher official position than they do. Since respect is a significant part of Nigerian culture, being aware of the person's age and official position is essential. Suppose you do not respect this aspect of Nigerian business culture. In that case, you risk sabotaging current or potential business relationships, as professionals will not want to continue participating in business discussions if they feel disrespected. As a rule of thumb, it pays to be respectful to everyone you encounter, from the admin assistant to the managing director (Aluko, KPA, 2018, online).

Fowler's experience did not initially recognize the concept below, as proposed by Nissi Ekpott. "I will tell you one little thing about doing business in Nigeria: time is like a slow river. If you can grasp this mindset and learn to manage it, you will do well in Africa" (Sand, 2021). Fowler concludes, "If I were to repeat my time in the West African states, I would be more open and honest in the presence of joint meetings where we would be forthcoming about each team's shortcomings. Regarding followership: the Americans' lack of patience and the African's lack of effort in meeting deadlines; it would be permissible to tactfully acknowledge both teams' weaknesses and also lead them gently to a compromise on a middle ground for the needed tasks and requirements" (2024, online). The lessons from followership (outputs) can help leaders know what inputs to add. This is an excellent example of learning from best practices in group dynamics, which leads to the intricacies of this new Teaming-Plus way.

Morale: Teaming-Plus for Dynamic Interdependence (G-R-O-U-P)

Now, we move on to a brief introductory summary of the Morale phase, including the specifics of each group dynamics step. The simple acronym is G-R-O-U-P. Often, people are <u>guarded</u> against one another. They do not know where they fit in or who their teams are. Moreover, when things go wrong, people often <u>resign</u> from team engagement due to frustration and conflict, which can lead to storming. However, with intervention and guidance, leaders help them through that, they reach the O phase, which is <u>operational</u>, and they start doing what they are asked.

If they can stay working together as a group, recruit for identified needs, and things begin to fall into place. If you are lucky, you get to the next phase, <u>utilization</u>. People are placed in areas where they are the most effective. For example, in baseball, a short, stubby person might be a good catcher, but a sleek, fast person might be better suited for center field or shortstop. Are the people placed in a way that leverages their individual strengths, creating a multiplier effect for the group? Effective utilization of each team member's unique strengths is key to team prosperity. And then ultimately, they get to P, the <u>production</u> phase, where members can complete each other's sentences. They understand one another, and results follow! Group dynamics or morale's lynchpin is interdependence.

It involves more than simply acknowledging that, as human beings, we are reliant on each other. It means letting go of our conception of (humanity) as autonomous individuals... that is, we are interdependent. This fundamentally challenges mainstream perspectives of leadership based on individual psychology and leadership development interventions, on narrow conceptions of power and what it means to be self-aware (Flinn, 2018; Flinn, 2024). ChatGPT notes that the quote is from O'Toole's work, entitled *"Interdependence and the Reimagining of Leadership* (i.e., Kezar & Holcombe, 2017).

Group morale measures (often subjectively) a group's bond, as seen in its unity and team spirit within the internal social structure (Klann & CCL, 2004). Strong social connections outside of work, such as those fostered through laughter, cooperation, coordination, commonality, and goal achievement, are evident. This extends to perspectives on work, colleagues, supervisors, and company goals (Whitaker & Whitaker, 2013). Morale feeds itself within the group and (when high) has its members focused on team objectives (Blum, 1998). Thus, it integrates individual feelings, group inputs and outputs, and the dynamics of belonging and partnering to achieve team goals (Deutser, 2023).

Observers of this phenomenon experience minimal conflict, smiling faces, smooth adjustments, cohesiveness, and positive attitudes (Guba, 1958). On the contrary, groups with low morale are clouded by apathy and resignation (Bardwick & Net Library, 2008). Establishing effective parties that leverage individual and group teaming competencies does not happen by accident. Teaming usually occurs when assumptions are suspended (Edmondson, 2012)—assumptions about the job classification norms, one's talent, and that of others. Ideal team members enhance hiring, employee skill assessment, advancement development, and embedding improvement into the culture (Lencioni, 2016). This evidence can be observed in the concept of "affect" (Owen, 2017), which is felt individually through "cognition and motivation" and collectively through "mood and emotions" (p. 79). One example: running a mass automotive production is hard. Significantly exceeding daily production is almost impossible. Fowler (2024) relays another relevant story on Teaming-Plus.

One day, while at Ford Motor Company (Kalamdani, 2006), we arrived for the night shift to find that the day shift had made a significant leap in production (765 engines in a 10-hour shift—a 26% increase over typical shift numbers). They were gloating and quite vocal about it. As soon as the day shift crew was out the door, I called over my night shift hourly team leader and asked him to gather our UAW members by the picnic table just before the line started. In the face of the challenge, I said, "Are we going to allow the day shift to get the spotlight?" I hoped to spark some motivation and perhaps solicit some insight (in Owen's words) into which operators knew our difficult production jobs/stations best. One such manufacturing process involved a lift-transfer job that utilized hydraulics to move a heavy engine block from one production line to another. It was the constraint/bottleneck (Goldratt & Cox, 2014) that no one wanted to work on. One member stepped up and said, "I can run the heck out of that job, I will do it all night" (where rotating was the norm). Long story short, we printed a "hoc report" in real-time that showed our night shift production numbers exceeded those of the day shift, time-stamped for proof.

We ran a hard copy of the report, folded it in half, and placed it on the same picnic table as the name of the most vocal day-shift operator, so she would see it first thing and spread the news. That night, when we arrived, the day-shift operators would not even look up at us. The qualitative night-shift relationships (Porras et al., 2010) established in the informal enabled an incredible performance in the formal, quantifiable setting. That record still stands today. It was achieved through mood and emotions (Owen, 2017). No matter what the business sign says on the street, it is about the people inside the building that matter" (Fowler, 2024, online).

Worksites are both organization and organism. "The people form a complex organism – rather like a hive of bees – with each person interacting with all the others to a greater or lesser extent, and each making its contribution to the good of the whole." ~Hannah Arendt (IL&M, 2007). Let us take a targeted look at each G-R-O-U-P phase in the interdependence of morale management. How can Teaming-Plus help your organization? At what stage do most new teams typically begin?

Guarded: Where do I fit?

Define Them. As teams, shifts, groups, committees, and other forums initiate joint efforts and relationships, individuals have numerous questions running through their minds. Will this group be successful? What does that look like? Do we have clear goals? What about roles and responsibilities? Where do I fit? Will I make worthy contributions? Will other members listen to me? Is this effort a priority for my boss? Or will they view this activity as a distraction from my primary mission? These and many other considerations make up the guarded stage. Hoover (2005) notes that the uncertainty surrounding these foundational questions creates undue obstacles to team cohesion.

Group formation is often quickly followed by a sense of storming (Lail, 2019). However, when these questions have clear, published answers on worker placement, they can enhance performance (Suswati, 2021). The guarded stage is often made up of several wanderers discussed earlier. What can a manager do to dilute some of the inertia and turn it into momentum? The answer to that question might include more conflict and uncertainty down the line, but for now, stability might be the prescription.

Enhance Them. DeVany (2010) suggests initiating a tactical approach by encouraging thorough 1) pre-planning, 2) monitoring, and 3) interactive checking. The planning includes assessing team member skills (both technical & interpersonal), establishing a meeting schedule (including expectations & cadence), and outlining a clear vision and goals. Answering for initial group members - what is my mission, and what is expected of me?

The monitoring phase involves the manager communicating team-lead roles and expectations, conducting regular check-ins, documenting priorities, and evaluating the overall group environment. The checking piece includes weekly, monthly, and quarterly updates to sustain the teams' efforts and eliminate obstacles. MIT (2018) suggests these activities can be conducted and even supported virtually, allowing executives to exert greater influence across functions without needing to be in multiple locations at once. Attention to these practical suggestions can help with the comfort and effectiveness of new team members. What usually happens next? Do conflicts arise? Most assuredly!

Resignation: Can I fit in?

Define Them: Storming is likely to occur across multiple groups at some point (Lail, 2019). Turnover (Kaye & Jordan-Evans, 2021) and quiet quitting can creep in when members ask themselves, 'Can I really fit in here, or do I even want to' (Sherwin & Sherwin, 2018)? The resignation phase is the likely reaction of groups and their members. Low morale can hit law enforcement (del Pozo et al., 2024), education (Williamson & Blackburn, 2023), transportation (Frock & Net Library, 2006), and even those in ministry

(Fields, 2002). Whenever human beings are involved, there is a risk of dysfunction (Lencioni, 2007). How can executives help their leaders move their team past this?

Enhance Them. To successfully pass through the resignation stage, the team lead "has a key role to play in modeling the behavior which will be most helpful to the group…the primary requirement (here) is an ability to confront conflict directly" (Laiken & OISE, 1994, p. 52). When the storm is confronted, "the good news is that if you can help the group weather this phase skillfully, members will become much more competent at handling conflict constructively in the future, and the group will become cohesive and compelling in ways that at this point seem like an unrealistic fantasy" (p. 52). Another way to say it is that teams can now start to operate!

Operation: Are we Good? Yes!

Define Them. Webster's defines 'operating' as performing a function, exerting influence, and carrying out a mission. Groups in the operational stage have successfully resolved (set aside) petty differences within their teams (Barnes, 2019), understand their roles, and generally collaborate with others to meet larger goals. They get down to work — nothing special per se — but avoid wasting time and resources. Many organizations never move past this stage. What can leaders do to at least get their teams to this point?

Enhance them. Rodriguez (2022) believes that attentive Employee Resource Groups can facilitate learning to improve operations. These HR services may, 1) align goals with stated priorities, 2) provide clarity with roles and responsibilities, 3) value its members, and 4) practice/expect continuous improvement with flexibility. How can we enhance these four team foundations to develop practical (tactical) Teaming-Plus steps that foster learning in organizations? More on each:

Foundation 1: Align Goals with Priorities.

Matching Teaming-Plus skill = Document Operational Definitions.

Simon (2015) contends that at times, words collide, confuse, and hinder understanding, separating knowledge within and between team members. Too often, jargon can cloud meaning. The focus on the planning portion of the P-D-C-A model allows for time, ensures a well-paced implementation, and secures that the t's are crossed and the i's are dotted (Realyvásquez et al., 2023). Planning, with clear written group clarity provided in advance, reduces the potential for misinterpretation or misapplication of goals and priorities (Hillier et al., 2016).

Foundation 2: Provide Clarity.

Teaming-Plus skill = Major on the Majors (Latham & Siegerman, 2022 - Audio) challenges leaders to ensure the message, policy, and/or intended leader expectations are well understood and received by members. They suggest "what you cannot see you do not understand" (Chapter One). This comprises 80% of worktime, figuring that part out, leaving little room for the actual work itself. Leaders must reinforce what matters most across multiple channels and media platforms (Chaturvedi & Chaturvedi, 2012).

Foundation 3: Value Team Members.

Teaming-Plus skill = Require Mission Values. Creelman & Kaiser (2009) take issue with diverse team composition, not in an ethnic sense, but rather in 'values' alignment. They propose homogeneous mission values must be a common denominator for team fitness, member selection, and outcome evaluation. Are the right people tactically where they need to be? Are attitudes creating a joint milieu of success? So, be public about the rationale/why things matter.

Foundation 4: Expect continuous improvement with flexibility.

Teaming-Plus Skill = Learn/Practice & Go-See.

Just as real-time data is more reliable than historical data, being present where the work is done is better for understanding than hearing about it afterward. Gemba (Márquez Figueroa et al.,

2024), popularized by Japanese auto workers, encourages leaders to see, show respect, and ask why. Gemba benefits leaders by increasing awareness and workers by providing the leader's presence and attention. It is a win/win. Practice Gemba to build knowledge, enable flexible interventions, and achieve floor-level targets (Holweg & Bicheno, 2023). These four Teaming-Plus skills, built on your four foundations, should ensure routine execution. Do leaders settle for this status quo? Or can teams reach greater heights?

Utilization: Now, we are humming!

Define Them. The utilization stage is when leaders are assigned, and resources are aligned to maximize the group's effectiveness (Sherf et al., 2018). Speed, strength, wisdom, and agility combined shape momentum for the mission in uncertain times (Alexander, 2024). Consider the coordinated art of speed sailing. In this exhilarating sport, momentum is generated when each crew member makes precise, on-the-fly adjustments to position the sails perfectly in the wind's path, creating powerful forward motion for the vessel. The Captain, from his unique vantage point, communicates real-time instructions to each crew member. While the individual shipmate may not immediately grasp the reasoning (pending storm?) behind a particular directive, their responsive action, applying the (timely) collective alignment with other crew members, sets the ship on a course toward victory (Jiminez, 2025). Summarily, managers and their teams can weather this paradox navigation (Lê & Pradies, 2023) to set sail. How can they (fall in) muster this call to quarters, effectively, so to speak?

Enhance Them. Utilization occurs when micros combine and align to form a macro. Businesses may view the concept of utilization in a physical sense, typically referring to space and storage (Ballerat-Busserolles et al., 2018); however, in this context, it refers to the alignment of people and processes within organizations. One of the world's top hospitals, the Cleveland Clinic's first pillar of system improvement ensures that resources are positioned so that all caregivers can make a difference on what matters most (Graban, 2016). Organization alignment "is not about forcing goals on people...it is about creating alignment...between goals and actions, from top to bottom, and across the organization. (The step to) identify and communicate what matters most. Even if executives have a brilliant strategy, it will...fail if the organization does not understand (the)...strategy and the need for change" (Graban, 2016, online blog).

Enabling utilization requires teams with ideal positioning, comprising humble, hungry, and intelligent individuals (Lencioni, 2016), working together through shared ideation (Folk, 2022; Sushil et al., 2016), within flexible work organizations (Kellerer et al., 2015; Sushil et al., 2016). "It has also been reflected in various connotations or dimensions of flexibility such as adaptiveness, adjustment, agility, amiability, autonomy, balance, compromise, customization, elasticity, liberalization, localization, malleability, mobility, openness, responsiveness, resilience, variability, versatility, and so on" (p.4). What do organizations see when this momentum takes hold?

Production: Cooking With Grease!

Define them. Fun fact: Gas stoves replaced conventional wood stoves in 1915. The phrase, 'cooking with grease,' was popularized by Hollywood writer Deke Houlgate for comedian Bob Hope. Hollywood has used the expression "Now you are cooking with gas" to mean that perfection has been achieved for some time (Ammer, 2013, 1940s slang). This captures the essence of teams moving beyond their individual goals to work towards further group objectives. Decisions and negotiations (Schoop et al., 2017) are made to build and solidify the best course of action (COA). Lawrence & Kirkham (2024) further explain,

> Design a COA for analysis, evaluation, and selection as the one to accomplish the mission most effectively. It includes

analyzing relative combat power, generating options, arraying initial forces, developing schemes of maneuver, assigning headquarters, and preparing COA statements and sketches. The commander may direct a specific course of action based on available time, staff proficiency, or other factors; FM 5-0 [*USACAC*, 2025].

Groups in the production stage utilize robust pre-planning, assimilating strategic and tactical maneuvering, to achieve mission success. Players are placed appropriately, plans are agreed upon, execution is monitored, and success is achieved. How can the C-suite establish this as a standard practice to support their vision and objectives?

Enhance Them. Leaders build high-performing teams (Skillshub Ltd., 2024) by understanding the lessons from the underachieving ones, fostering team building, establishing core values, norms, and behaviors through a culture of self-assessment that adapts to the ebbs and flows of the environment. Savvy executives today help their teams tap into artificial intelligence (AI) for problem-solving (Tang et al., 2019). Production excellence manages change by focusing on both organizational and individual motivation, ensuring that change is aligned with how individuals perceive their jobs and organizations (Black & Gregersen, 2003). They must understand their workers' mental maps. "If leaders cannot change individuals' mental maps, they will not change the destinations people pursue or the paths they take to get there" (Chapter 1, Para. 2). Morale is enhanced, the group's interdependence is achieved, and goals are met through the G-R-O-U-P dynamics explained above.

Are you ready to walk your teams through this process? Are you ready to win? What will be your first step?

Result: Teaming + Alliances

When individuals and teams are healthy—not necessarily conflict-free but working through issues—diversity (in ethnicity and problem-solving skills) can be a huge enabler. The concept of alliances at work (Kuglin & Hook, 2002) and even in society (Sullivan et al., 2017) can be rare. Nevertheless, there are examples. The early 1900s partnership between Carnegie Steel and the Federal and National Steel companies led to the creation of the first billion-dollar company, capturing 67% of the market share - to the Warner Communications to Time, Inc. 1980s merger - on to the Irish company AerCap ($35B) purchase of the American GE Electric business (Reuters, 2021), alliances have propelled companies to even greater profits. But what about on a smaller scale? How can mature, savvy individuals (senior workers) effectively partner with other workers to form teaming alliances? Are there examples of this?

Yes, Pixar, a struggling new movie maker, shaped an internal team, i.e., the "Braintrust" (2014), made up of diverse creatives that ultimately delivered the animated hit *Toy Story* [Film], which saved the new company. Additionally, diverse armed services (Special Forces groups) have excellent mission interoperability, often without even speaking to one another; near telepathic communication is required in security environments that necessitate silence (NRC, 2009). High-functioning teams in business, too, often need this same performance interoperability. Poor communication hurts the bottom line for both large and small companies, to the tune of $62 million annually for companies with more than 100,000 employees (Grossman, 2011) and an average of over $420,000 in losses per year for smaller companies with 100 employees (Hamilton, 2010). Effective teaming leverages strong communication skills, drives growth, and positions companies for greater success. Human resources should help leaders stay attuned to the pulse of communications today.

Morale (Dynamic Teams) Workbook
Pass this out to your team members for some unfiltered insight.
Three questions, i.e., a Teaming-Plus Summary: 1) **How to build individual *team players*?** Parker (2008) defines effective players as contributors, collaborators, communicators, and challengers. Lencioni (2016) characterizes them as humble, hungry, and politically and socially intelligent. Dubinskaya (2022) found that the potential for self-actualization among employees persists well into their seventies, provided they can continue working. Organizations that are sensitive to this in their workers can create environments where employees can thrive. Studer (2020) found that the best leaders were sensitive to this in their workers because they saw themselves as followers, willing to learn, and adaptable. Peters and Haslam (2018) saw this firsthand in Marine recruits who found favor and future leadership roles were unassuming at first, although the other recruits, "who considered themselves ... natural leaders (could not convince their peers that this was the case. Instead,...saw themselves (and were seen by commanders) as followers who ultimately emerged as leaders. In other words, it seems those who want to lead are well served by first endeavoring to follow" (Section 3). What does your organization need to do to build better team players?

____

===

2) How to build high-performing *teams*? Individuals and teams go through developmental phases (Egolf & Chester, 2013). Some robust characteristics include members with verbal and nonverbal communication skills, as well as proficiency in listening, ne-gotiation, problem-solving, decision-making, and assertiveness (Quizlet, 2015). Additionally, managers who understand utilization/human factors (Van Cott et al., 1992) position workers to make the most impact. Teams can be true enablers of success. How can your organization better support teams?

---

3) How can we build on our accomplishments to achieve even greater heights? Managers can do a few things: catch people doing things right (Blanchard, 2002), respond in real-time to employee concerns (Romero, 2009), honor standards as a baseline for improvement, educate workers for promotion (Tracy, 2016), circulate their winner's influence (Bustamante et al., 2022), and lastly buffer noise from working environments (Scott, 2022). We will amplify this list in the C-H-E-C-K section later.

Another confirmation of teaming is the increase in real-world problem-solving (Rittel & Webber, 1973). One such technique used by teams is brainstorming, in which individuals and teams consider various approaches, issues, and solutions to problem resolution, while categorizing potential causes in an Ishikawa diagram (Yazdani & Tavakkoli-Moghaddam, 2012) - see Figure 2.

Figure 2
Fishbone Diagram

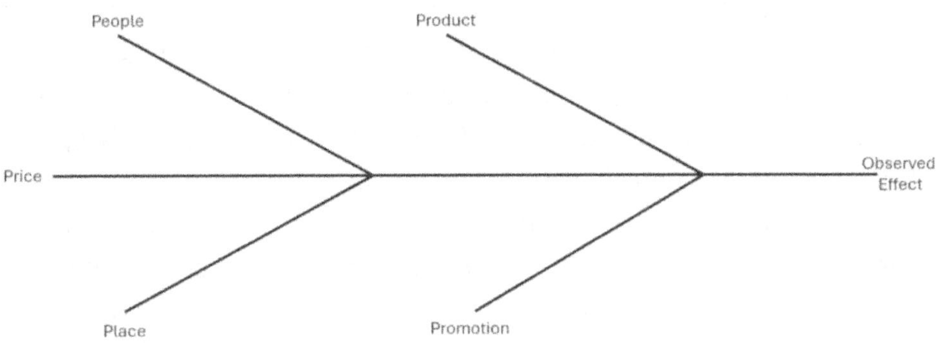

What problem (effect) is your team currently going through? Work through this fishbone to categorize potential causes (i.e., by people, product, price, place, and promotion). Then, pick the top three and perform a 5-why exercise. You may find some counterintuitive answers (Gross, 2014). See it explained here (Edginton, 2017): https://www.youtube.com/watch?v=N7cR2gArCFE (cut and paste).

To facilitate growth and development, we suggest that leaders be open and encourage uniqueness. "As differences are welcomed, people begin finding...ways of connecting. Instead of sticking to culturally defined...interactions or fear-driven avoidance, people (can) find...areas of commonality" (Network, 2012, p. 388). This brings Blanchard's truth to life that none of us is as smart as all of us (Bouwhuis, 2012), attacks problems with strength in numbers (Laughlin, 2011), and ingrains continuous improvement in the culture (Nakane & Darga, 1997). Let us expand these three.

•Collective Smartness: Momentum is created with multiple minds working together to find solutions. The team's IQ increases when multiple perspectives are considered. Creativity is born from diversity of opinion (Paulus & Nijstad, 2003). Rather than promoting groupthink, which can suppress prudent individual ideas, encouraging collaboration helps generate practical solutions by building on each other's input (Milliken & Martins, 1996).

•Group Problem Solving (GPS): Laughlin's (2011) approach harnesses team members in many ways – being complementary to one another, being conflictive with one another (iron sharpens iron), and by balancing intellective (mathematical) and judgmental (intuitive) skills in soliciting solutions. This technique seeks a practical answer, not merely group consensus.

•Culture of Improvement: The Ford Production System philosophy (Webdeveloper, 2025), an internal division challenging the status quo manufacturing operations in the late 1990s, taught that structure drives behavior, which defines the culture (Mar, 2024). The phrase *culture change* may be an oxymoron. It is like asking oranges to become apples... for actual change to occur, the farmer must move upstream to "structure" and add/change the new (different) apple seeds. In the same way, business structure, leadership models, and expectations shape behavior, which, in turn, fashions the observed culture.

Group *Morale* is both an input and an output of effective teaming (Klann, 2004). It serves as an incentive to continue making impactful contributions and encourages greater involvement. It is "the time spent together in shared experiences and the communication among members. It is the quality and quantity of both time and communication that bring success" (p. 14). It does not come naturally for most. Workers tend to be self-protective and default to predictability. Vaananen et al. (2008), too, even draw the lack of it (at work) as a contributing factor to employee heart attacks.

Managers must persist in addressing the challenges workers face. Klan and Klan (2004) encourage leaders to:

• Be constant, open, honest, and safe with communication (Rate yourself 1-10) __.
• Offer consistent expectations/explanations with storytelling (1-10) __.

- Leverage creative meetings, formal/informal, to pass on information (1-10) ___.
- Use communication to resolve conflict (p. 14) (1-10) ___.

Teaming effectiveness is tied directly to communication (King-Sears et al., 2015). When communication breaks down, team cohesion suffers. "Routine self-evaluation or reflection..." (p. 73) from group members can be an effective tactic for enhancing team effectiveness. Fleming and Monda (2001) first highlighted the lack of cohesion as a known process variable that reduces group teaming, primarily through a lack of respect for teammates, a lack of celebration of successes, and an ego-centric view of work.

Healthcare (as an example) can be a lonely business. Crossing inter-professional and cultural healthcare boundaries (demarcations) is a challenge. Providers are trained in subspecialties and tend to stay within their areas of expertise. Providers want to work on top-of-license, which may present difficulties for teaming applications. Those caregivers who demonstrate discipline in process rigor to the extent they do in their specialty seem to be better cross-teaming facilitators (Hubbard, 2011). Doctors Without Borders, among the Afar (Ethiopia) people, learned firsthand the power of acquiring new skills and paying attention to areas of weakness. The 'all-hands-on-deck approach' was necessary in the harshness of back-bush Africa.

Surprisingly, knowledge (expertise) can adversely affect teaming and team results. Dr. Hubbard (Borders, 2011) cites one team member, who knew the Afar culture the best, ultimately hurt team cohesion. "When the team was left alone, we operated smoothly, but when Milton was around, we were no longer a team, just disciples...(yet) he did know the Afar people far better than we did..." (p. 39). How do you deal with know-it-alls?

How do you best leverage skills across diverse teams?

____

____

In what ways can talent development, coupled with group morale, facilitate continuous improvement?

____

____

In summary, Teaming-Plus is a team sport guided by strong leadership. It works best when everyone "is capable, empowered and expected to make improvements every day…(being) a leader in continuous improvement, in healthcare, and beyond" ~ Dr. Lisa Yerian, Cleveland Clinic Foundation (LEI, 2019). How can we further bridge Teaming-Plus with system improvement? Moving forward may involve checking the rear-view mirror from time to time. It begins by building on our past.

History of Organizational Performance
Lean as a System

Henry Ford, one of the world's founding fathers of organizational performance, wrote in his book *Today and Tomorrow* (1926) that standards (although not romantic) provided the springboard for improvement. If you visited Toyota (2014) in Japan, you would see his picture displayed in the lobby. They honor Ford as the founder of many of their principles. Toyota took process improvement to the next level (TPS, 2025), which is undergirded by the dignity of work, enhances society, promotes improvement, and celebrates human worth, all while balancing strategy with innovative tactics (Fowler, 2025)—more on this symphony below.

Lean Thinking

When Michael George, an innovator in his own right, first wrote *Lean Six Sigma* (2002), he attempted to mix/align two powerful improvement approaches (lean and six sigma) for leverage, but an unintended, false dichotomy emerged. Sadly, it continues to be perpetrated by the uninformed.

Remember, over the years, process improvement efforts have undergone significant changes. From Henry Ford's centralized production to the Shewhart/Deming PDSA Cycle (Sayah & Khaleel, 2022), Toyota's Production System (Monden, 2012), and on to today's Lean Six Sigma (2010), successful companies have done a good job building upon prior methodologies. LSS brings together various approaches from the past, which were at times applied in a vacuum. The strength of this evolution lies in its' system approach, rather than a mere process approach. Few companies today apply the strict traditional Total Quality Management (Amasakaa, 2012) alone; yet no one would argue that quality is not important. Instead, quality is one piece, one facet of enterprise management (FOWLER, 2025).

Before highlighting the interconnectedness, let us establish the traditional definitions of each of our subjects. Lean Manufacturing (Wang, 2011), often referred to simply as 'lean,' is a production strategy (LEI, 2022). It considers the exploitation of resources and/or materials for any goal other than creating customer-perceived value as wasteful and targeted for elimination. At its core, lean drives value while maintaining excellence.

Six Sigma (2018) is a mathematical calculation tied to the standard deviation's distance from a data distribution's mean. It seeks to improve the quality of output by identifying/removing the cause of errors and variability (Santander Romero et al., 2024). It combines quality management methods and statistics to assign competence levels to practitioners within an organization (e.g., Black Belts, Green Belts). In the past, many companies had both lean experts and Six Sigma black belts, who reported to different lines of communication and command chains. Fowler (2015) elaborates on the implications of mature system thinking.

> In the industries we work in, we have observed this (separation) dividing resources, creating unnecessary competition, and fostering division. Other successful companies also began to combine the two approaches into a single methodology. Thus, Lean Six Sigma was born (2010).

> Applying the System: For years, we had the privilege of working alongside some of Toyota's former leaders, who had transferred to the consulting business. We would travel the country together, spending weeks with plant managers and floor-level workers. We would ask the hard questions, encourage successes, and point out opportunities for improvement. As we observed their approach, we noticed that many organizations adopting 'lean' did so by narrowly applying the philosophy. It turned into an application exercise with a new tool, rather than fostering an integrated culture. Even today, many companies view Lean Six Sigma solely as a set of tools, achieving only limited and sporadic improvements, and wonder why.

> We should not deceive ourselves. The primary goal of Lean Six Sigma (LSS) is to save and/or generate more money—plain and simple. It will be effective only when understood as a comprehensive system. When applied correctly, you will utilize various tools; however, if the foundational principles are overlooked or never learned, the approach will likely fade away as just another management trend. The mindset precedes the toolset (Fowler, 2015, online).

What are the structural specifics of this Lean Six Sigma thinking? Take a coin as an example. How many sides does it have? Side 1, HONOR Standards: Not necessarily only writing, publishing, editing, or distributing them, but honoring them (FOWLER, 2025, Slide 113). In the spirit of the late 90s ISO 9001 mantra (Tricker & Sherring, 2005), document what you do, do what you document, then prove it in practice. Standards build opportunities. Automotive entrepreneur, Henry Ford, said, "Today's standardization is the necessary foundation on which tomorrow's improvement will be based. If you think of 'standardization' as the best you know today, but which is to be improved tomorrow, you get somewhere" (Ford, 1926, p. 30). Later, Toyota Production System creator Taiichi Ohno (2009) reaffirmed that without a standard, there can be no kaizen (i.e., lasting improvement). So, the first side of the LSS coin is to take your written regulations, procedures, and audits seriously; they are the baseline for your company's stability.

Side 2, HONOR People's Good ideas: People want to be in on things; they want to have a 'say.' Allow your workers to really contribute. Here is the fun part. Workers are less skeptical of management when they know their business culture values (upholds) standards. In this environment, workers are more likely to provide input because they know that if their opinions are accurate, backed by data, the organization's culture is mature enough to implement their good ideas (Rizzardo, 2025). This is a tremendous motivating factor. Collaboration and empowerment are true enablers for improvement and the second side of LSS (FOWLER, 2025, Slide 114).

Side 3/Edge, HONOR the Customer: The edge uniquely links both sides of a coin. The customer should be the central reason for all your standards and improvement efforts. They should touch all aspects of your business plan and execution (Madhwacharyula & Ramdas, 2023). Perhaps if more company leaders applied the three sides, more of those coins would go into the 'profit' bin instead of the 'cost' one. (Fowler, 2015; FOWLER, 2025, Slide 115). More on this LSS thinking:

In 1998, we from a major American auto company took a detailed tour of a Toyota assembly facility. Bells and lights were going off, group leaders were running around like chickens with their heads cut off, and the line kept stopping and starting. One of the confident American vice presidents said to a young Toyota group leader, "You all are really messed up today!" To which the kid paused, stopped, and stared up at the executive, calmly saying, "Yes, Sir, but at least we know it" (Jiminez, 2025).

I am celebrating my twentieth year of learning the principles (in 2015), concepts, tools, and, most importantly, the (correct) thinking of the Japanese manufacturing approach called the Toyota Production System, which by no means is limited to the American translation of "production." It was probably the wrong word used anyway. It should have been "business," "enterprise," or "holistic" system. I came across a post on LinkedIn and other business sites that claims, 'Get your black belt in 5 days of class for $299.00.' Alternatively, 'Become a lean tool expert in one month after taking our course and test.' Sadly, people are buying it. PLEASE! The more I learn, the more I realize I do not know.

No committed martial arts student expects to get a black belt in a month, nor should those curious about performance improvement. As we were leaving the tour, during the final Q&A period, a question was asked of a Toyota executive: "Why do you divulge all your business secrets for the world to see?" He politely and humbly replied, "Because you will never get it, the tool is simple, but the application as a system has complexities. Do you really have the patience (Fowler, 2015; Liker & Meier, 2021)?

Humility, respect for people, systems thinking, honoring standards, and building cadences around customer takt (demand) are just a few of the interconnected concepts to learn (Kramer, 2024, video). The problem lies not in the individual tools, but in their harmony as a whole — that is the hard part. If you are an aspiring Lean Six Sigma practitioner, my first advice is to slow down, read and listen more, and speak less! "The key to the Toyota Way and what makes Toyota stand out is not any of the individual elements; however, what is important is having all the elements together as a system. It must be practiced every day in a very consistent manner, not in spurts" (Ohno, 1998; Fujio Cho, TMC Chairman, 2025).

What about problems? Are they seen as a good thing to be found ... or a bad thing to hide? Once upon a time, there was a frustrated plant manager (Glover, WIGL, 2021). At times, his production team shipped products with defects, including missing parts in the packaging. His quality team often hid the ugly data and highlighted only the good news when company executives visited. The plant manager was desperate, so he hired a costly black belt consultant to address his quality issues.

This so-called expert reviewed the defect rate on the missing parts. After a few weeks of studying the particulars, he suggested to the plant manager that the company buy an industrial scale to weigh the parts in the shipping containers at the end of the line. If the weight were below the required amount (with some parts missing), the line would stop, prompting the team to investigate and replace. After a few weeks of data collection, the plant manager and black belt felt confident about their progress. So, they decided to expand the improvement effort by requiring 5S (workplace organization) on the production floor (Stern, 2024, Section 12.3).

The following week, the plant manager conducted a floor audit and noticed a fan out of place. It was in the 'wrong' spot just off the production line. The plant manager went over and pulled the fan off the line. To which the operator just upstream from the fan yelled, "Why are you moving that?" The manager replied, "We are doing our 5S audit now, and this fan should not be here; why is it here anyway?" The operator replied, "I got tired of walking to the end of the line when the scale shut us down, so I moved the fan right next to me, turned it on high, and it blows the box off the line if it is too light – then we just replace the parts here. So put it back, please, and you should return that expensive scale and consultant because we do not need either!" Lean thinking loves simplicity. Do you? (Fowler, 2015; Glover, 2021).

One final story to bring this home. Problems are not about people; they are always about process (*LinkedIn*, 2025). There was once an operator who installed a hose clamp at a manufacturing facility. Moreover, the quality manager was responsible for ensuring the hose clamp was tight before the product left the zone, under the plant manager's supervision, who oversaw all aspects of the process. There was also a Vice President of Warranty who tracked all of this. If the clamp were not secured and properly installed (by pulling a plastic tab), it would eventually leak, leading to customer claims down the line. This was not a good thing. Brands' reputations go down, and costs go up!

The VP was made aware of the large number of warranty claims for leaking ACs, and he was not pleased. He makes a regularly scheduled visit to the site, where he meets with both plant and quality managers. This time, however, he takes them to the station where the clamp is secured. He then pulls the Andon cord (stops the line), walks over to the operator, and (surprisingly) says...?

"We are sorry and need to apologize to you! We failed to provide you with an air-tight process, one that prevents or at least detects poor hose quality. We noticed there is no standard for installation between shifts. Here is what I plan to do: I will give you two days off (with pay) to design an error-proofed process that ensures these clamps are securely tightened. You can have the quality and plant manager (and their teams) as resources. I am confident you and your night-shift counterpart will figure this out. I am looking forward to seeing the solution. You add value, we are overhead, please help us address this quality problem, and protect the customer, okay?"

Many times, traditional manufacturing leaders would have reamed the operator for shipping bad quality and quite possibly disciplined him. However, this mature lean leader led in a much different way. He focused on the 'bad' process, invited the 'good' operator to get involved, and took responsibility for the errors. That is what lean leadership is all about - honoring people and eliminating variability. The question is: What would you have done? How would you have reacted? How do you think those operators felt?

Back to the story. After two days, the lineman had designed an innovative funnel with a light actuator at the bottom. The new process involved pulling the tab, dropping it through the funnel, and activating the sensor, which kept production. After a specific time, synced to the station cycle time, if the sensor was not actuated, it would automatically stop the line, alerting the operator to a potential missing step. The Quality Manager loved it; the Plant Manager appreciated it — and the VP led the way! "If you cannot describe what you are doing as a process, you do not know what you are doing" - W. Edwards Deming (Acquate, 2019). What can we do to instill this thinking and these practices in our people? It starts with *checking* in on them ... just like this seasoned VP modeled (Fowler, 2015).

Enabling Operational Excellence (C-H-E-C-K)

Improvement labels come in many forms, including CI, Agile, Lean, BPM, QC/QA, Lean Six Sigma, and process or system improvement, among others. All these methodologies share a few commonalities. They all want to get better, cheaper, and faster (Hammer et al., 2010). Perhaps not always in that order, or all three at once, but quality, cost, and timing are usually at the forefront of most improvement efforts, regardless of the methodology's name.

Another common denominator (variable) is that all these methods utilize human intellect. Humans are at the center of improvement. So, the first thing we can do is to **catch people doing things right.** Every success in business and life came from a human idea. How do leaders spark those ideas (Christfort & Vickberg, 2024)? What can organizations do with and for individuals to generate robust ideas, reduce cycle times, achieve higher quality, and lower costs? What do humans need to engage in their workplace consistently? What needs to be done to prevent or at least mitigate employee turnover? Are there proven techniques or approaches?

Brady Barr, PhD (2020), National Geographic's resident herpetologist, studied the effects of animals in the classroom on students' levels of engagement/learning and found that when students focus less on themselves and invite the external world into their minds, a spark of desire to know more is born. A survey (AHA, 2015) of 1200 teachers found increased "students' responsibility/leadership, compassion, empathy, and respect (with) an enhanced ... traditional academic lessons, decreased stress (and) increased ... comfort levels, making them more engaged" (p. 15). We are not recommending bringing an alligator into the break room. However, perhaps more executives would understand and expose their employees to more than just themselves, their work, and routine expectations. What leaders would not want their people to be more responsible, compassionate, empathetic, respectful, and comfortable at work? All of them, of course! So, let us first take seriously the task of exposing potential up-and-comers to the great big world we are blessed to live in.

Sticking briefly with the animal kingdom, Fielde (1904) found that an ant worker's tenacity for accomplishment was tied to being recognized. We believe the same phenomenon applies to people as well. Social media experts (Mosley, 2013) recommend utilizing real-time data to provide assessments on employee performance through crowdsourcing and other forms of immediate feedback, thereby enhancing awareness and future planning. The customer metrics cannot be ignored. Employees who are open to this type of data have demonstrated improved performance. Legendary management guru Ken Blanchard et al. (2009) acknowledged, "People who feel good about themselves produce good results" (secret #1). What is the best way for leaders to do this? What is more effective? Positive or negative feedback (Brink & Owen, 2007)?

The power of recognition is intricately linked to how individuals view themselves. Honneth (2022) postulates this in three ways. He terms them self-confidence, self-respect, and self-worth. Self-confidence is tied to meeting one's physical needs; self-respect is tied to standing one's ground in matters of judgment; and lastly, self-worth/esteem is tied to issues of accomplishment. Honneth demonstrates that the more positive reinforcement one receives, the greater their internal self-appreciation. He maintains workers' hope for recognition, leading them toward greater autonomy/emancipation. Freedom to design one's own work is a significant enabler. Small victories and confidence breed success in future endeavors; when a good fit for the task and the worker is present, epiphanies occur, and results follow.

The next step to enhance performance is to **honor and refine standards with ideas**. Standards provide a baseline for improvement (Protzman et al., 2023) and are grounded in individual and group ideas. Advances in brain lateralization have shown "the left hemisphere needs certainty and needs to be right ... (yet) the right hemisphere makes it possible to hold several ambiguous possibilities in suspension together without premature closure on one outcome" (McGilchrist, 2019, p. 82). Leveraging standards brings stability, enabling the formation and development of ideas for improvement. It is an effort in tandem, multiplied by both hemispheres.

Answers and epiphanies often come from the right hemisphere, and openness is where solutions are born. At times, the left hemisphere's goal is to enable us to manipulate things, whereas the goal of the right hemisphere is to relate to things and understand them as a whole. Two ways of thinking that are both needed but are fundamentally incompatible at the same time" (McGilchrist, 2019, pp. 62, 70). Legendary character from the famous Monty Python stories, actor John Cleese (Divided Brain, 2016), relies heavily on his right brain when acting. Standards may be boring, but they provide a practical foundation for activating creativity (Kühn et al., 2019).

In a paradoxical truth, being autocratic about standards allows executives to be participative with their people and their ideas. It is a little-known counterintuitive secret that takes us full circle back to the wisdom of Ohno and Ford.

Multiple studies of employees confirm that people desire to learn and contribute to their workplaces (De Grip & Sauermann, 2012). Success often breeds success (Morgulev, 2023). The next step to boost performance is to **educate team members for advancement.** Individuals seek empowerment. Do my efforts matter? Am I perceived as valuable?

Employers who recognize that change is constant (Turner, 2022) continually pursue innovations to enhance their team members' performance. From the formation of the Royal Society of London,

> founded in 1660 and often referred to as 'the invisible college', the society was orchestrated …in order to encourage the exchange of scientific and philosophic ideas and theories. The society's motto, 'Nullius in verba,' is translated as 'take nobody's word for it'. The motto was upheld as a manifestation of the members' drive to verify all statements through

scientific facts and experimental research findings (Allen, 2018; ChatGPT notes: *this can be found in historical accounts or discussions regarding the Royal Society, particularly in academic texts on the history of science*) ...

... to the birth of present-day artificial intelligence, creative managers over the centuries have looked for ways to make their teams better through technology and science. Educating usually comes before advancement. Often, giving people responsibility is what makes them responsible (Vukotich & Booksx, 2010). The International Society of Performance Improvement emphasizes the importance of knowing your colleagues, particularly the value of relationships (Hale, 2021). Fostering collaborative learning enhances performance. Allison Rossett (1999) details this linkage.

> Performance analysis is a process by which you partner with clients to identify and respond to problems and opportunities, study individuals and the organization, and determine an appropriate cross-functional solution system. A systematic and systemic approach to engaging with the client; this is the process by which you determine when and how to use education and information resources (p. 227).

Acumen development comes from a robust 1) Training Needs Assessment. Rossett contends, "a systematic study that incorporates data and opinions from varied sources to create, install, and evaluate educational and informational products and services. The effort commences as a result of a handoff from the performance analysis. It should concentrate on those needs that are related to skill, knowledge, and motivation" (p. 230; also, Knowledge Academy, 2019; Likert, 2021); and 2) a Needs Analysis: The breaking down of an identified need to determine its basis, causes, and the relationships among (other) identified needs (Kaufman, 1985, p.

88). In an educated workforce, creativity becomes contagious (Ng et al., 2022). Therefore, if you want your team members to be engaged and your group to thrive, make learning a priority (Kaufman & Russell, 2001).

Workers trained in one area can also be cross-trained in others. In this way, they will become more valuable. So, let us, next, **circulate their influence.** Broaden their scope of control and release them on the identified problems. Watch and see the fireworks of worker versatility (Kamada, n.d.). As individuals become empowered and find their best fit within the group (the Utilization Stage of group development), they still need to boost their productivity. This can happen by granting them more influence. Greater responsibility presents new challenges. In many large corporations, talented individuals can get lost in the crowd. If you want someone to take responsibility, provide them with opportunities to do so. Leaders will inevitably rise to the top, often embodying the labels assigned to them. The power of expectations (Weinstein, 2002) resonates not only in the classroom but also powerfully within the halls of business (Schmidt & Posner, 1982).

However, reaching the final step in many organizations remains rare. This pivotal leap involves intricately tying individual and departmental goals to the organization's overarching objectives, all of which are rooted in the corporate vision or mission. In its purest form, the "Production" mode takes the values set at the highest levels and cascades them down through the ranks. When a company successfully attains this significant milestone (launching a new product/reaching a revenue target), a manager's role becomes vital in inspiring individuals for learning and teams to aim even higher (Smith, 2011). The last step lies in **minimizing distractions** to free (and foster) leaders' focus and determination (i.e., Jiminez's (2025) "overwatch" concept). In this environment, leaders lead, organizers organize, thinkers innovate, and visions transform into reality.

The performance phase is the pinnacle of the preceding stages and should guide every decision made within the organization. While technology will undoubtedly shape our future, let us not forget that a machine or computer never negotiated or inspired a decision or landmark business deal. Every impactful move, every financial triumph, and every satisfied customer springs from a human being making a needed choice at just the right moment. Performance-driven employees recognize that if they fail to treat their customers with respect, someone else will be more than happy to do so. Today's innovators leverage digital customer service (Michaeli, 2021) to measure what matters most. Remember, if everything is a priority, then nothing is. In this empowered environment, an effective leader removes obstacles that stifle or distract the group's ability to run the business. A competent manager can buffer unwanted roadblocks and ensure their team is working on the right things. Leaders must reduce noise for their teams (Scott, 2022).

"Coming Together is a Beginning; Keeping Together is Progress;
Working Together is Success"
- Henry Ford (2021).

Performance Workbook (Value-Added Teaming-Plus)

The *CEO's S-T-A-M-P of Approval* is taking shape (Jiminez, 2025; O'Neil, 2025). (**S**upport) - flexible leaders who place workers according to their strengths with teaming considerations (**T**eamwork) - give workers a fighting chance at self-actualization (**A**ptitude) and become influencers in the group (**M**orale), hopefully leading to positive results in (**P**erformance). The value of Teaming-Plus in healthcare (Gittell, 2009) (for example) is evident in caregiver resilience, improved patient outcomes, and operational efficiency through strong co-worker relationships. Let us expand this list.

1 - Resilience: Long hours and minimal instant gratification can wear down sincere workers (Thom-Mayer, 2021). Teaming-Plus sensitivities can provide the boost-tired caregivers desire when they need a break. The geese rotation (Saatchi & Saatchi, 2012) comes to mind (team leaders recognize when individuals need a break and are moved to the back of the flight pattern for respite). What are a few ways Teaming-Plus can help address your current resilience gaps?

---

2 - Patient Quality: Outcomes result from teaming excellence (Sorbero & Rand Corporation, 2008). "Process-of-care and (patient) outcome measures" (p. 43) were studied through a teaming lens, informed by clinical judgment, and claimed to be the first healthcare study to link teamwork and teaming to measures. The findings were spread across three clinical areas. The study panel rated "54 of the 108 candidate process measures (50 percent) and 33 of the 97 candidate outcome measures (34 percent) as highly related to teamwork" (p. 43).

How can the quality in your industry be improved through robust Teaming-Plus?

---

3 - Operational Efficiency: Gittell (2009) measured a teaming component (relational coordination) for surgical performance. Nine nonprofit hospitals and orthopedic centers were studied (Hoffer et al., 2000). Findings were binned in two areas: quality and efficiency of care. Was the work performed as intended and completed in the standard surgery time? Teaming coordination proved influential in the results. Quality of care meant less joint (replacement) pain and increased mobility, and efficiency was measured by the reduction in surgical time compared to the average. Relational coordination realized a 33% reduction in patient pain complaints and a 26% reduction in surgical time. Performance was enhanced. How about you? Are your teams getting better? How so?

In summary, performance teaming is evident in activities that customers (patients) perceive as value-added (Protzman et al., 2023), i.e., teams that achieve it right the first time and apply process rigor to modify the form, fit, and function of a product or service. This requires teaming across multiple lines of demarcation, where the sum of the parts is greater than the whole (McGuire & Rhodes, 2009) and where Teaming-Plus approaches are always centered on the voice of the customer (Denove and J.D. Power, 2006). Is this enough? Value-added customer perspectives are seen as experiences – more on that dynamic from Pine & Gilmore (1999):

> Experiences are (another) economic (customer) offering, as distinct from services as services are from goods, but one that has until now mainly gone unrecognized...When a

person buys a service, he purchases a set of intangible activities carried out on his behalf. However, when he buys an experience, he pays to spend time enjoying a series of memorable events that a company stages—as in a theatrical play—to engage him personally (p. 3). The newly identified offering of experiences occurs whenever a company intentionally uses services as the stage and goods as props to engage an individual. While commodities are fungible, goods are tangible, and services are intangible, experiences are memorable. Buyers of experiences...value being engaged by what the company reveals...experiences are events that engage individuals in a personal way (p. 12).

How can your organization better enhance your customers' experience? ____

Conclusion

Talent development from Teaming-Plus takes organizations to the next level. It "is a way of working that brings people together to generate new ideas, find answers, and solve problems" (Edmondson, 2012, p. 26). As individuals and teams begin to organize for learning (Edmondson, 2012), utilizing day-to-day lessons that formalize this learning as they execute their mission, leadership must be aware of two detractors to Teaming-Plus:

Two Detractors: The breakdown of communication (Garber, 2010) and punitive managers (Strasser et al., 1981) hinder the birth and effectiveness of teaming. Leaders who mishandle failures create a culture that discourages risk-taking and success. However, when focusing on the five *S-T-A-M-P of Approval* enablers for effective Teaming-Plus practices, a group can reach new heights in:

1. **S**upport: Leadership in action...

2. **T**eamwork: Workers who are placed appropriately... (Jiminez, 2025)
3. **A**ptitude: Individuals who look to contribute and grow...
4. **M**orale: Groups who coordinate themselves... and bring
5. **P**erformance: Value-added, sustained improvement.
   See Figure 3 on the next page.

In what ways can your organization display better Teaming-Plus?

____

____

This may sound simple to some, but it requires members who are determined to learn as they go and leaders who model humility, patience, and a commitment to the group's success. Do you have what it takes to ensure teaming success in your business? Are you willing to take the Teaming-Plus challenge to improve your customers' experience? We would love to hear your success stories. CEO's grasp the macro here, do you?

Figure 3
Talent Development and Teaming-Plus for Performance

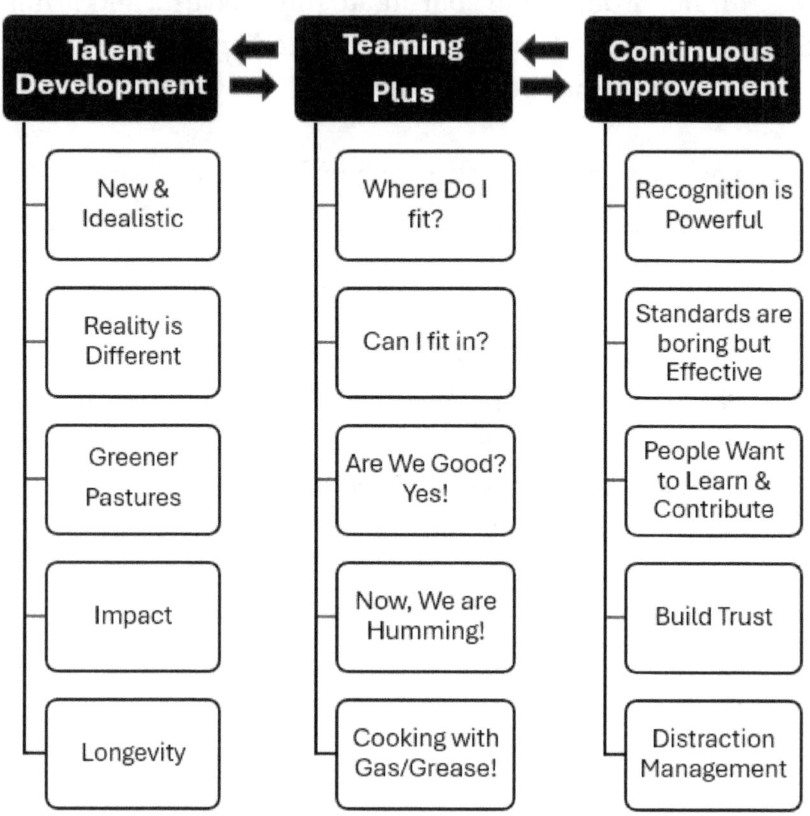

Appendix B References

$522,000,000 MERGER OF UTILITIES FORMED; Control of American Light and Traction Acquired by United Light and Power. DEAL CLOSED SE-CRETLY Koppers and Mellon Interests Said to Have Engineered Move- Earnings Improve. LOCAL COMPANY AFFECTED Brooklyn Borough Gas 90 Per Cent. Owned by a Subsidiary of the Dominant Corporation. Aided by Mellon Interests. Gas System Rivalry Seen. (10 September 1928). *The New York Times*. https://www.ny-times.com/1928/09/10/archives/522000000-merger-of-utilities-formed-control-of-american-light-and.htmlLinks to an external site.

Acquate. (2019). *The W. Edwards Deming Institute*. Deming.org. https://deming.org/

Alexander, M. (2024, March 26). *Resource Utilization: What It Is & A Simple Way To Calculate It*. The Digital Project Manager. https://thedigitalproject-manager.com/project-management/resource-utilization/

Allen, V. (13 April 2018). *Teams That Changed The World - WorkStyle*. Www.workstyle.io. https://www.workstyle.io/top-performing-team-case-studies

Allen, D. G., & Vardaman, J. M. (Eds.). (2021). *Global talent retention : understanding employee turnover around the world*. Emerald Publishing Limited

Amasakaa, K. (2012). *Science TQM, New Quality Management Principle : The Quality Management Strategy of Toyota*. Bentham Science Publishers.

Amir, M., Ali, K., Ali, D., & Ali, A. Z. (2022). Human Resource Practices and Employee Performance: Mediating Role of Work Engagement and Training Sessions. *JISR Management and Social Sciences & Economics*, *20*(1), 187–208. https://doi.org/10.31384/jisrmsse/2022.20.1.10

Ammer, C. (2013). *The American Heritage Dictionary of Idioms* (2nd ed.). Houghton Mifflin Harcourt.

Andrew Carnegie Quote. (2025). A-Z Quotes. https://www.azquotes.com/quote/407525

Appraisal 2006 - let us do it differently. (2006). Businessline (Islāmābād, Pakistan), 1–.

Argyris, C. (1990). Overcoming Organizational Defenses: Facilitating Organizational Learning. Upper Saddle River, N.J.: Prentice Hall.

ART 5.1.1.1.3 Develop Courses of Action. (n.d.). Retrieved 17 August 2025, from https://rdl.train.army.mil/catalog-ws/view/100.ATSC/C281D17E-9DCE-413B-8494-2B59E3BCD531-1361429772893/report.pdf

Bader, B., Gielnik, M. M., & Bledow, R. (2022). How transformational leadership transforms followers' affect and work engagement. European Journal of Work and Organizational Psychology, 1–13. https://doi.org/10.1080/1359432x.2022.2161368

Ballerat-Busserolles, K., Wu, Y., & Carroll, J. J. (2018). *Cutting-edge technology for carbon capture, utilization, and storage* (1st ed.). Scrivener Publishing.

Bardwick, J. M., & NetLibrary, I. (2008). *One foot out the door: How to combat the psychological recession that's alienating employees and hurting American business.* AMACOM. https://search.ebscohost.com/login.aspx?direct=true&scope=site&db=nlebk&db=nlabk&AN=210998

Barnes, B. K. (2019). *Building better ideas : how constructive debate inspires courage, collaboration and breakthrough solutions* (First edition.). Berrett-Koehler Publishers, Inc.

Barone, S., & Lo Franco, E. (2012). Statistical and managerial techniques for Six Sigma methodology, theory, and application (1st edition). Wiley.

Barr, B. (2020). *Whatever happened to the classroom turtle? : how animals spark student engagement and a love of learning.* Solution Tree Press.

Biech, E. (2021). *Skills for Career Success : Maximizing Your Potential at Work.* Berrett-Koehler Publishers, Incorporated.

Biech, E., & Association for Talent Development, publisher. (2018). *Starting a talent development program* (1st edition). Association for Talent Development.

Beissmann, T., & Ford, introducing One Manufacturing's global production system. (8 August 2012). Drive. https://www.drive.com.au/news/ford-introducing-one-manufacturing-global-production-system/

Bellomo, T. (2021). *Teamwork in Talent Development.* ATD Press.

Benson JC. (2022). Followership and exemplary follower characteristics: A middle–level management perspective. [Order No. 30372302]. Texas A&M University.

Black, J. S., & Gregersen, H. B. (2003). Leading Strategic Change: Breaking Through the Brain Barrier (1st edition). Financial Times/Prentice Hall.

Blanchard, K. (2002). *Whale Done! : The Power of Positive Relationships.* Simon & Schuster.

Blanchard, K. H., Carew, D., & Parisi-Carew, E. (2009). *The One-Minute Manager Builds High-Performing Teams (Third Edition).* William Morrow.

Benzaghta, M. A., Elwalda, A., Mousa, M., Erkan, I., & Rahman, M. (2021). SWOT Analysis applications: an Integrative Literature Review. Journal of Global Business Insights, 6(1), 54–72. https://doi.org/10.5038/2640-6489.6.1.1148

Block, P. (1993). Stewardship: Choosing service over self-interest. San Francisco: Berrett-Koehler.

Blum, E. (1988). Continental survey: most employees report morale. *Travel Weekly, 47*(52), 27-.

Booksx, I., & Harvard Business School Press. (2001). *Harvard business review on managing diversity.* Harvard Business School Press.

Bouwhuis, M. (2012). "None of us is as smart as all of us…" (Van Vugt, 2003, p.5). Fontys.

Branham, L. (2000). *Keeping the people who keep you in business : 24 ways to hang on to your most valuable talent.* AMACOM.

Brink, B. van den, & Owen, D. (2007). *Recognition and power : Axel Honneth and the tradition of critical social theory*. Cambridge University Press.

Brown, S. E. (2022). *Lead upwards : how startup joiners can impact new ventures, build impressive careers, and inspire great teams*. John Wiley & Sons, Inc.

Burchell, M., Robin, J., & Great Place to Work Institute. (2011). *The great workplace : how to build it, how to keep it, and why it matters* (1st ed.). Jossey-Bass.

Burns, J.M. (1978). Leadership. New York, NY: Harper & Row.

Burt, C. D. B. (2015). *New Employee Safety : Risk Factors and Management Strategies* (1st ed. 2015). Springer International Publishing. https://doi.org/10.1007/978-3-319-18684-9

Bustamante, S., Martinovic, M., Saltevo, E., & Schmitz, M. (2022). *Shaping a Sustainable Future: Innovative Teaching Practices for Educating Responsible Leaders*. Nomos Verlagsgesellschaft mbH & Co. KG. https://doi.org/10.5771/9783748933090

Calarco, A., Gurvis, J., & Center for Creative Leadership. (2006). *Adaptability : responding effectively to change* (1st ed.). Center for Creative Leadership.

Calvin, J. (1536). Institutes of the Christian Religion - Christian Classics Ethereal Library. Www.ccel.org. Retrieved 29 September 2023, from https://www.ccel.org/ccel/calvin/institutes.iii.xix.html

Canfield, J. V. (1990). *The looking-glass self : an examination of self-awareness*. Praeger.

Carey, M. (2020). Creating Leaders: A Pilot SoTL Study of an Ontological / Phenomenological Leadership Course. International Journal for the Scholarship of Teaching and Learning, 14(2). https://doi.org/10.20429/ijsotl.2020.140205

Carsten, M. K., Koonce, R., Bligh, M. C., & Hurwitz, M. (Eds.). (2016). Followership in action : cases and commentaries. Emerald.

Carter, P. J. (2010). *IQ and psychometric tests : assess your personality, aptitude, and intelligence* (2nd ed.). Kogan Page.

Chaturvedi, P. D., & Chaturvedi, M. (2012). *Fundamentals of Business Communication.* (0 ed.). Pearson India.

Cheema, D. S. (2010). *Knowledge Management: Analysis, Design and Implementation* (Rev. ed.). Abhishek Publications Claxton, J. (Ed.). (2014). *Employee engagement*. Emerald.

Christfort, K., & Vickberg, S. (2024). *The Breakthrough Manifesto : Ten Principles to Spark Transformative Innovation* (First edition.). John Wiley & Sons, Inc.

Cleveland Clinic. (2020). *Patient Safety Program | Cleveland Clinic*. Cleveland Clinic. https://my.clevelandclinic.org/departments/patient-experience/depts/quality-patient-safety/patient-safety-program

Cleveland Clinic. (2022). Access Anytime Anywhere | Cleveland Clinic. Cleveland Clinic. https://my.clevelandclinic.org/

Cohen, W. A. (2010). Heroic leadership leading with integrity and honor. Jossey-Bass.

Cook, M. F., & American Management Association. (1992). *The AMA handbook for employee recruitment and retention*. American Management Association.

Creelman, D., & Kaiser, R. B. (2009). In focus : acquiring talent - the value of hiring for team fit. Center for Creative Leadership.

Crosby, R. (2012). *The Team Church: Ministry in the Age of Collaboration*. Abingdon Press.

Currid, J. D., & Chapman, D. W. (Eds.). (2017). *ESV Archaeology Study Bible : English Standard Version*. Crossway.

Dalton, M. A., & Hollenbeck, G. P. (1996). How to design an effective system for developing managers and executives (1st edition). Center for Creative Leadership

Daniels, A. C. (2000). *Bringing out the best in people : how to apply the astonishing power of positive reinforcement* (New&updated ed.). McGraw-Hill.

Davila, N., & Pina-Ramirez, W. (2023). *Effective onboarding* (1st edition). Association for Talent Development.

Davis, A. (Alison B., & Shannon, J. (2011). *Set new hires up for success with the proper orientation program* (1st edition). FTPress Delivers.

De Grip, A., & Sauermann, J. (2012). *The effects of training on own and co-worker productivity: Evidence from a field experiment.* The Economic Journal, 122(560), 376–399. https://doi.org/10.1111/j.1468-0297.2012.02500.x

DellaVecchio, D. (n.d.). Gift test [Review of gift test]. Gift Test; Gift Test. Retrieved 9 September 2023, from https://www.gifttest.org/ministry/

DellaVecchio, D. & Winston, B. (2015).International Journal of Leadership Studies, Vol. 9 Iss. 1, 2015. School of Business & Leadership, Regent University ISSN 1554-3145

Del Pozo, B., Rouhani, S., Clark, M. H., Atkins, D., Andraka-Christou, B., & Martins, K. F. (2024). Understaffed and beleaguered: a national survey of chiefs of police about the post-George Floyd era. *Policing : An International Journal of Police Strategies & Management*, 47(5), 846–860. https://doi.org/10.1108/PIJPSM-12-2023-0171

Denove, C., & Power, J. D. (2006). *Satisfaction : How every great company listens to the voice of the customer*. Portfolio.

Detert, J. R. (2023). *Let us call quiet quitting what it often is : calibrated contributing : for employees who are rationally matching their effort at work to what they get in return in an increasingly unbalanced system, quiet quitting is not the correct term* ([First edition]). MIT Sloan Management Review.

Deutser, B. (2023). *Belonging Rules: Five Crucial Actions That Build Unity and Foster Performance* (1st ed.). BenBella Books.

DeVany, C. (2010). *90 days to a high-performance team, a complete problem-solving strategy to help your team thrive in any environment*. McGraw-Hill.

https://search.ebscohost.com/login.aspx?direct=true&scope=site&db=nlebk&db=nlabk&AN=291593

Dionne, K.-E., & Carlile, P. (2016). Le pouvoir transformationnel des hackathons. *Gestion (HEC Montréal)*, *41*(2), 62–63. https://doi.org/10.3917/riges.412.0062

The Divided Brain – THE DIVIDED BRAIN documentary based on the book THE MASTER AND HIS EMISSARY by Iain McGilchrist. (2016). Thedividedbrain.com. https://thedividedbrain.com/

DUAN, J., LI, C., XU, Y., CHIA-HUEI, W. (JUNE 2017). Journal of Organizational Behavior, Vol. 38, No. 5. pp. 650-670 (21 pages) https://www.jstor.org/stable/26610642

Dubinskaya, A. N. (2022). SELF-ACTUALIZATION OF OLDER WORKERS IN PROFESSIONAL ACTIVITIES: SOCIAL AND PSYCHOLOGICAL RATIONALE. *Научное Обозрение. Экономические Науки (Scientific Review. Economic Sciences)*, *4 2022*, 30–34. https://doi.org/10.17513/sres.1110

Durett, J. (2006). GE hones its leaders at Crotonville. *Human Resource Management International Digest, 14*(7). https://doi.org/10.1108/hrmid.2006.04414gad.005

Edginton, J. (2017). The Jefferson Memorial and the 5 Whys - by Jerilyn Edginton. On *YouTube*. https://www.youtube.com/watch?v=N7cR2gArCFE

Edmans, A. (2011). Does the stock market fully value intangibles? Employee satisfaction and equity prices. *Journal of Financial Economics, 101*(3), 621–640. https://doi.org/10.1016/j.jfineco.2011.03.021

Edmondson, A. C. (2012). *Teaming: How organizations learn, innovate, and compete in the knowledge economy.* Jossey-Bass Pfeiffer; Chichester.

Edmondson, A. C. (2013). *Teaming to innovate* (1st ed.). Jossey-Bass.

Edmondson, A. C., College, H., & Henry William Chesbrough. (2017). *Extreme teaming: lessons in complex, cross-sector leadership.* Emerald Publishing.

Edmondson, A. C., & Harvey, J.-F. (2017). *Extreme teaming : lessons in complex, cross-sector leadership* (1st ed.). Emerald Publishing Limited.

Eikenberry, K. (2025). *Flexible Leadership: Navigate Uncertainty and Lead with Confidence* (1st ed.). BenBella Books.

Eisenberger, R., & Stinglhamber, F. (2011). *Perceived organizational support : fostering enthusiastic and productive employees.* American Psychological Association.

Egolf, D. B., & Sondra L. Chester. (2013). *Forming, storming, norming, performing : successful communication in groups and teams* (Third edition.). iUniverse.

Elizaphanian. (6 February 2023). *LLF: a left-brain car crash.* Elizaphanian. https://elizaphanian.com/?p=7808

El-Shamy, S. (2003). *Dynamic induction : games, activities, and ideas to revitalize your employee induction process* (1st ed.). Gower.

Epitropaki, O., Sy, T., Martin, R., Tram-Quon, S., & Topakas, A. (2013). Implicit Leadership and Followership Theories "in the wild": Taking stock of information-processing approaches to leadership and followership in organizational settings. The Leadership Quarterly, 24(6), 858–881. https://doi.org/10.1016/j.leaqua.2013.10.005

Everly, G. S., Strouse, D. A., & Everly, G. S. (2010). The secrets of resilient leadership : when failure is not an option : six essential skills for leading through adversity. DiaMedica Publishing.

Ferdman, B. (2014). Diversity at work : the practice of inclusion (B. M. Ferdman & B. Deane, Eds.; 1st edition.). Jossey-Bass, A Wiley Brand.

Ferris, G. R. (2000). *Research in personnel and human resources management. Vol. 19*. Emerald.

Fielde, A. (1904). *Three odd incidents in an ant's life. [Reactions of ants to material vibrations. Tenacity of life in ants. Power of recognition among ants.*

Fields, D. (2002). *Your first two years in youth ministry : a personal and practical guide to starting right.* Youth Specialties Books published by Zondervan, Grand Rapids, MI.

Flinn, K. (2018). *Leadership Development*. Routledge. https://doi.org/10.4324/9781315678269

Flinn, K. (2024). Rethinking Leadership Development. In *Leadership Development in Practice* (2nd ed., Vol. 1, pp. 53–78). Routledge. https://doi.org/10.4324/9781003341727-4

Folk, L. S. (2022). *The Hidden Barriers and Enablers of Team-Based Ideation* (1st ed., 2022). Springer International Publishing. https://doi.org/10.1007/978-3-031-16795-9

Ford, H. (1926). *Today and tomorrow*. Routledge. *"Coming Together is a Beginning; Keeping Together is Progress; Working Together is Success"…Henry Ford. (2021). International Journal of Regional Anaesthesia, 2*(1). https://doi.org/10.13107/ijra.2021.v02i01.015

FOWLER, T. W. (17 June 2015). *Do you see problems as a good thing … to be found or a bad thing … to hide? (A fun short story from the lean vantage point) Once upon a time, there was a frustrated plant manager. His production team regularly shipped products with defects, including missing parts in the packaging.* Linkedin.com. https://www.linkedin.com/pulse/do-you-see-problems-good-thing-found-bad-hide-timothy-fowler/?trackingId=QRr1c6HQQmutb7xwJ2VE7A%3D%3D

Fowler, T. *LinkedIn*. (2015). Linkedin.com. https://www.linkedin.com/pulse/did-you-know-takes-20-years-learn-lean-timothy-fowler/?trackingId=QRr1c6HQQmutb7xwJ2VE7A%3D%3D

FOWLER, T. W. (30 September 2015). *There was once an operator who installed a hose clamp at a Toyota manufacturing facility. And a quality manager whose job was to ensure the hose clamp was tight before leaving the plant.* Linkedin.com. https://www.linkedin.com/pulse/lean-leadership-its-never-people-problem-timothy-fowler/?track-ingId=QRr1c6HQQmutb7xwJ2VE7A%3D%3D

Fowler, T. (2024). Academic [Unpublished Paper]. School of Business and Leadership. Regent University.

FOWLER, T. (2025). *Right-Brain Problem Solving In A Left-Brain Business World*. SlideShare; Slideshare. https://www.slideshare.net/slideshow/right-brain-problem-solving-in-a-left-brain-business-world/7487230 (Also searchable on the archived InternetMedicine website).

Free Online Ambition Test: Mind Help Assessment. (2023). Retrieved 18 September 2023, from https://mind.help/assessments/ambition-test/

Friend, M., & Cook, L. (2007). *Interactions: Collaboration skills for school professionals. 5. ed*. Pearson A and B.

Frock, R., & NetLibrary, I. (2006). *Changing how the world does business: FedEx's incredible journey to success : the inside story* (1st ed.). Berrett--Koehler. https://search.ebscohost.com/login.aspx?direct=true&scope=site&db=nlebk&db=nlabk&AN=260692

Fujio Cho | *Automotive Hall of Fame*. (2025). Automotivehalloffame.org. https://www.automotivehalloffame.org/honoree/fujio-cho/

Furlong, W., & Crossan, M. (2021). Character-Infused, Social Value Purpose for Aspirational Leaders. Business Law International, 22(3), 235.

Garber, P. R. (2007). *Retention.* (1st edition). HRD Press.

Garber, S. (2010). *Alternative litigation financing in the United States : issues, knowns, and unknowns* (1st ed.). RAND.

George, M. L. (2002). *Lean Six Sigma : combining Six Sigma quality with lean speed* (1st edition). McGraw-Hill.

Gittell, J. H. (2009). *High performance healthcare : using the power of relationships to achieve quality, efficiency, and resilience*. McGraw-Hill. https://search.ebscohost.com/login.aspx?direct=true&scope=site&db=nlebk&db=nlabk&AN=280297

Glanz, J. (2022). "Personal Reflections on Supervision As Instructional Leadership: From Whence It Came and To Where Shall It Go?" https://core.ac.uk/download/519802501.pdf.

Glover, A. - *WIGL*. (2021). WIGL. https://wi-gl.com/team/dr-ahmad-glover/

Glover, S., & Hannum, K. (2008). *Leadership in Action: Learning Respect: Showing and Earning Esteem is Crucial for Leaders*—Center for Creative Leadership.

Goldratt, E. M., & Cox, J. (2014). *The goal : a process of ongoing improvement.* HighBridge Audio.

Gordon, S., Feldman, D. L., & Leonard, M. (Eds.). (2014). *Collaborative caring : stories and reflections on teamwork in health care* (1st ed.). ILR Press. https://doi.org/10.7591/9780801454639

Graban, M. (19 January 2016). *Cleveland Clinic Improvement Model, Part 1: Alignment & Visual Management*. Lean Blog. https://www.leanblog.org/2016/01/the-cleveland-clinic-improvement-model-part-1/

Grossman, D. (2011). "The Cost of Poor CommunicationsLinks to an external site.," The Holmes Report.

Guba, E. G. (1958). Morale and Satisfaction: A Study in Past-Future Time Perspective. *Administrative Science Quarterly, 3*(2), 195–209. https://doi.org/10.2307/2391017

Guerin, L., & DelPo, A. (2017). *Create your own employee handbook: a legal & practical guide for employers* (8th edition): Nolo, Law of all.

Hailey, L. (22 September 2022). *Employee Retention: 12 Strategies to Retain Employees.* Science of People. https://www.scienceofpeople.com/employee-retention/

Hale, J. (2021). KNOW YOUR COLLEAGUES. *Performance Improvement, 60*(9-10), 30–32. doi:https://doi.org/10.1002/pfi.22004

Hamilton, D. (2010). "Top Ten Email Blunders That Cost Companies Money. " Links to an external site." Creative Communications & Training.

Hammer, M., Hershman, L. W., & Wilson, G. K. (2010). *Faster, cheaper, better* [Broadcast]. Tantor Media, Inc.

Hampel, B., & Lamont, E. (2011). *Perfect phrases for new employee orientation and onboarding : hundreds of ready-to-use phrases to train and retain your top talent* (1st edition). McGraw-Hill.

Hannah, S. T., & Avolio, B. J. (2011). Leader character, ethos, and virtue: Individual and collective considerations. *The Leadership Quarterly, 22*(5), 989–994. https://doi.org/10.1016/j.leaqua.2011.07.018

Hapsari, I. D., Qomariah, N., Putu Martini, i. N., & Nursaid, N. (2022). Recruitment and Competence: Its Influence on Employee Performance through Employee Placement. *JOURNAL OF ECONOMICS, FINANCE AND MANAGEMENT STUDIES, 5*(11). https://doi.org/10.47191/jefms/v5-i11-09

Harbott, K. (2021). *The 6 Enablers of Business Agility : How to Thrive in an Uncertain World.* (1st ed.). Berrett-Koehler Publishers, Incorporated.

Harrin, E. (2013). *Managing Project Scope Shortcuts to Success*. BCS, The Chartered Institute for IT.

Hays-Thomas, R. (2017). Managing Workplace Diversity and Inclusion: A Psychological Perspective. Routledge.

Hernandez, S. (2013). Collaboration in special education: Its history, evolution, and critical factors necessary for successful implementation. *US-China Education Review B, 3*(6), 480–498. https://files.eric.ed.gov/fulltext/ED544122.pdf

Hetrick, S. (2023). *Toxic organizational cultures and leadership : how to build and sustain a healthy workplace.* Routledge. https://doi.org/10.4324/978100333038

Hickman, S., & American Society for Training and Development. (1999). *Successful orientation programs : career development.* American Society for Training & Development.

Hidayat et al., S. E. (2018). Students' Level of Awareness of Accreditation Process: A Case of University College of Bahrain. *International Journal of*

Pedagogical Innovations, 6(1), 13–22.
https://doi.org/10.12785/ijpi/060102

Hillier, J., Roo, G. de, & Wezemael, J. van. (2016). *Complexity and planning : systems, assemblages and simulations* (1st ed.). Routledge.
https://doi.org/10.4324/9781315573199

Hollander (1992). Hollander, E. P. (1992). Leadership, followership, self, and others. The Leadership Quarterly, 3, 43-54. Doi:10.1016/1048-9843(92)900005-Z

Home. (1986). Youth for Tomorrow. Retrieved 13 September 2023, from
https://www.youthfortomorrow.org/

Honneth, A. (1 November 2022). Pedagogy4Change. https://www.pedagogy4change.org/axel-honneth-recognition-theory-in-social-pedagogy/

Hoover, J. D. (2005). *Effective small group and team communication* (Second edition). Thomson/Wadsworth.

Heffernan, M. (6 August 2012). Dare to disagree. Www.ted.com.
https://www.ted.com/talks/margaret_heffernan_dare_to_disagree?awesm=on.ted.com_ Heffernan

Hill, T., & Westbrook, R. (1997). SWOT analysis: It is time for a product recall. Long Range Planning, 30(1), 46–52.

This study was reported in Jody **Hoffer**. Gittell, Kathleen Fairfield, Ben Bierbaum, Robert Jackson, Michael Kelly, Richard Laskin, Stephen Lipson, John Silisji, Thomas Thornhill, and Joseph Zuckerman (2000), Impact of Relational Coordination on Quality of Care, Post-Operative Pain and Functioning, and Length of Stay: A Nine Hospital Study of Surgical Patients,' *Medical Care*, 38 (8): 807-819

Hohlbein, P. J. (2015). "The Power of Play in Developing Emotional Intelligence Impacting Leadership Success: A Study of the Leadership Team in a Midwest Private, Liberal Arts University." https://core.ac.uk/download/288854005.pdf.

Holweg, M., & Bicheno, J. R. (2023). Gemba. In *The Lean Toolbox Sixth Edition*. Picsie Books.

House, R. J., Hanges, P., Ruiz-Quintanilla, S. A., Dorfman, P. W., Javidan, M., Dickson, M., Gupta, V., Koopman, P. L., Arnold, V., & Gesner, M. J. (1999). Cultural influences on leadership and organizations: Project GLOBE. JAI Press. USA. pp. 171-233

Humphrey, J. (2018). Impromptu : leading in the moment (1st edition). Wiley.

Hunt, P., Soto, G., Maier, J., & Doering, K. (2003). Collaborative Teaming to Support Students at Risk and Students with Severe Disabilities in General Education Classrooms. *Exceptional Children*, 69(3), 315–332.
https://doi.org/10.1177/001440290306900304

Hurwitz, M. & Koonce, R. (2016). The Practice of Followership: From Theory to Application. J Leadership Studies, 10: 41–44.
https://doi.org/10.1002/jls.21491

International journal of lean six sigma (Online). (2010). Emerald.

International journal of conflict management (Online). (1990). Center for Advanced Studies in Management.

Institute of Leadership & Management (2007). Building the Team (5th ed.). Routledge. https://doi.org/10.4324/9780080548371

Jaye, T., Garuba, D., & Amadi, S. (2011). *ECOWAS and the dynamics of conflict and peace-building* (1st ed.). Codesria.

Jiminez, R. (2025). Paper [Unpublished] School of Business and Leadership. Regent University.

Johnson, D. W. (1986). *Reaching out : interpersonal effectiveness and self-actualization* (Third edition.). Prentice-Hall.

Jones, A. (2025). ARMY FUTURES COMMAND'S CONTESTED LOGISTICS CROSS-FUNCTIONAL TEAM: Transforming for Future Sustainment. *Army Sustainment, 57*(2), 94.

Kalamdani, R. S. (n.d.). *Application of Taguchi methods and waste minimization.*

Kalamdani, R., Khalaf, F., Thomas, A. S., De Pennington, A., & McKay, A. (2006). Application of Design for Six Sigma to manufacturing process design at Ford PTO. *International Journal of Product Development, 3*(3–4), 369–387. https://doi.org/10.1504/IJPD.2006.009917

Kamada, S. (n.d.). *Lean Institute Brasil Using the Help Chain to Maintain Production Stability*. Retrieved 20 October 2025, from https://www.lean.org.br/comunidade/artigos/pdf/artigo_35_ingles.pdf

Katzenbach, J. R. (1998). *Teams at the top : unleashing the potential of both teams and individual leaders*. Harvard Business School Press.

Kaufman, G. (1985). *Shame, the power of caring* (Second edition revised.). Schenkman Pub. Co.

Kaufman, R., & Russell, J. D. (2001). [Rev. of *Strategic thinking: A guide to identifying and solving problems*]. *Performance Improvement (International Society for Performance Improvement), 40*(1), 49–50. https://doi.org/10.1002/pfi.4140400112

Kaye, K. (1994). *Workplace Wars and How to End Them: Turning Personal Conflicts into Productive Teamwork*. American Management Association. https://search.ebscohost.com/login.aspx?direct=true&scope=site&db=nlebk&db=nlabk&AN=2458

Kaye, B. L., & Jordan-Evans, S. (2003). *Love it, do not leave it : 26 ways to get what you want at work* (1st edition). Berrett-Koehler.

Kaye, B., & Jordan-Evans, S. (2021). *Love 'Em or Lose 'Em, Sixth Edition : Getting Good People to Stay* (Sixth edition.). Berrett-Koehler Publishers, Inc.

Keegan, S. (2015). *The psychology of fear in organizations : how to transform anxiety into well-being, productivity, and innovation*. Kogan Page.

Kellerer, W., Basta, A., & Blenk, A. (2015). *Flexibility of Networks: a new measure for network design space analysis?* https://doi.org/10.48550/arxiv.1512.03770

Kezar, A., & Holcombe, E. (2017). *Voices from the field: Viewpoints on shared leadership in higher education: Important lessons from research and practice*. https://www.acenet.edu/Documents/Shared-Leadership-in-Higher-Education.pdf

King-Sears, M. E., Janney, R., & Snell, M. E. (2015). *Collaborative teaming* (Third edition.). Paul H. Brookes Publishing Co.

Klann, G., & Center for Creative Leadership. (2004). *Building your team's morale, pride, and spirit* (1st edition). Center for Creative Leadership.

Kohlberg, L. (1981). *The philosophy of moral development : moral stages and the idea of justice* (First edition.). Harper & Row.

Kohlberg's Theory of Moral Development 1 (1958). Kohlberg's Stages of Moral Development. Retrieved 17 September 2023, from https://openlab.bmcc.cuny.edu/ece-110-172/wp-content/uploads/sites/1578/2021/05/Kohlberg-Moral-Development.pdf

Kotter, J. (1995). Leading change: Why transformation efforts fail. Harvard Business Review, 73(2): 61– 7.

Kouzes, J. M., & Posner, B. Z. (1999). *Encouraging the heart : a leader's guide to rewarding and recognizing others* (1st ed.). Jossey-Bass. https://search.ebscohost.com/login.aspx?direct=true&scope=site&db=nlebk&db=nlabk&AN=26054

Kouzes, J. & Posner, B. (2017). The Leadership Challenge: How to Make Extraordinary Things Happen in Organizations. San Francisco, CA: Jossey-Bass. ISBN-10: 0470651725.

KPA. (2 April 2018). *Business Culture in Nigeria 101 - Understanding & scaling up*. KPA. https://kpakpakpa.com/business-culture-101-understanding/

Kramer, S. (2024). *"Takt" time considerations for customer satisfaction* [Video recording]. Henry Stewart Talks.

Richard P. Kropp Jr, & Glenn M. Parker. (1992). *50 Activities for Team Building, Volume I*. HRD Press.

Kuglin, F. A., & Hook, J. (2002). *Building, leading, and managing strategic alliances : how to work effectively and profitably with partner companies*. AMACOM.

Kuhnert, K.W. (1994). Transforming leadership: Developing people through delegation. In B. M. Bass & B. J. Avolio (Eds.) Improving organizational leadership through transformational leadership (pp.10–25). Thousand Oaks, CA: SAGE.

Kühn, S., Sader, R., & Rieger, U. M. (2019). "Without standards, there can be no improvement"—Taiichi Ohno. *Gland Surgery*, 8(6), 591–592. https://doi.org/10.21037/gs.2019.11.23

Kumar, V. (2010). HD - Rocky Balboa (2006) - inspirational speech. On YouTube. https://www.youtube.com/watch?v=D_Vg4uyYwEk

Laiken, M., & Ontario Institute for Studies in Education. (1994). *The Anatomy of High-Performing Teams : A Leader's Handbook* (1st ed.). The Ontario Institute for Studies in Education. https://doi.org/10.3138/9781442680494

Lail, J. (2019). Between Forming and Storming: Interstage Awareness in Group Formation. *Academy of Educational Leadership Journal*, 23(3), 1–7.

Larkin, T., & Larkin, S. (1994). *Communicating change : how to win employee support for new business directions*. McGraw-Hill.

Larue, O. (2023). *The Toyota economic system : how leaders create true prosperity through financial congruency, dignity of work, and environmental stewardship*. Routledge. https://doi.org/10.4324/9781003348627

Latham, A., & Siegerman, R. (2022). The power of clarity : unleash the true potential of workplace productivity, confidence, and empowerment. Ascent Audio.

Laughlin, P. R. (2011). Group problem solving (Course Book). Princeton University Press. https://doi.org/10.1515/9781400836673

Lawrence, E., & Kirkham, J. (2024). COURSE OF ACTION (COA) FORMAT. In the *Small Unit Leaders Operational Planning Guide*. eBookit.com.

Lawson, K. (2016). *New employee orientation training* (1st edition). ATD Press.

Lê, P., & Pradies, C. (2023). Sailing through the storm: Improvising paradox navigation during a pandemic. Management Learning, 54(1), 56–76. https://doi.org/10.1177/13505076221096570

LEI, Lean Enterprise Institute. (2022). *What is lean?* Lean Enterprise Institute. https://www.lean.org/explore-lean/what-is-lean/

LEI (2019). *Stop Asking Your Leaders to "Support" Your Lean Transformation - Lean Enterprise Institute*. Lean Enterprise Institute. https://www.lean.org/the-lean-post/articles/stop-asking-your-leaders-to-support-your-lean-transformation/

Lencioni, P. (2007). *The Five Dysfunctions of a Team: Participant Workbook* (1st edition). Pfeiffer Imprint.

Lencioni, P. (2016). The ideal team player : recognizing and cultivating the three essential virtues : a leadership fable (1st ed.). Jossey-Bass, a John Wiley & Sons, Inc. imprint

Lesley University. (2019). *Perception is reality: The looking-glass self*. Lesley University; Lesley University. https://lesley.edu/article/perception-is-reality-the-looking-glass-self

Li, Y. (2019). *The Etymology of "Talent" and the Comparison of "Origins" Between Chinese and Western Views on Talent*. https://doi.org/10.2991/iccese-19.2019.35

Liang, S. -G., & Chi, S. -C.S. (2013). Transformational leadership and follower task performance: The role of susceptibility to positive emotions and follower positive emotions. Journal of Business and Psychology, 28(1), 17– 29. https://doi.org/10.1007/s10869-012-9261-x

Liborius, P. (2017). What Does Leaders' Character Add to Transformational Leadership? *The Journal of Psychology*, *151*(3), 299–320. https://doi.org/10.1080/00223980.2016.1270889

Liddell, H. G., Robert Scott, A Greek-English Lexicon, Preface (1925). (2023). Tufts.edu. https://www.perseus.tufts.edu/hopper/text?doc=Perseus%3Atext%3A1999.04.0057%3Afrontmatter%3Dpref.

Liker, J. K. (2021). *The Toyota Way : 14 Management Principles from the World's Greatest Manufacturer (Second edition)*. McGraw-Hill.

Liker, J. K., & Meier, D. (2021). The Toyota Way Fieldbook. In Amazon (Unabridged edition). McGraw-Hill, Ascent, and Blackstone Publishing. https://www.amazon.com/Toyota-Way-Fieldbook-Jeffrey-Liker/dp/B0BX7FX5SV

LinkedIn. (2015). Linkedin.com. https://www.linkedin.com/pulse/why-many-ceos-dont-like-lean-consultants-false-dichotomy-fowler/?trackingId=QRr1c6HQQmutb7xwJ2VE7A%3D%3D

LinkedIn. (2025). Linkedin.com. https://www.linkedin.com/pulse/lean-leadership-its-never-people-problem-timothy-fowler/

Little, J., Palepu, R., & Higgins, M. (2024). Disillusionment amongst clinical staff experiencing repeated change. *Australasian Psychiatry : Bulletin of the Royal Australian and New Zealand College of Psychiatrists*, *32*(4), 290–292. https://doi.org/10.1177/10398562241261263

Lombardi, V. (2019). *Forbes*. https://www.forbes.com/quotes/9453/

Lord, R. & Maher, K. (1991). Leadership and information processing: Linking perceptions and performance. Unwin Hyman, Boston, MA

Lurie, A. (2009). *Five Minutes on Mondays: Finding Unexpected Purpose, Peace, and Fulfillment at Work* (1st edition). Pearson.

Madhwacharyula, C., & Ramdas, S. (2023). *Scaling Customer Success : Building the Customer Success Center of Excellence* (1st ed. 2023). Apress. https://doi.org/10.1007/978-1-4842-9192-4

Manz, C. C., & Neck, C. P. (1999). *Mastering self-leadership : empowering yourself for personal excellence* (2nd ed.). Prentice Hall.

Manz, C. C., & Sims, H. P. (2001). The new super leadership leading others to lead themselves (1st edition). Berrett-Koehler Publishers, Inc.

Mar, K. (2024, September 30). Culture vs. Structure: Why Larman's Laws Suggest Structure Always Wins. Agile Federation. https://www.agilefederation.com/post/culture-vs-structure-why-larman-s-laws-suggest-structure-always-wins

Mariani, G., Greggio, F., & Reolon, G. (2017). M&A and value creation : a SWOT analysis. G. Giappichelli Editore.

Márquez Figueroa, L. J., García Alcaraz, J. L., Díaz Reza, J. R., Quintana Alvarado, J., Realyvásquez Vargas, A., & Robles, G. C. (2024). Gemba. In Lean Manufacturing in Latin America (pp. 385–408). Springer. https://doi.org/10.1007/978-3-031-70984-5_17

Maslow, A. H. (1962). *Toward a psychology of being*. Princeton: D. Van Nostrand Company.

Mattone, J., & Xavier, L. F. (2012). *Talent leadership : a proven method for identifying and developing high-potential employees* (1st edition). American Management Association.

Mayer, T. (2021). *Battling Healthcare Burnout : Learning to Love the Job You Have, While Creating the Job You Love* (First edition.). Berrett-Koehler Publishers, Inc.

McGilchrist, I. Master and His Emissary. (2019). Retrieved 29 September 2023, from https://channelmcgilchrist.com/master-and-his-emissary/

McGuire, J. B., & Rhodes, G. B. (2009). *Transforming your leadership culture* (First edition.). Jossey-Bass

Merriam-Webster. (2021). *Definition of Teamwork*. Merriam-Webster.com. https://www.merriam-webster.com/dictionary/teamwork

Michaeli, D. (2021). *Digital customer service: transforming the customer experience in an on-screen world*. Wiley.

Milliken, F. J., & Martins, L. (1996). Searching for common threads: Understanding the multiple effects of diversity in organizational groups. Academy of Management Review, 21, 402–433

Monden, Y. (2012). *Toyota production system : an integrated approach to just-in-time* (Fourth edition.). CRC Press. https://doi.org/10.1201/b11731

Morgulev, E. (2023). Success breeds success: Physiological, psychological, and economic perspectives of momentum (hot hand). Asian Journal of Sport and Exercise Psychology, 3(1), 3–7. https://doi.org/1

Mosley, E. (2013). *The crowdsourced performance review : how to use the power of social recognition to transform employee performance* (1st edition). McGraw-Hill Education.

Munro-Hay, Stuart. *Aksum: An African Civilization of Late Antiquity*. Edinburgh University Press, 1991.
– Comprehensive academic work on Aksumite statecraft, economy, architecture, and trade networks.

Nakane, H., & Darga, R. (1997). Continuous improvement culture : to the next generation. Gold Leaf Press.

National Research Council. Standing Committee on Research, D., & U.S. Special Operations Command. (2009). *Sensing and supporting communications capabilities for special operations forces : abbreviated vision* (1st ed.). National Academies Press.

Network, O. D. (2012). Handbook for Strategic HR: Best Practices in Organization Development from the OD Network, AMACOM. ProQuest Ebook Central, http://ebookcentral.proquest.com/lib/regent-ebooks/detail.action?docID=1043643. Created from regent-ebooks on 2025-06-27 13:21:41.

New International Version Bible. (2011). Zondervan. (Original work published 1973)

Nikita, N., & Singh, A. (2025). A process improvement study on patient flow from the emergency department to the intensive care unit. *International Journal of Health Care Quality Assurance*, 38(3), 144–157. https://doi.org/10.1108/IJHCQA-03-2024-0039

Nishii, L. H., & Mayer, D. M. (2009). Do Inclusive Leaders Help to Reduce Turnover in Diverse Groups? The Moderating Role of Leader-Member Exchange in the Diversity to Turnover Relationship. Journal of Applied Psychology, 94(6), 1412–1426. https://doi.org/10.1037/a0017190

Norris, F. (5 March 1989). "Time Inc. and Warner to Merge, Creating Largest Media Company" Links to an external site. *The New York Times*.

Northouse, P.G. (2013). Leadership Theory and Practice. Thousand Oaks, CA, Sage. Chapters 5—10.

Ng, T. W. H., Koopmann, J., & Parker, S. K. (2022). Promoting idea exploration and harmonization in the creative process: cultivating interdependence and employees' perspective-taking is key. European Journal of Work and Organizational Psychology, 31(4), 567–582. https://doi.org/10.1080/1359432X.2021.2014454

Offermann, L., J.K. Kennedy, P.W. Wirtz (1994). Implicit leadership theories: Content, structure, and generalizability. The Leadership Quarterly, 5 (1) (1994), pp. 43-5

Oksanen, M. (2025, November 17). What is new in Teams Free | October 2025 - Teams Insider. Teams Insider. https://insider.teams.com/blog/whats-new-in-teams-free-october-2025/

O'Neil, P. (2025). Paper [Unpublished] School of Business and Leadership. Regent University.

Ono, T. (1988). *Toyota production system : beyond large-scale production* (1st edition). CRC Press.

Owen, C. (2017). *Human Factors Challenges in Emergency Management : Enhancing Individual and Team Performance in Fire and Emergency Services* (First edition.). Taylor and Francis.

Palus, C. J., & Horth, D. M. (2002). The leader's edge: six creative competencies for navigating
complex challenges (1st ed.). Jossey-Bass.

Papke, E. (2016). *The elephant in the boardroom : how leaders use and manage conflict to achieve greater levels of success* (1st edition). Career Press.

Parker, G. M. (2008). *Team players and team work : new strategies for developing successful collaboration* (2nd ed.). Jossey-Bass.

Pearson, A. H. (2022). Situational Leadership Theory: Do Followers Have a Preference? Press Ganey. (2019). *Press Ganey Associates*. Pressganey.com. https://www.pressganey.com/ProQuest Dissertations Publishing

Perera, A. (2024). Self-Actualization In Psychology: Theory, Examples & Characteristics. *Simply Psychology*. https://www.simplypsychology.org/self-actualization.html

Peters, K. & Haslam, A. (2018). "Research: To Be a Good Leader, Start by Being a Good Follower," Harvard Business Review, https://hbr.org/2018/08/research-to-be-a-good-leader-start-by-being-a-good-follower.

Petruska, R. (2012). *Gemba walks for service excellence : the step-by-step guide for identifying service delighters* (1st edition). CRC Press.

Phillips, J.B. (1958). Phillips New Testament (PHILLIPS) - Version Information - BibleGateway.com. (n.d.). Www.biblegateway.com. Retrieved 17 September 2023, from https://www.biblegateway.com/versions/JB-Phillips-New-Testament/

Phillips, J. J., & Connell, A. O. (2003). *Managing employee retention : a strategic accountability approach* (1st ed.). Butterworth-Heinemann.

Phillips, J. J., & Edwards, L. (2009). *Managing talent retention : an ROI approach* (1st edition). Pfeiffer.

Pine, B. J., & Gilmore, J. H. (1999). *The experience economy : work is theatre & every business a stage.* Harvard Business School Press. https://search.ebscohost.com/login.aspx?direct=true&scope=site&db=nlebk&db=nlabk&AN=7795

Pixar (2014). INSIDE THE PIXAR BRAINTRUST. *Fast Company, 184,* 67.

Podsakoff, P. N., MacKenzie, S. B., Moorman, R. H. & Fetter, R. (1990). *Transformational leader behaviors and their effects on followers, trust in leader, satisfaction, and organizational behaviors—The Leadership Quarterly I. (107–142).*

POP. (2024). POP. https://www.performance-on-purpose.com/

Porras, J. I., Thompson, M., & Emery, S. (2010). *Recruiting your dream team, relationships built to last, leads to success built to last* (1st edition). FT Press.

Potoker, E. S. (2011). International human resource development : a leadership perspective (2nd ed.). Routledge. https://doi.org/10.4324/9780203843420

Project Gutenberg eBook of The Measure of a Man, by Randall Garrett. (n.d.). Www.gutenberg.org. Retrieved September 18, 2023, from https://www.gutenberg.org/files/24135/24135-h/24135-h.htm

Protzman, C., Whiton, F., & Kerpchar, J. (2023). *Sustaining lean : creating a culture of continuous improvement.* Routledge. https://doi.org/10.4324/9781003186090

Quizlet. (2015). Quizlet. https://quizlet.com/au

Realyvásquez Vargas, A., García Alcaraz, J. L., Satapathy, S., & Díaz-Reza, J. R. (2023). The PDCA Cycle for Industrial Improvement: Applied Case Studies (1st ed.). Springer. https://doi.org/10.1007/978-3-031-26805-2

Reichheld, F. F., & Teal, T. (1996). *The loyalty effect : the hidden force behind growth, profits, and lasting value.* Harvard Business School Press. https://search.ebscohost.com/login.aspx?direct=true&scope=site&db=nlebk&db=nlabk&AN=7253Reuters. (2021). "AerCap to buy GE's aircraft leasing unit in $30 billion deal"Links to an external site. *Reuters. March 10, 2021 – via www.reuters.com.*

Riggio, R. E., Chaleff, I., & Lipman-Blumen, J. (2008). The art of followership : how great followers create great leaders and organizations (First edition.). Jossey-Bass.

Rizzardo, D. (2025). *5 Best Practices for Boosting Lean Engagement.* Industryweek.com. https://www.industryweek.com/operations/continuous-improvement/article/55130479/5-best-practices-for-boosting-lean-engagement

Rodriguez, R. (2022). *Employee resource group excellence : grow high performing ERGs to enhance diversity, equality, belonging, and business impact.* Wiley.

Romero, D. B. (2009). *The Business of Listening.* Axzo Press LLC.

Ross, S. C. (2014). "A conceptual model for understanding the process of self-leadership development and action-steps to promote personal leadership development," Journal of Management Development, Vol. 33 No. 4, pp. 299–323. https://doi.org/10.1108/JMD-11-2012-0147

Ross, S. C. (2015). The Road to Self-Leadership Development : Busting Out of Your Comfort Zone. Emerald Group Publishing Limited.

Rossett, A. (1999). Knowledge management meets analysis: training *& Development (Alexandria, Va.), 53*(5), 62.

Saatchi & Saatchi. (2012). *Lessons from geese* [Video recording]. Seven Dimensions.

Sammis, J. (1887). Trust and Obey. Hymnary.org. https://hymnary.org/text/when_we_walk_with_the_lord

Sand, D. (2021). Nigerian Business Culture. Nigerian Business. https://www.howwemadeit inafrica.com/nigerian-business-culture-and-incentives-an-inside-perspective/47005/

Santander Romero, W., Moyano Alulema, J., Guamán Lozano, A., & García Cabezas, E. (2024). Six Sigma as a Methodology to Reduce Weight Variability: Antonio Dairy Case Study. *ESPOCH Congresses, 3*(3), 281–301. https://doi.org/10.18502/espoch.v3i3.16709

Saundry, R., Latreille, P., & Ashman, Ian. (Eds.). (2016). *Reframing Resolution : Innovation and Change in the Management of Workplace Conflict.* Palgrave Macmillan UK. https://doi.org/10.1057/978-1-137-51560-5

Sayah, H., & Khaleel, A. (2022). THE APPLICATION OF ACCREDITATION STANDARDS IN INSTITUTIONAL IRAQI UNIVERSITIES USING DEMING CYCLE (PDSA)" AN APPLIED STUDY IN THE COLLEGES OF SUMER UNIVERSITY – IRAQ". *Proceedings on Engineering Sciences (Online), 4*(1), 23–32. https://doi.org/10.24874/PES04.01.004

Schindler, J. H. (2015). *Followership : what it takes to lead* (First edition.). Business Expert Press.

Schleien, S. J., Miller, K. D., Walton, G., & Pruett, S. (2014). Parent Perspectives of Barriers to Child Participation in Recreational Activities. *Therapeutic Recreation Journal, 48*(1), 61.

Schmidt, W. H., & Posner, B. Z. (1982). *Managerial values and expectations : the silent power in personal and organizational life.* AMA Membership Publications Division, American Management Association.

School of Business and Leadership. (2025, May 2). Regent University. https://www.regent.edu/school-of-business-and-leadership/

Schoop, M., & Kilgour, D. Marc. (Eds.). (2017). *Group Decision and Negotiation. A Socio-Technical Perspective : 17th International Conference, GDN 2017, Stuttgart, Germany, August 14-18, 2017, Proceedings* (1st ed. 2017). Springer International Publishing. https://doi.org/10.1007/978-3-319-63546-0

Schyns, B. & Mohr, G. (2004). Nonverbal elements of leadership behavior. German Journal of Human Resource Research, 18, pp. 289-305

Scott, K. H. (2022). *A Qualitative Study of Teachers as Path-Goal Leaders with an Emphasis on Clearing the Path of Distraction*. ProQuest Dissertations & Theses. Studer, Q. (2020). *The busy leader's handbook : how to lead people and places that thrive* (1st edition). Wiley.

Shaw, R. B. (2017). *Extreme teams : why Pixar, Netflix, AirBnB, and other cutting-edge companies succeed where most fail* (1st edition). AMACOM, American Management Association.

Sherf, E. N., Sinha, R., Tangirala, S., & Awasty, N. (2018). Centralization of Member Voice in Teams: Its Effects on Expertise Utilization and Team Performance. *Journal of Applied Psychology*, *103*(8), 813–827. https://doi.org/10.1037/apl0000305

Sherwin, D., & Sherwin, M. (2018). *Turning people into teams : rituals and routines that redesign how we work* (1st ed.). Berrett-Koehler Publishers, Inc.

Silber, K. H., & Foshay, W. R. (2010). *Handbook of improving performance in the workplace. Volume one, Instructional design and training delivery* (K. H. Silber & W. R. Foshay, Eds.; 1st ed.). International Society for Performance Improvement.

Simon, P. (2015). Message not received : why business communication is broken and how to fix it (1st edition). Wiley.

Singh, D. (2006). *Emotional intelligence at work : a professional guide* (Third revised edition.). Response Books.

Singh, P., & Kumar, N. (2010). *Employee Relations Management* (1st edition). Pearson India.

Seneca, On Benefits, (2011). Miriam Griffin and Brad Inwood (trs.), University of Chicago
Press, 2011, 222pp., $45.00 (hbk), ISBN 9780226748405.

Senge, P. M. (2006). *The fifth discipline : the art and practice of the learning organization* (Revised and updated.). Doubleday/Currency. https://search.ebscohost.com/login.aspx?direct=true&scope=site&db=nlebk&db=nlabk&AN=717326

SLII® - A Situational Approach to Leadership. (2023). BLANCHARD. https://www.blanchard.com/our-content/programs/slii

Sorbero, M. E., & Rand Corporation. (2008). *Outcome measures for effective teamwork in inpatient care : final report* (1st ed.). RAND Corp.

Skillshub Ltd., instructor, & Packt Publishing, publisher. (2024). *Building high-performance teams.* ([First edition].) [Video recording]. Packt Publishing.

Sloan. (2018). *Getting dispersed teams right: Successfully managing remote teams requires an understanding of the benefits and challenges of virtual workers; there are tactics managers can use to help both them and the company thrive.* MIT Sloan Management Review.

Smith, R. H., Parrott, W. G., Diener, E., Hoyle, R. H., & Kim, S. H. (1999). Dispositional
Envy. Personality and Social Psychology Bulletin, 25, 1007-1020.

Smith, R. M. (2011). *Strategic learning alignment : make training a powerful business partner*. American Society for Training & Development.

Snell, M. E., Janney, R., & Elliott, J. (2005). *Collaborative teaming* (Second edition.). P.H. Brookes Pub.c.
http://www.loc.gov/catdir/toc/ecip057/2005002210.html

Staff, U. D. (2023, June 21). *Drink From A Fire Hose: Definition, Meaning, and Origin*. US Dictionary. https://usdictionary.com/idioms/drink-from-a-fire-hose/

Stallone, S. (1976, December 3). Rocky. IMDb. https://www.imdb.com/title/tt0075148/

Sternberg, L., & Turnage, K. (2017). *Managing to make a difference : how to engage, retain, and develop talent for maximum performance* (1st edition). Wiley.

Stewart, G. L., & Carson, K. P. (1997). Moving beyond the mechanistic model: An alternative approach to staffing for contemporary organizations. *Human Resource Management Review, 7*(2), 157–184.
https://doi.org/10.1016/S1053-4822(97)90021-8

Strasser, S., Dailey, R. C., & Bateman, T. S. (1981). Attitudinal Moderators and Effects of Leaders' Punitive Behavior. *Psychological Reports, 49*(3), 695–698. https://doi.org/10.2466/pr0.1981.49.3.695

Studer, Q. (2020). *The busy leader's handbook : how to lead people and places that thrive* (1st edition). Wiley.

Sullivan, R., Warner, M., & Natural Resources Cluster of Business Partners for Development. (2017). *Putting partnerships to work : strategic alliances for development between government, the private sector, and civil society* (R. Sullivan & M. Warner, Eds.; 1st ed.). Greenleaf Pub. https://doi.org/10.4324/9781351281249Links to an external site.

Study.com. (2022). https://study.com/academy/lesson/pygmalion-effect-definition-examples-quiz.html

Sushil, C., Julia, & Burgess, J. (Eds.). (2016). Flexible Work Organizations: The Challenges of Capacity Building in Asia (1st ed. 2016). Springer India. https://doi.org/10.1007/978-81-322-2834-9

Suswati, E. (2021). Work Placement Affects Employee Performance Through Work Motivation. *Jurnal Aplikasi Manajemen, 19*(2), 394–403. https://doi.org/10.21776/ub.jam.2021.019.02.15

Suwarto, F. X., & Subyantoro, A. (2019). The Effect of Recruitment, Selection, and Placement on Employee Performance. *International Journal of Computer Networks and Communications Security, 7*(7), 126–134.

身份中台. (2025). Sxu.edu.cn. http://sdsfzt-443.webvpn.sxu.edu.cn/auth/#/login?service=http://webvpn.sxu.edu.cn/users/auth/cas/callback?url

Tang, C.-B., Zhang, Y., Wang, L., & Zhang, Z. (2019). What can AI learn from bionic algorithms?: Comment on "Does being multi-headed make you better at solving problems? A survey of Physarum-based models and computations" by Chao Gao et al. *Physics of Life Reviews*, *29*, 41–43. https://doi.org/10.1016/j.plrev.2019.01.006

Tang, J., Abbass, H. A., & Leu, G. (2019). *Simulation and Computational Red Teaming for Problem Solving*. Wiley. https://doi.org/10.1002/9781119527183

The Knowledge Academy. (2019). *Training Needs Analysis Course*. Theknowledgeacademy.com. https://www.theknowledgeacademy.com/vn/courses/learning-and-development-courses/training-needs-analysis-course/

Thom-Mayer (2021). [Rev. of *Battling Healthcare Burnout: Learning to Love the Job You Have, While Creating the Job you Love*]. *ProtoView*.

Thomas, D. (2020). God's Sovereignty and Our Responsibility. Ligonier Ministries. https://www.ligonier.org/learn/articles/gods-sovereignty-and-our-responsibility

Thompson, G., & Glasø, L. (2018). Situational leadership theory: a test from a leader-follower congruence approach. Leadership and Organization Development Journal, 39(5), 574–591. https://doi.org/10.1108/LODJ-01-2018-0050

Thompson, G., & Vecchio, R. P. (2019). Situational leadership theory: A test of three versions. The Leadership Quarterly, 20(5), 837–848. https://doi.org/10.1016/j.leaqua.2009.06.014

Thompson, S. (2025). Creating a New Hire Orientation Schedule Template. In *Newstex Entrepreneurship Blogs*. Newstex.

Thoms, P. (2004). *Driven by time : time orientation and leadership*. Praeger.

Thorpe, D. (2018, February 12). *HeadwayExec LLC - Doug Thorpe*. Business Advisor and Executive Coach | Doug Thorpe. https://dougthorpe.com/major-minors-minor-majors/

Toyota Motor Corporation MarketLine Company Profile. (2014). MarketLine, a Progressive Digital Media business.

TPS. (2025). *Toyota Production System*. Toyota Motor Corporation Official Global Website; global.toyota. https://global.toyota/en/company/vision-and-philosophy/production-system/

Tracy, B. (2016). *Personal success* (1st edition). AMACOM, American Management Association Council.

Treat, Shaun Robert. (2004). "The Myth of Charismatic Leadership and Fantasy Rhetoric of Crypto-charismatic Memberships." https://core.ac.uk/download/217389758.pdf.

Tricker, R., & Sherring-Lucas, B. (2005). *ISO 9001 : 2000 in brief* (2nd ed.). Butterworth-Heinemann. https://doi.org/10.4324/9780080478814

Tuckman, B. W. (1965). *Developmental sequence in small groups*. Psychological Bulletin, 63(6), 384–399.

Tulgan, B. (2015). *Bridging the soft skills gap : how to teach the missing basics to today's young talent* (1st edition). Jossey-Bass.

Turnbull, A. P., Turbiville, V., Schaffer, R., & Schaffer, V. (1996). "Getting a Shot at Life" through Group Action Planning. https://core.ac.uk/download/213391256.pdf

Turner, J. R. (2022). Change is a constant. Performance Improvement Quarterly, 34(4), 323–326. doi:https://doi.org/10.1002/piq.21379

Uhl-Bien, M. (2006). Relational Leadership Theory: Exploring the social processes of leadership and organizing. The Leadership Quarterly, 17(6), 654–676. https://doi.org/10.1016/j.leaqua.2006.10.007

US Army Combined Arms Center. (2025). Usacac.army.mil. https://usacac.army.mil/

VA Office. (2020). *VA.gov | Veterans Affairs.* Va.gov. https://www.va.gov/adr/

Van Cott, H. P., Huey, B. M., & National Research Council. Panel on Human Factors Specialists' Education and Utilization. (1992). *Human factors specialists' education and utilization : results of a survey.* National Academy Press.

Van Velsor, E., McCauley, C. D. (Cynthia D., & Ruderman, M. N. (2010). The Center for Creative Leadership handbook of leadership development (3rd ed.). Jossey-Bass, a Wiley Imprint.

Vogelsang, J. (Ed.). (2013). *Handbook for strategic HR. Section 2, Consulting and partnership skills : best practices in organizational development from the OD network.* AMACOM.

Vukotich, G., & Booksx, I. (2010). *Breaking the chains of culture : building trust in individuals, teams, and organizations—*Information Age Pub.

Walker, A. N. (2022). *Training and Development: The Key to Employee Longevity.* University of Dayton / OhioLINK.

Wang, J. X. (2011). *Lean manufacturing is business bottom-line-based.* CRC Press. https://search.ebscohost.com/login.aspx?direct=true&scope=site&db=nlebk&db=nlabk&AN=337556

Wang Q, Wang J, Zhou X, Li F, Wang M. How Inclusive Leadership Enhances Follower Taking Charge: The Mediating Role of Affective Commitment and the Moderating Role of Traditionality. Psychol Res Behav Manag. 2020 Dec 1;13:1103-1114. Doi: 10.2147/PRBM.S280911. PMID: 33299363; PMCID: PMC7720287.

Wealleans, D. (2017). *The Organizational Measurement Manual.* (1st ed.). Taylor and Francis.

Webdeveloper. (2025). *The Ford Production System | Operations Case Studies.* Ibscdc.org. https://www.ibscdc.org/Case_Studies/Operations/Operations/The%20Ford%20Production%20System-Operations%20Management.htm

Weber, M. (1947). The theory of social and economic organizations (T. Parsons, trans.).New York, N.Y.: Free Press.

Weinstein, R. S. (2002). *Reaching higher : the power of expectations in schooling* (1st ed.). Harvard University Press. https://doi.org/10.4159/9780674045040

Weiss, H. M., & Cropanzano, R. (1996). Affective Events Theory: A theoretical discussion of the structure, causes, and consequences of affective experiences at work. In B. M. Staw & L. L. Cummings (Eds.), Research in organizational behavior: An annual series of analytical essays and critical reviews (Vol. 18, pp. 1–74). Elsevier Science/JAI Press. https://psycnet.apa.org/record/1996-98665-001

Welch, M. (2018). *The street savvy sales leader : a guide to building teams that consistently win new business* (1st ed.). Figure 1.

Welsby, Derek A. *The Medieval Kingdoms of Nubia: Pagans, Christians, and Muslims along the Middle Nile.* British Museum Press, 2002.

Westchester County Economic Development. (2025). Countyoffice.org. https://www.countyoffice.org/westchester-county-economic-development-white-plains-ny-a24/

Whitaker, T., Lumpa, D., & Whitaker, B. (2013). *Motivating and inspiring teachers : the educational leaders' guide for building staff morale* (Second edition.). Routledge. https://doi.org/10.4324/9781315856445

Williamson, R., & Blackburn, B. R. (2023). *Improving Teacher Morale and Motivation: Leadership Strategies that Build Student Success* (1st ed.). Taylor & Francis. https://doi.org/10.4324/9781003310471

Wingard, J., & Farrugia, C. A. (Eds.). (2021). *The great skills gap : optimizing talent for the future of work.* Stanford Business Books. https://doi.org/10.1515/9781503628076

Winston, B. (2009). The Romans 12 Gifts: Useful for Person-Job Fit. Regent University. https://www.regent.edu/journal/journal-of-biblical-perspectives-in-leadership/romans-12-spiritual-gifts/

Without Standards, There Can Be No Kaizen. (2009, January 13). The Lean Thinker. https://theleanthinker.com/2009/01/12/without-standards-there-can-be-no-kaizen/

Womack, J. (2007, December 20). Respect for People. Lean Enterprise Institute. https://www.lean.org/the-lean-post/articles/respect-for-people/

World Mental Health Care (WMHC). (2021, June 24). https://wmh.care/

Wright, T. A., & Quick, J. C. (2011). The role of character in ethical leadership research. *The Leadership Quarterly, 22*(5), 975–978. https://doi.org/10.1016/j.leaqua.2011.07.015

Writer, S. (2025, March 4). *A Deep Dive into the Efficiency Principles Behind the Henry Ford Assembly Line.* Reference.com; amg. https://www.reference.com/business-finance/deep-dive-efficiency-principles-behind-henry-ford-assembly-line

WSJ. GE Sells Crotonville, a Training Ground for Generations of Managers -- WSJ. (2024, Apr 14). *Dow Jones Institutional News* https://go.openathens.net/redirector/regent.edu?url=https://www.proquest.com/wire-feeds/ge-sells-crotonville-training-ground-generations/docview/3038235136/se-2

Yerian, L., (2018). How to Create a Culture of Continuous Improvement. Consult QD. https://consultqd.clevelandclinic.org/how-to-create-a-culture-of-continuous-improvement/

Yin, R.K. (1994). Case Study Research: Design and Methods, 2nd ed., Sage, Thousand Oaks, CA.

Yukl, G. A., & Lepsinger, R. (2004). Flexible leadership : creating value by balancing multiple challenges and choices. Jossey-Bass.

Chapter Five | Retreat References

Anurag Tiruwa, Ph.D. (2025, April 27). *In 2025, organizations are no longer judged solely by their market value — they are judged by how they treat their people. Human-centered leadership is no longer optional; it is a business imperative.* Linkedin.com. https://www.linkedin.com/pulse/novatechs-leadership-transformation-why-approaches-tiruwa-ph-d--zpvrc/

Biostrategenix. (2025). Biostrategenix. https://biostrategenix.com/

Boyce, I., DeVoe, J., Norsen, L., Smith, J. A., Anson, E., McGregor, H. A., & Singh, R. (2024). The Financial Impact of an Employee Wellness Program Focused on Cardiovascular Disease Risk Reduction. Healthcare, 12(23), 2358–2358. https://doi.org/10.3390/healthcare12232358

Developing Confident Leaders through Transformation at Atos. (2025, August 14). Harvard Business Impact. https://www.harvardbusiness.org/client-story/developing-confident-leaders-through-transformation-at-atos/

Frankena, W. K. (1965). *Philosophy of education*. Macmillan.

INDUSTRY- LEADING CASE STUDIES 2024. (2024). https://businesscultureawards.com/wp-content/uploads/2024/12/case-studies-2024.pdf

Mill, J. S., & Magid, H. M. (1965). *On the logic of the moral sciences : a system of logic, book VI*. Bobbs-Merrill Company, Inc.

Rubber Stamp It. *AI video production | LTX*. (2025). Ltx. studio. https://app.ltx.studio/projects/c5e1655f-a800-4dbc-a336-e9ca32554215/gen-workspace?sessionId=a09504c1-a680-4aa6-a233-c52e500e296

Contributors ...

Project Manager: T. Wiles Fowler
Proofreader: Dr. Chip Palmer
Designer: Yu Yang
Audiobook: Cory Stoutner
Spanish: Rafael Frontaura
Final Design/Edit: Tim Schulte

About the Author …

T. Wiles Fowler, known as the "Right Brain," is honored to serve as the Continuous Improvement Director at the Cleveland Clinic's Diagnostics Institute. He earned a Master's Degree in International Leadership from York University and walks for a Doctorate in Strategic Healthcare Leadership from Regent in May 2026. With several decades of experience in federal and commercial sectors, he specializes in strategic planning, executive coaching, budget management, and operational excellence. He is focused on enhancing efficiency and eliminating waste, having led international teams for the U.S. Department of Defense and the Department of State. His work has taken him to various countries, including contributions to the POTUS Air Force One refueling process. He has been married to his wife, Terri, for 42 years, and they have four children and six grandchildren (and counting!)

www.ingramcontent.com/pod-product-compliance
Lightning Source LLC
Chambersburg PA
CBHW072354110726
47909CB00003B/703